Microsoft®
Excel® 2010
Core Certification

Courseware 3243-1

Exam 77-882

September 2010

CCI Learning Solutions Inc.

Microsoft® Office Excel 2010

Courseware Developer: Kenny Lee

Microsite Developer: Lorin Ledger

Editors: Lynne Melcombe, Wes Bergen

CCI Publishing Team: Kelly Hegedus, Sue Wong, Kevin Yulo

CCI Learning Solutions Inc. would like to acknowledge the financial support of the Government of Canada through the Book Publishing Industry Development Program for our publishing activities.

Working With the Data Files

The exercises in this courseware require you to use the data files provided for the book. Follow the instructions shown to download the data files for this courseware.

1   Launch your browser and navigate to the CCI Web site location http://www.ccilearning.com/data.

2   Enter: *3243* in the **Courseware #** box and click Find Data .

3   Click **Run** in the File Download – Security Warning window. (Alternatively, you can choose to **Save** the file to a location on your computer.)

4   In the Internet Explorer – Security Warning window click **Run** again.

5   In the **WinZip Self-Extractor** dialog box, use the **Browse** button to specify the Windows Desktop as the location to unzip the file and then click **Unzip**.

5   The **3243 Student Files** folder containing the required student work files has now been downloaded to your desktop. It is recommended that you rename the folder using your own name before starting the exercises in this courseware. You can reinstall and use the work files as many times as you like.

What is the Microsoft ® Office Specialist Program?

The Microsoft Office Specialist Program enables candidates to show that they have something exceptional to offer – proven expertise in certain Microsoft programs. Recognized by businesses and schools around the world, over 4 million certifications have been obtained in over 100 different countries. The Microsoft Office Specialist Program is the only Microsoft-approved certification program of its kind.

What is the Microsoft Office Specialist Certification?

The Microsoft Office Specialist certification validates through the use of exams that you have obtained specific skill sets within the applicable Microsoft Office programs and other Microsoft programs included in the Microsoft Office Specialist Program. The candidate can choose which exam(s) they want to take according to which skills they want to validate.

The available Microsoft Office Specialist Program exams include*:

- Using Windows Vista®
- Using Microsoft® Office Word 2007
- Using Microsoft® Office Word 2007 - Expert
- Using Microsoft® Office Excel® 2007
- Using Microsoft® Office Excel® 2007 - Expert
- Using Microsoft® Office PowerPoint® 2007
- Using Microsoft® Office Access® 2007
- Using Microsoft® Office Outlook® 2007
- Using Microsoft SharePoint® 2007

The Microsoft Office Specialist Program 2010 exams will include*:

- Microsoft Word 2010
- Microsoft Word 2010 Expert
- Microsoft Excel® 2010
- Microsoft Excel® 2010 Expert
- Microsoft PowerPoint® 2010
- Microsoft Access® 2010
- Microsoft Outlook® 2010
- Microsoft SharePoint® 2010

What does the Microsoft Office Specialist Approved Courseware logo represent?

The logo indicates that this courseware has been approved by Microsoft to cover the course objectives that will be included in the relevant exam. It also means that after utilizing this courseware, you may be better prepared to pass the exams required to become a certified Microsoft Office Specialist.

For more information:

To learn more about Microsoft Office Specialist exams, visit www.microsoft.com/learning/en/us/certification/mos.aspx

To learn about other Microsoft approved courseware from CCI Learning Solutions, visit http://mos.ccilearning.com

* The availability of Microsoft Office Specialist certification exams varies by Microsoft program, program version and language. Visit www.microsoft.com/learning for exam availability.

Table of Contents

About This Courseware

Lesson 1: Introducing Excel

Lesson 2: Constructing Cell Data

Lesson 3: Using Formulas

Lesson 4: Formatting the Worksheet

Lesson 5: Viewing and Printing Workbooks

Lesson 6: Working with Charts

Lesson 7: Working with Graphics

Lesson 8: Analyzing, Organizing and Sharing Workbooks

Appendices

Course Description

Microsoft® Excel® 2010 Core teaches the information worker how to work with different types of documents using a variety of core and intermediate features to create and edit professional-looking spreadsheets for a variety of purposes and situations. Some topics may appear to be basic skill sets but are discussed in more detail, exploring at a higher level different options that can be chosen or applied for that skill set.

Students who complete this course will have reviewed all of the exam objectives and be on their way to preparing for Microsoft Excel 2010 Core Exam #77-882.

Course Series

This *Microsoft Excel 2010 Core* courseware is one of nine courses in CCI's Microsoft Office Specialist 2010 series. Other courses available in the series include:

- Word 2010 Core
- Access 2010
- PowerPoint 2010
- Outlook 2010
- Word 2010 Expert
- Excel 2010 Expert

The Microsoft Office Specialist 2010 Series contains exercises that students can use to learn each of the features discussed. Additional resources to practice and apply the skill sets are available from the CCI Office 2010 Microsite. Students are encouraged to register at http://2010.ccilearning.com in order access these additional activities both during and after completing the course.

Instructor Resources are available and are produced specifically to help and assist an instructor in preparing to deliver the course using the CCI materials. Contact your coordinator or administrator, or call your CCI Account Manager for information on how to access these resources.

Course Prerequisites

This course is designed for students who are familiar with personal computers, using a keyboard and using a mouse. The course assumes that students have completed the *Microsoft Windows* course or have equivalent Microsoft Windows knowledge and experience.

☐ start and run Windows	☐ use Minimize, Restore Down/Maximize, or Close
☐ use the taskbar	☐ use the left and right mouse buttons appropriately
☐ use the Start button	☐ understand file management techniques
☐ use the Help feature	☐ navigate between files, folders, or drives

System Requirements

According to the Microsoft Office System User's Guide, you must have the following in place prior to using the program:

- personal computer with a 500 megahertz (MHz) processor or higher

- 1 gigabyte (GB) hard disk drive to save the files used in this courseware

- 256 megabytes (MB) RAM or higher

- 1024x 768 or higher resolution monitor

- Windows XP with Service Pack (SP) 3 (32-bit), Windows Vista with SP1 (32-bit or 64-bit), Windows Server 2003 R2 (32-bit or 64-bit) with MSXML 6.0 installed, Windows Server 2008 with SP2 (32-bit or 64-bit), Windows 7 (32-bit or 64-bit)

- mouse or other pointing device compatible with Windows

In the materials contained in this courseware, we assume that you have met these criteria, and that you have successfully installed both Windows and Excel on your computer.

Classroom Setup

The features and exercises shown in this courseware were developed using the standard installation of Microsoft Office 2010 on a system with Windows 7.0. If your computers have Windows Vista installed, you will need to adjust accordingly to accommodate for the differences in dialog boxes when saving or opening files.

It is likely your instructor set up the classroom computers based on the system requirements to run the software for this course. Most software configurations on your computer are identical to those on your instructor's computer. However, your instructor may use additional software to demonstrate network interaction or related technologies.

MMM
More Materials on the Microsite!

The Microsoft Office Specialist Series contains exercises that students can use to learn each of the features discussed. More materials to practice and apply the skill sets are available from the CCI Office 2010 Microsite. Students are encouraged to register at http://2010.ccilearning.com in order access these additional activities both during and after completing the course.

Course Design

This course book was developed for instructor-led training and will assist you during class. Together with comprehensive instructional text and objectives checklists, this course book provides easy-to-follow hands-on lab exercises and a glossary of course-specific terms.

This course book is organized in the following manner:

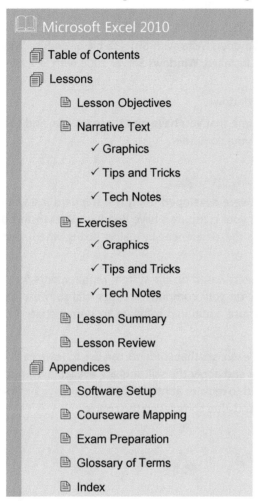

When you return to your home or office, you will find this course book to be a valuable resource for reviewing exercises and applying the skills you have learned. Each lesson concludes with questions that review the material. Lesson review questions are provided as a study resource only and in no way guarantee a passing score on a certification exam. Appendices in the back of this course book provide additional information.

Course Objectives

This course book teaches the skills you will need to successfully complete the Excel 2010 Core exam. These skill sets are introduced using a fictional company named Tolano Adventures, a travel service that is a department within Tolano Environmental Consulting. Tolano Adventures offers tours to the public that are friendly to the environment.

You will use Excel to create and edit professional-looking spreadsheets for a variety of purposes and situations. As you begin to build your skills, you will then create a variety of flyers and other promotional materials as well as explore different ways to share the information with internal and external customers.

After completing this course, you will be able to:

- understand and describe the concept of electronic spreadsheets
- identify the basic components of Excel
- enter data, symbols, and special characters into a worksheet
- move around in a workbook
- create, open, save, and close a workbook
- save a workbook in a previous Excel version format
- select a range of cells
- change and undo changes to the contents of cells
- cut, copy, and paste data in a worksheet using the Windows and Office Clipboard
- adjust column widths and row heights
- hide and unhide rows and columns
- insert and delete rows, columns, or cells
- find and replace data in a worksheet
- use AutoFill to copy or fill data or set up a series of data
- rename, insert, delete, copy or move worksheets
- create and edit simple formulas using math operators and cell references
- use commonly-used functions and conditional functions
- use absolute and relative cell references
- display and print formulas
- format numbers and decimal places
- enhance the worksheet using fonts, alignment, lines, borders, colors or patterns
- use the Format Painter
- clear cell contents and formatting
- apply themes, styles, and conditional formatting
- create and arrange worksheet windows
- split and freeze panes
- zoom in and out of worksheets
- print and preview worksheets
- use different workbook views
- add and preview page breaks
- change margins, orientation, or layout for printing a worksheet
- set headers and footers for a worksheet
- change Excel options
- create, edit, format and print charts
- create, customize, and remove Sparkline charts
- insert, modify and format clip art images, pictures, shapes, WordArt, and SmartArt objects
- sort data
- use the AutoFilter
- work with named ranges
- create, modify or remove a hyperlink
- use Office Backstage to share workbooks with others

Conventions and Graphics

The following conventions are used in CCI learning materials.

File Names or Database Field Names	File names or database field names are indicated in *italic* font style.
Exercise Text	Content to be entered by the student during an exercise appears in `Consolas` font.
Procedures	Procedures and commands you are instructed to activate are indicated in **bold** font style.
Features or Command Options	Menu options and features are listed in the left hand column and corresponding descriptions are in the right hand column.

The following graphics are used in CCI learning materials.

 Specific Keyboard Graphics to easily identify the key to press on the keyboard.

 This icon indicates the numbered objective from the Microsoft Office Specialist exam being covered in this topic. Refer to the Appendix for a complete listing of exam objectives.

 Technical Notes point out exceptions or special circumstances that you may find when working with a particular procedure, or may indicate there is another method to complete the task.

Notes, tips or tricks or alternative ways to accomplish a task are shown as memo notes.

MMM
See:
Understanding
Basic
Terminology

Whenever you see this icon, navigate to http://2010.ccilearning.com for **M**ore **M**aterials on the **M**icrosite. These additional activities include online exercises, creative application exercises, fun activities and additional review. They're designed to give you more practice using Excel 2010. Use the microsite in class or at home to practice some of the skills you are having trouble mastering, or to try your skills using different materials.

Learn the Skill

Learn the Skill graphics signal the start of step-by-step, hands-on exercises.

Microsoft®
Excel® 2010
Core Certification

Lesson 1: Introducing Excel

Lesson Objectives

The objectives of this lesson are to introduce the Excel program, learn how it works, and understand how to move in the program, create a workbook, enter data into a worksheet, and work with files. Upon completion of this lesson, you should be able to:

☐ understand what an electronic spreadsheet is

☐ understand what Excel is and what it can do

☐ identify elements on the Excel screen

☐ understand some basic terminology

☐ use the Quick Access Toolbar

☐ move around in Excel

☐ use keyboard shortcuts

☐ enter text, numbers, dates, and times

☐ insert symbols or special characters

☐ move around a worksheet

☐ use Backstage to save, create new, open, and close a workbook

☐ switch between workbooks

☐ save in a previous version Excel format

☐ manage files and folders

☐ select cells

What is an Electronic Spreadsheet?

An electronic spreadsheet is a software program that is primarily designed to perform any number of mathematical calculations simultaneously, replacing the tedious work of using pencils, paper, and calculators. Spreadsheets are extremely useful for solving financial and statistical problems, performing "what-if" analyses, and displaying charts and graphs.

You might imagine an electronic spreadsheet as a large piece of paper divided into rows and columns. The intersection of a single row and a single column is called a cell. To build a spreadsheet, you enter information into the individual cells. You can also perform calculations within each cell that depend on the values in other cells of the spreadsheet.

What is Excel?

Excel is an electronic spreadsheet program developed by Microsoft for the Windows environment. A powerful tool for analyzing and presenting information, Excel actually consists of three programs in one:

Spreadsheet	Use for entering and analyzing data, such as financial forecasting, cash flow, and auditing. Excel uses the term worksheet in place of spreadsheet.
Graphics	Use for creating charts to represent numeric data.
Database	Use for compiling and sorting lists.

Some of Excel's advantages are:

- It is relatively easy to learn. All Windows programs, such as Word, Excel, and PowerPoint, operate similarly. Many of the skills you learn in one Windows program carry over to others.

- Windows allows an exchange of data between programs. For example, you can create a chart in Excel and insert it into a memo you are writing in Word.

- Excel can produce output of print-shop quality using features such as the spelling checker and other tools that enhance your work and provide it with a truly professional look.

- Excel has a large selection of built-in mathematical, financial, statistical, and database functions. It includes 11 basic chart types, with each chart type having two or more subtypes. There are also some tools for forecasting or analysis, and a function helper to help you work with these built-in functions.

- Worksheets can be grouped together in a single file rather than separate files. In Excel, these files are called workbooks. Inside a workbook, there are several ways (such as renaming worksheet tabs) to manage the multiple worksheets.

- Excel uses AutoFill to fill selected cells with data that follows from the information in the first of the selected cells. For example, if you select four cells, and the first cell contains Qtr 1, AutoFill will fill in the next three cells with Qtr 2, Qtr 3, and Qtr 4.

- By default, editing occurs directly in the cell; this includes formatting portions of text and making font changes. Alternatively, you can perform edits in the formula bar.

Although Excel is a very large program, it is enjoyable to learn and use. Most people find it takes them less time to become competent and productive with Excel than they initially anticipated.

Looking at the Screen

When Excel starts, a new workbook opens and the screen displays as follows:

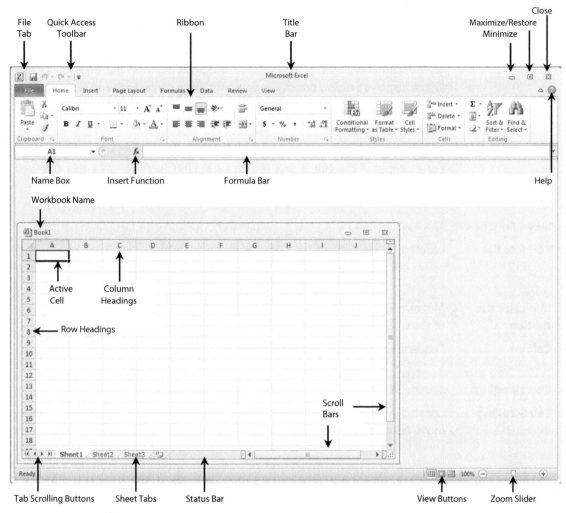

File Tab	When clicked, this displays the Backstage view from which you can select commands for a file (e.g., Save, Open, Close, etc.). A panel at the left displays commands that may include tabs with a set of sub-commands to manage the file.
Quick Access Toolbar	Located above the Ribbon, this provides quick access to frequently used commands. You can customize the toolbar to contain commands you use regularly.
Title Bar	Located at the top of the screen, the title bar indicates the contents of the window (e.g., Book1, Department Budget - Microsoft Excel). It may also show the text [Compatibility Mode] if the workbook you are using has been saved to be compatible with a previous version of Excel. If more than one window is open on the screen, the one with a title bar that is a darker color or intensity is the active window.
Microsoft Office Excel Help	Displays the Help window to obtain the latest help on a feature; Microsoft's Help option links to the Microsoft Web site for the latest information. Alternatively, you can also use the Help topics installed with Office.
Minimize, Maximize, Restore, or Close the Window	Located in the upper right-hand corner of the window, these buttons enable you to minimize (–) the application window to a button on the taskbar, maximize (☐) the program to full screen, restore (☐) the window to its original size, or close (✕) the application window.

Ribbon	A collection of tabs (e.g., File, Home, Insert, Page Layout, etc.) that provide quick access to commands you need to complete a task.
Ribbon Tab	Each Ribbon tab relates to a type of activity, such as inserting objects in a worksheet, or modifying the format of data in a worksheet. You will see extra tabs when applicable; for example, you will see the Chart Tools tab when you insert a chart.
Ribbon Group	Each tab contains groups of related commands to edit, format, or enhance items in your documents. Some groups have a Dialog box launcher button at the bottom right, which displays a dialog box or window with more commands and options.
Workbook Name	If the workbook is displayed in its own window, the title bar specifies the name of the current workbook.
Name Box	Located on the left below the Ribbon, this displays the cell address of the active cell. For example, if the Name Box displays A21, this indicates that A21 (the cell at the intersection of column A and row 21) is the active cell. In the example on the previous page, cell A1 is selected and the cell address is displayed in the Name Box.
Insert Function	This tool opens a dialog box to help you choose and insert a built-in function.
Formula Bar	Located to the right of the Name Box, the formula bar displays the contents of the active cell. Under certain circumstances, the formula bar can be used to make entries into the worksheet.
Minimize the Ribbon	Minimizing the Ribbon displays the Ribbon Tabs only, enabling you to see more rows of the worksheet on the screen.
Column Headings	Sequential letters at the top of each column enable you to track columns.
Row Headings	Sequential numbers on the left side of each row enable you to track rows.
Tab Scrolling Buttons	Located in the bottom left corner of the workbook window, these buttons allow you to move between the worksheet tabs. Buttons with a single triangle move the view one sheet for each click. Buttons with vertical lines before or after the triangles move the view to the first or last worksheet in the workbook. Note that this does not change the sheet you are viewing, only the tabs displayed at the bottom of the screen.
Scroll Bars	The vertical scroll bar located on the far right of the screen enables you to scroll up and down in the worksheet. The horizontal bar is located on the bottom right of the screen and enables you to scroll to the left or right in the worksheet.
Status Bar	This bar displays the current cell mode, auto calculations, the View buttons, and the Zoom slider. You can customize the Status bar to display keyboard locks and other features.
View Buttons	With these buttons, you can change quickly between alternate views for the worksheet on the screen. The views are Normal, Print Layout, and Page Break Preview.
Zoom Slider	The buttons at either side of the slider allow you to increase or decrease the zoom by 10%, or you can drag the slider button to choose a particular zoom percentage. Excel displays the current zoom percentage in the Zoom level button, at the right of the View buttons. You can also click this button to set a custom or specific zoom percentage.

The previous screen shot displays various commonly used areas of the Excel screen. Because you can customize the screen's appearance, not all parts always appear. For instance, some people like to have the workbook displayed (or restored) as a window on the screen, while others prefer to maximize the workbook. It is also possible to change the color scheme used for the program within Excel, not just by changing the option in Windows.

ScreenTips help identify buttons or elements on the tabs of the Ribbon and the screen. To view a ScreenTip, position the mouse cursor on the item. A tip then displays the name of the button along with a description of the purpose of this item. For some items, a keyboard shortcut may also display as an alternative for activating this feature.

A number of the elements shown in this section can be set to show or hide, as you prefer. In most cases, set items by clicking the **File** tab, clicking **Options,** and then clicking the **Popular** or **Display** categories.

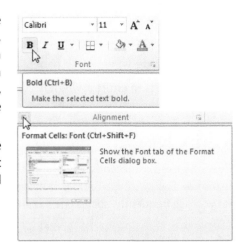

Understanding Basic Terminology

A worksheet is similar to an extremely large sheet of paper divided into rows and columns. In Excel, the rows are numbered from 1 to 1,048,576. Each of the 16,384 columns is named with a letter combination starting with A to Z, then AA to ZZ, then AAA to AZZ, and so on up to column XFD.

Workbook	A single Excel file containing one or more worksheets (e.g. Sheet1, Sheet2, Sheet3) is called a workbook You can have more than one workbook open at any time, but you can only work in one of them at any one time.
Worksheet	A worksheet is a two-dimensional arrangement of cells in rows and columns. When you use a workbook with multiple worksheets, you can only use one worksheet at any given time.
Cell	Located at the intersection of every row and column, a cell holds a single value, label, or formula. It may also contain comments, formatting, and other related data.
Cell Address	Excel has more than 17 billion (x 10^9) cells available per worksheet (1,048,576 rows x 16,384 columns). Each cell has its own distinct address (its point of column-by-row intersection), such as B7 (column B at row 7).
Active Cell	The cell where you are entering data or the current location of the cell marker is the active cell.
Sizing	When the worksheet is not maximized, the sizing button appears at the bottom right of the active window. Use the mouse to drag the corner to the desired size. In addition to this button, you can size any window by pointing to the border of the window; when the double-headed arrow ( ) is displayed, drag the mouse to change the width or height of the window.

Mouse Symbols

This section introduces some of the more common mouse symbols and their purposes:

⊕	Select a cell or range of cells in the worksheet.
⇗	Move or copy selected cells by dragging and dropping.
⇖	Select items, command buttons, and menu options.
↔ ↕ ↖	Size objects.
I	Edit text within the formula bar or a cell.
+	Indicates the use of the AutoFill feature to copy the contents of cells.

+	Provides a guide for the top left and bottom right corners when creating objects.
✛ ✚	Change the column width or row height.
✚ ✛	Split the window into panes.
→ ↓	Select an entire row/entire column.

Using the Quick Access Toolbar

The Quick Access Toolbar is located at the left of the title bar above the Ribbon and contains buttons for frequently used commands. By default, this toolbar contains the Excel control icon, Save, Undo, Redo, and Customize Quick Access Toolbar buttons. Use the right-most button to customize or display commands that you use frequently, such as new blank workbook, print, or spell check.

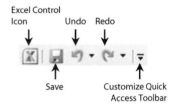

To customize the Quick Access Toolbar, use one of the following methods:

- Click **Customize Quick Access Toolbar** and click a button from the displayed list or click **More Commands**; or

- click **File**, click **Options**, and then click **Quick Access Toolbar**; or

- right-click anywhere on the Ribbon, click **Customize Quick Access Toolbar,** and click a button from the list or click **More Commands**.

You can also move the Quick Access Toolbar to a different position below the Ribbon using one of the following methods:

- Click **Customize Quick Access Toolbar** and then click **Show Below the Ribbon**; or

- right-click the Ribbon, click **Customize Quick Access Toolbar,** and then click **Show Quick Access Toolbar Below the Ribbon**.

Using the Ribbon

The Ribbon can help you quickly find commands you require to complete a task. Commands are grouped on tabs with each tab relating to a type of activity, such as inserting items into a document, changing the view of your document, formatting text in the document, and so on. You can customize the Ribbon to display commands you use frequently in a particular order, or to add or remove commands for a Ribbon tab.

To reduce screen clutter, contextual tabs appear only when they are applicable (e.g. Picture Tools, Header and Footer Tools, Table Tools, etc.)

The active button is the one that appears in a different color or has an outline around it; many of these deactivate when you click the same button or click another choice. For instance, the **Bold** command can be applied to selected text by clicking that button; to turn off the boldface, click the same button again. If you want text to be larger, click the down arrow for the **Size** button and choose the required size. When you need to change the font size again, click the down arrow for **Size** and then select the new size.

When the Ribbon displays different choices (as shown in the Shape Styles list in the screen above), one item has a border around it to indicate it is active. To see how the text would appear with another style, point the mouse on one of the other items; Excel previews the effect that will take place if it is selected.

Each tab on the Ribbon contains groups with similar commands. For example, the **Home** tab has a group called **Font** that contains buttons for formatting text characters, and the **Insert** tab contains a group with different types of graphics or illustrations that can be inserted into a worksheet.

If a group shows a feature with a vertical scroll bar, it also has a button below the bottom scroll button, a triangle with a bar above it, which you can click to display the full list or gallery for that option.

This is the **More** button and, when clicked, it displays a gallery with more options, as seen at the right. As you point the mouse cursor at an option, Excel displays a **Live Preview** for how the selected item will appear if you apply this feature. You can turn off this feature in Excel Options.

Click the **Dialog box launcher** button at the lower right of a group to show the corresponding dialog box with more options for this feature. In some cases, a task pane may appear at the left or right side of the screen instead of a dialog box. The **Dialog box launcher** button displays the name of the dialog box or task pane window that will appear when clicked.

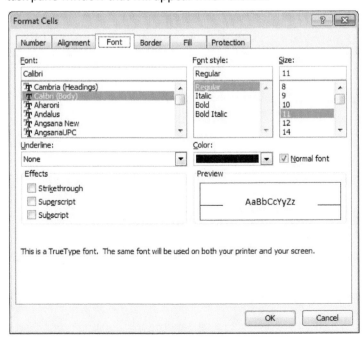

Dialog Box   Window/Task Pane

Within the dialog box, you can select items from the lists, use the arrow for a list box to display more choices for that list, or click a command to turn the feature on or off. It may display a preview of the changes.

A dialog box displays the various options that you can select to perform a change to a worksheet, or cells within a worksheet. Once you click OK to perform the change, the dialog box closes. A task pane is similar to a dialog box because it is used to make changes to parts of the worksheet, except that it remains open until you close it. An example of a task pane is the Office Clipboard, which collects and displays the items selected when the Cut or Copy command is used.

If you want to show more lines on the screen or you do not want the display the Ribbon, you can minimize it. To minimize the Ribbon, use one of the following methods:

- Use the ⌃ button at the far right of the top of the Ribbon; or
- right-click anywhere on the Ribbon and then click **Minimize the Ribbon;** or
- double-click on any Ribbon tab; or
- press Ctrl + F1.

Using the Keyboard

You can also access commands in Excel using the keyboard; some users consider the keyboard to be a faster method for accessing commands. There is also the benefit of consistency between Windows programs, in that some keyboard shortcuts are the same in all Windows programs, such as pressing Ctrl + C to copy, Ctrl + S to save, or Ctrl + P to print.

These keyboard shortcuts are also known as *Hot Keys*. The following lists many of the commonly used hot keys in Excel. Note that different commands are activated when the keyboard key is combined with the Shift, Ctrl, or Alt key:

Key	Command	With Shift key	With Ctrl key	With Alt key
F1	Help		Show/hide Ribbon	
F2	Edit			Save As
F4	Redo			Exit Excel
F10	Activate menu			
Delete	Clear	Cut	Clear	
B			Bold	
C			Copy	
F			Find	
G			Go to	
H			Replace	
I			Italic	
P			Print	
S			Save	
U			Underline	
V			Paste	
X			Cut	
Y			Redo	
Z			Undo	

To access the Ribbon using the keyboard, press Alt or F10 to display the keyboard buttons for the commands in the Ribbon.

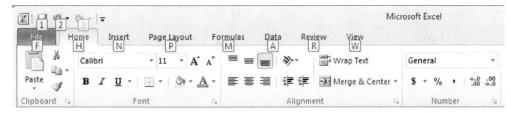

When you press the key for the appropriate feature, Excel displays the next set of keys you can use to select a command or feature. For example, pressing P displays the **Page Layout** tab.

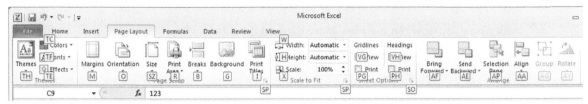

Pressing B will allow you to access the **Breaks** command, which, in this case, displays a menu with more options.

You can also use the keyboard to perform the following actions:

- To access another tab, with the Ribbon active, press ← or → to move to the appropriate tab.
- To show or hide the Ribbon, press Ctrl + F1.
- To change the highlight or focus from the active tab, the status bar, or your worksheet, press F6. For example, to switch view modes, press F6 to move the focus from the worksheet to the status bar. Then press Tab to move to the Page Layout button and, when it is highlighted, press Enter.
- To display a shortcut menu, press Shift + F10.
- To move from the tab to the command in the first group, press Tab. Continue pressing Tab to move to the next command, or Shift + Tab to move to the previous command. This only occurs once you press Alt or F10 to display the keyboard shortcuts on the Ribbon.

To activate the selected command, press Enter.

- To exit or cancel a selection at any time, press Esc. You may need to press Esc more than once to return to your worksheet.

 ## Learn the Skill

In this exercise, you will start Excel and access some of the tools to see how they work.

1 Start Microsoft Excel, if not already open.

2 Click the **File** tab and review the contents of this screen.

3 Click the **File** tab once more to exit this screen.

4 Use the mouse pointer to point to the **View** tab.

Notice how the **View** tab highlights, even though you have not clicked it.

5   Click the **View** tab to activate it.

6   Point to **Page Layout** in the Workbook Views group and notice how the color of the button changes.

7   Click **Page Layout** to see how the view changes.

8   On the **View** tab, in the Workbook Views group, click **Normal** to switch to the default view.

9   Move the cursor to the Zoom slider at the bottom right of the screen. Click and drag the slider to the right until you see the zoom percentage change to approximately **200%**.

10   At the top right of the Ribbon, click the **Minimize the Ribbon** button.

Notice how you now can see a few more rows on the screen.

11   Click and drag the slider the other way so the percentage changes to 50%, then drag the slider to return the zoom to **100%**.

12   Click **Expand the Ribbon** once more to re-display the Ribbon.

13   Now move the cursor to the top of the screen and click some of the tabs to see how the commands are categorized and grouped on the tabs.

14   Press (Alt) to display the keyboard shortcuts on the tab.

15   Press (P) to display the **Page Layout** tab.

16   Then press (M) to display the **Margins** options.

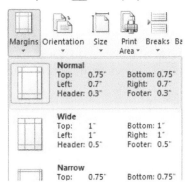

17   Press (Esc) to cancel this option.

Notice that the keys are still displayed on the tab, so you can continue to use the keyboard to choose another command.

18   Press (Esc) again until the shortcut keystrokes no longer appear.

Identifying Screen Symbols

Occasionally you may see different types of symbols appear after performing a task or activating a command. These symbols are visual clues provided within Excel to help you identify a particular status or recognize that other options may be available to you for this command.

Some of these symbols include:

Circular References: D6	The Circular indicator appears in the status bar if Excel finds a circular reference in the current worksheet. A circular reference occurs when a formula in one cell references another cell. The second cell, in turn, will also contain a formula that refers back to the first cell, directly or indirectly. Excel will display the double-headed blue arrow between these offending cells.

(AutoFill options)	This appears when you use the AutoFill feature to copy data or formulas into adjacent cells. Excel provides you with options for this item. When you point to this button, it appears with a drop-down arrow. Click the arrow to display more options for this item.
(Paste Options)	Excel identifies that you have pasted an item and provides other options for the paste action. When you point to this button, it appears with a drop-down arrow. Click the arrow to display more options for this item.

We discuss more options for using many of these buttons later in this courseware. If you would like more information at this point, use the Help feature in Microsoft Office Excel, or refer to the User's Guide.

Entering Data in a Worksheet

2.1

If you design and build it in a logical manner, an Excel worksheet is a very powerful tool. The basic building block of every worksheet is entering data into the cells.

Types of Data

You can make three main types of entries when you are inserting data into worksheet cells:

Numeric	Numeric data form the core of all spreadsheets. This type of data consists of number, date, or time values that you enter directly into a worksheet cell. These numbers can not only show information in a worksheet, but can be used to calculate other values on the same or other worksheets. By default, numeric values align to the right.
Text	Text data consist of alphabetic and numeric characters and most printable symbols. Text data are usually labels or titles used to describe and explain the data in adjoining cells. Text is seldom included in calculations, but Excel does include several functions that apply to text data. If you enter a text value that is wider than the cell, it will flow into the adjacent cells as long as those cells are empty. By default, text data align to the left.
Formulas	Formulas, which you enter in individual cells, are composed of values, cell references, arithmetic operators, and special functions for calculating and displaying result. These results may then become part of other formulas located in other cells. The ability to use formulas is what differentiates spreadsheets from word processing software like Microsoft Word.

Entering Text

3.3

To enter data, move your pointer to the desired cell, click in it, and type the entry. If you make a typing error while still entering information in a cell, press the (Backspace) key to erase your mistake. When you have finished entering data in a cell, press the (Enter) key to move the cell pointer automatically to the next cell down. Alternatively, use your mouse to click another cell (or press any arrow key), which performs the same result of storing the data in that cell and moving the cell pointer to the new location.

The best way to begin any worksheet is to enter column and row titles that identify the purpose of the numeric data. When you enter titles for the worksheet, you are creating an outline of the relationships you will later represent mathematically.

When typing information, notice that Excel displays the text in two places:

- You can enter or edit data directly in the active cell where the pointer appears, or you can enter or edit it in the formula bar. The latter method is especially useful for very long data entries. In either case, the data is displayed in both places.

- Text entries can be up to 32,767 characters, although a maximum of 255 characters are displayed. If a text entry is longer than the width of the cell, it will extend past the column border after you have pressed ⟨Enter⟩, as long as there is nothing entered in the adjoining cells. Entries in adjoining cells truncate the display of the text at the border. The entire entry goes into the cell, but only that portion of it that fits in the available space is visible. By default, Excel aligns text data on the left side of the cell. You can easily change the appearance and alignment of a text entry.

Learn the Skill

This exercise demonstrates how to enter text data into a worksheet cell, which will serve as a label or title for other cells containing numeric data.

1   In a new blank workbook, click in cell A2.

2   Type: Price Quote and press ⟨Enter⟩.

Notice the current active cell is now **A3**. When you press ⟨Enter⟩, Excel completes the entry of data in the current cell, then moves the cell pointer to the next cell down.

3   Press ⟨Enter⟩ twice to move down two rows.

4   In cell **A5**, type: Airfare and press ⟨Enter⟩.

5   In cell **A6**, type: Hotel and press ⟨Enter⟩.

6   In cell **A7**, type: Car Rental and press ⟨Enter⟩.

7   In cell **A8**, type: Taxes and press ⟨Enter⟩.

If you entered the wrong value into a cell, simply select the cell and type the correct entry again to replace the incorrect value.

Now try a feature called AutoComplete, in which Excel determines whether you are repeating the same text as in a previous cell and completes it for you. If it is the text you want, you simply press ⟨Enter⟩ to accept it.

8   In cell **A9**, type: A.

Notice that Excel automatically offers you a text label, based on your previous entry. You can now press the ⟨Enter⟩ key to accept it or continue typing the value that you want.

9   Ignore the suggested label and continue typing the rest of the text: irport Fees.

Notice that the text extends further than the default column width for this text entry. If you enter data in the next column, the part of this new label that overflows into the next column will appear to be cut off.

10   In cell **A12**, type: Airline:

Notice this time that the AutoComplete feature did not turn on. This is because of the blank cells (**A10** and **A11**) that are preventing Excel from "looking up" a previous similar value in this column.

11   Enter the following in the remaining cells:

Cell	Text
A13	Hotel:
B12	Great West Airline
B13	Hotel Zathura

Your screen should look something like the following example:

Entering Numbers

2.1

Numbers, such as those representing dollar and percentage values, are constant—that is, they do not change. They are typically used as part of calculations, with results appearing in other parts of the workbook.

By default, Excel aligns numeric values to the right side of a cell. They are displayed with no commas unless you enter them at the same time. Extraneous zeroes are not displayed, even if entered at the same time. You can format the values to your preference at a later time.

If you enter a value that contains a mixture of alphabetic and numeric digits (e.g., part numbers such as T-1000), Excel treats the entire entry as text and aligns it to the left of the cell.

Learn the Skill

This exercise demonstrates how to enter text data into a worksheet cell, which will serve as a label or title for other cells containing numeric data.

1 In cell **B5** of the workbook, type: 450.

2 In cell **B6**, type: 1,050.

3 In cell **B7**, type: 225.

4 In cell **B8**, type: 46.50.

5 In cell **B9**, type: 9.9.

6 Click in cell **A9**.

Notice in cell A9 that the part of the text entry that had overflowed into cell B9 is now hidden because a value was entered into cell B9. However, the formula bar shows that the data in cell A9 is unchanged.

7 Click in cell **D8**, and type: 3.1%.

Excel interprets the entered values as numeric and aligns them on the right of their cells. However, if you enter any non-recognizable characters, or insert any commas or decimal points in the wrong position, Excel will treat the entire contents of that cell as a label, and align it on the left side of the cell.

8 In cell **D9**, type: 2,2% (including the comma).

Your screen should look something like the following:

⊿	A	B	C	D	E
1					
2	Price Quote				
3					
4					
5	Airfare	450			
6	Hotel	1,050			
7	Car Rental	225			
8	Taxes	46.5		3.10%	
9	Airport Fe	9.9		2,2%	
10					
11					
12	Airline:	Great West Airline			
13	Hotel:	Hotel Zathura			
14					

Notice that Excel aligned the data on the left side of the cell. Because you entered a comma instead of a period, Excel assumes that the cell entry is a text value.

9   Move back to cell **D9** and type: 2.2% to replace the incorrect contents of that cell.

Entering Dates and Times

2.1

Excel is also capable of handling date and time values. When entering dates, note the following:

- If you enter a full date value including the month, day, and year value, the date value will display as dd-mmm-yy by default.

- The date value does not have to be the full day, month, and year. It can be just the day and month (format is dd-mmm), or the month and year only (format is mmm-yy).

- If you enter only the name of a month, Excel will treat it as a text value. If you enter only a day or year value, Excel will treat it as a numeric value. In these cases, Excel will not recognize that you intended to enter a part of a date value.

- When entering the date, Excel attempts to interpret what you have entered. For example, the following are acceptable date values:

  September 15, 2010 (you must include the comma followed by a space)

  Sep 15, 10

  15-Sep-10

  09/15/10 (month, day, year sequence — see next bullet)

  9-15-10

  Sep 2010

  Sep 15

- If you enter the date using only numeric values (e.g., 09/15/10 as shown above), the sequence of the values must match the date sequence specified in the Windows Control Panel, Regional and Language Options. For the United States, the normal date sequence is month/day/year. For Canada and the United Kingdom, the sequence is day/month/year. If Excel is not able to interpret the date value, it will appear as a text label (left aligned in the cell).

When entering time values, note the following:

- The time must consist of hours and minutes, as a minimum, in the format of hh:mm. You can also add seconds and the AM/PM indicator. The alternative to the latter is to use the 24-hour clock format.

- The following are acceptable time values:

   1:15 PM (be sure to add a space before the AM/PM indicator)

   13:15

   13:15:01

   1:15:01 PM

   1:15

Learn the Skill

This exercise demonstrates the use of dates.

1   In cell **A3**, type: `As of:` and press [Tab].

2   In cell **B3** type: `Jun 30` and press [Enter].

   Notice that Excel puts the date in the default format and aligns it to the right.

Step 2 works correctly only if your computer's region setting specifies a date sequence of month/day/year. If the date sequence is day/month/year (as in Canada and the UK), you must enter the full date including year—Jun 30, yyyy. Doing step 2 above with your region setting as English (Canada) will cause Excel to interpret the date as June 1, 1930.

3   In cell **D3** type: `Expires:` and press [Tab].

4   In cell **E3** type: `Jul 15, 2010` and press [Enter].

	A	B	C	D	E	F
1						
2	Price Quote					
3	As of:	30-Jun		Expires:	15-Jul-10	
4						
5	Airfare	450				
6	Hotel	1,050				
7	Car Rental	225				
8	Taxes	46.5		3.10%		
9	Airport Fe	9.9		2.20%		
10						
11						
12	Airline:	Great West Airline				
13	Hotel:	Hotel Zathura				

5   Select cell **E3**.

   The date value for this cell also appears in the formula bar. The date value sequence corresponds to the setting in the Windows Control Panel.

6   Select cell **B3**.

   Because you have not included a year in this date value, Excel assumes it is the current year and adds it for you. If you want a different year, you have to enter it as part of the date.

Inserting Symbols and Special Characters

2.1

There may be instances when special characters are required. Because the standard QWERTY keyboard is limited to about 96 characters (including upper and lower case characters), Excel provides shortcut keys to create many commonly used characters. You must select other characters from a specific font family. To insert a symbol, on the **Insert** tab in the **Text** group, click **Symbol**.

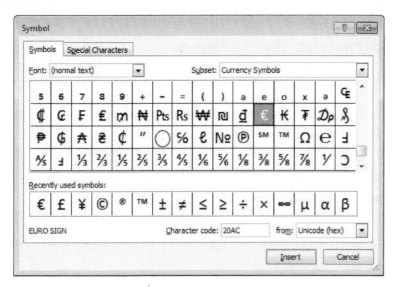

Font	Select the font that contains the characters you want to insert. There are thousands of special characters to use. Many typefaces or fonts are classified as "symbol" fonts and offer special characters, such as animals, arrows, bullets, or Wingdings and Zapf Dingbats. Other fonts contain primarily alpha character types.
Subset	If Unicode is selected in the from box, the subset type is shown. For instance, with Times New Roman, as you scroll through the list of characters, the subset changes from Basic Latin to Basic Greek, Hebrew, and so on.
Recently used symbols	This box displays a list of the most recent symbols used. To use one of these symbols again, click on it in this list.
Character code	This box displays the ASCII character code for the selected symbol in hexadecimal format or decimal format, depending on the setting in the from box.
From	This enables you to select between the Unicode (expanded) character set or the Standard ASCII character set. ASCII codes can be displayed in either decimal or hexadecimal notation.

You can also insert special character symbols—symbols that are commonly used in documents—instead of searching through the symbols for the font that contains the particular character you need. When you click on the **Special Characters** tab, you should see a screen similar to the following example:

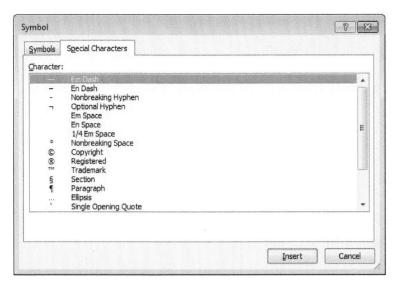

Many characters have shortcut keyboard methods assigned to them, making it easy to enter the symbol. You can also insert a symbol by typing its decimal ASCII code on the numeric keypad while holding down the (Alt) key.

Once you have inserted a symbol into a document, you can be treat it in the same manner as a text character (i.e., format it to your preferences by changing the color, size, position, etc.)

Learn the Skill

This exercise demonstrates the use of symbols and special characters.

1   In cell **A1**, type: Tolano Adventures but do **not** press the (Enter) key yet.

2   On the **Insert** tab, in the **Symbols** group, click **Symbol**.

3   Click the **Special Characters** tab.

4   Select the ™ **Trademark** symbol, and click **Insert**.

5   Click **Close** to exit the Symbol dialog box.

6   Press (Enter) to complete the entry into this cell.

7   Select cell **A14**. On the **Insert** tab, in the **Symbols** group, click **Symbol**.

8   In the Symbol dialog box, select the **Symbols** tab and click the Subset down arrow, and select **Currency Symbols**.

9   Select the € **Euro Sign** symbol and click **Insert**.

10   Click **Close** to exit the Symbol dialog box.

11   Type: 25 local resort fee to be paid on arrival at hotel. and press (Enter).

Your document should look similar to the following example:

	A	B	C	D	E	F
1	Tolano Adventures™					
2	Price Quote					
3	As of:	30-Jun		Expires:	15-Jul-10	
4						
5	Airfare	450				
6	Hotel	1,050				
7	Car Rental	225				
8	Taxes	46.5		3.10%		
9	Airport Fe	9.9		2.20%		
10						
11						
12	Airline:	Great West Airline				
13	Hotel:	Hotel Zathura				
14	€25 local resort fee to be paid on arrival at hotel.					
15						

Moving Around the Worksheet

1.1

You can move around the cells of a worksheet very quickly by either using the keyboard or scrolling with the mouse. Use one of the following methods to move around in the worksheet:

Scroll Bars	Click the arrow buttons at either end of the scroll bars to move one row or column at a time. Click on the scroll box (the size will vary depending on the zoom percentage) and drag to display another location in the worksheet.
←, →, ↑, ↓	Press one of these directional keys to move one cell at a time.
Home	Press this key to move to column A in whichever row the active cell is.
Ctrl + Home	Press this key combination to move to cell A1, regardless of where you are in the worksheet.
Ctrl + End	Press this key combination to move to the last cell in the data table.
Ctrl + G / F5	Display the Go To dialog box so you can move quickly to a cell reference, range name, or bookmark, or use the Special button to find specific types of information (e.g., comments, blanks, etc.)

Working with Workbooks

As you begin using workbooks, you need to consider how to organize your files for quick and easy access. This includes considerations such as how you name the file, where you save it, whether it needs to be saved as a specific file type, and whether you want to add or change the file properties to make it easier to find at a later date. The Save commands are located in Backstage via the **File** tab.

Saving Workbooks

To be able to recall your work later, you must save your workbook before exiting Excel or turning off your computer. The saved file also provides an excellent fall-back option if you try something in your worksheet that does not work as you expected, and you are unable or unwilling to undertake all the necessary steps to correct the problem.

When naming a workbook, keep the following in mind:

• Workbook names must follow the same basic rules as naming files in Windows: a maximum of 255 characters (including the drive and folder path), and none of these characters: / \ : * ? " < > |

• File names should be descriptive so that you can identify the contents quickly.

- Excel automatically assigns a .xlsx extension or file type at the end of the file name, so you need not do this. You only have to type in the name for the workbook.

- Files can be saved with two different types of save commands:

  - Use **Save As** to save a new document or to save an existing document with a new name or new location.

  - Use **Save** to save changes to the active workbook but retain the existing name and keep the file in the existing location.

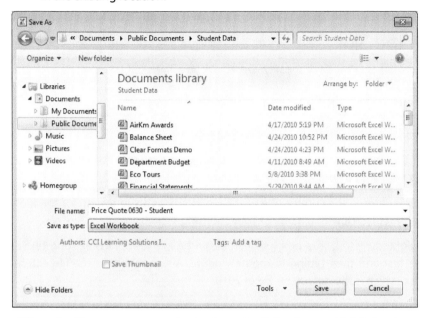

- When the file name appears in the Save As dialog box as highlighted text, begin typing the new file name to insert the new file name for this workbook. Use the arrow direction keys to move anywhere in the existing file name to add or delete text to the file name.

- To save a workbook as a different file type, such as an earlier version of Excel, use **Save as type** in the Save As dialog box to find the file format you need.

- By default, Windows sets up the Documents library to store files. Excel draws on this, but you are not restricted to this folder. You can:

  Libraries are available only with Windows 7.

  - Create your own folders to help organize files by clicking **New folder** on the command bar in the Save As dialog box.

  - Save in any location that you can access (hard drive, thumb drive, flash disk, network drive, etc.)

If you are unsure whether you have saved a file previously, look at the workbook name in the title bar to see if it is the default name of *Book1* (or *Bookx* where the *x* is a number). Alternatively, use **Save As** to give the workbook a different name, thereby ensuring you do not accidentally overwrite the workbook currently stored on the hard drive with the one on your screen.

Even if the file already exists in one location, you can save the same file to another location. Be careful with having files with the same name in different locations, as it may be difficult to determine which is the most current or valid version to use.

To view the file type (the extension part of the file name), you need to turn on this option using Windows Explorer. Click **Organize**, **Folder and search options**, and on the **View** tab, deselect **Hide extensions for known file types**. Showing the file types can be helpful when determining which file you want to use; for example, two files may have the same name, but the file extensions show that one is in Excel 2010 format (.xlsx) while the other is in Excel 2003 format (.xls).

To save changes made to the current workbook using the same file name, use one of the following methods:

- Click **File** and then **Save;** or
- on the Quick Access Toolbar, click **Save;** or
- press $\boxed{\text{Ctrl}} + \boxed{\text{S}}$.

You can use **Views** in the Save As dialog box to help display the folders and files in the way you prefer (e.g., list, thumbnails, etc.)

Learn the Skill

In this exercise, you will save the new workbook you have just created.

1   In the Quick Access Toolbar, click **Save**.

2   In the left pane of the Save As dialog box, navigate to where the student data files are located for this courseware. Check with your instructor if you are unsure of the location.

Notice that Excel has entered the current title of the workbook as a suggestion for the file name. You can use this name, or replace it with a name of your choosing.

Whenever text is highlighted (Book1) in a box, you can begin typing to replace existing text rather than deleting the characters first and then typing in the new name. Also notice that the file extension in the **Save as type** box is .xlsx, which is the default for Excel 2010.

3   Click in the **File name** field, and type: Price Quote 0630 -Student where Student is your name.

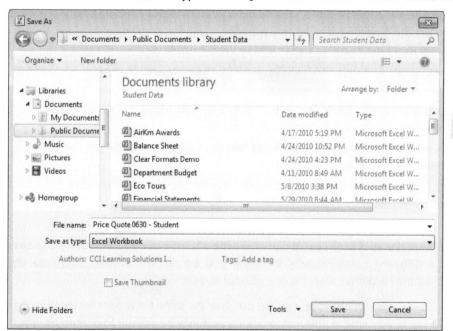

You can also press ENTER after entering the file name to save the file.

The 0630 in the workbook name helps to differentiate this file from the many other price quote files that this user may have stored on the same drive.

4   Click **Save**.

Notice that the title bar now contains the new file name as visual confirmation that the file is now saved.

Creating a New Workbook

When you start up Excel, you open a new blank workbook by default. You can also create a new workbook at any time and you can have more than one workbook open and on the screen at any time.

Each time you create a new workbook in a current session, Excel numbers it sequentially, starting at 1 as *Book#*, with # representing the number of new workbooks created during this session of Excel. When you exit Excel and later reopen the program, the numbering begins at 1 again.

To create a new blank workbook, use one of the following methods:

- For a new blank document, click **File**, click **New**, click **Blank workbook**, and then click **Create;** or
- press Ctrl + N ; or
- to choose from a variety of pre-designed documents called templates, click **File**, click **New**, click a template, and then click **Create**.

Instead of starting with a blank workbook, you can create a workbook using a template. A template is simply a pre-designed workbook that may already contain data, formulas, and other objects, which saves you time and effort. Examples of common templates are sales invoices, balance sheets, and loan amortization schedules. Additional templates are also available from the Microsoft Office.com website.

Learn the Skill

In this exercise, you will create a new workbook using different methods.

1 Press Ctrl + N .

You should now have a new blank workbook titled as *Book2* on the screen.

2 If necessary, click Restore Window for the *Book2* window so that both *Book1* and *Book2* appear together in the Excel application window.

Two workbooks are now visible on your screen.

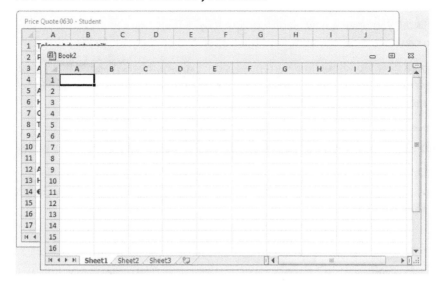

Notice that the Windows Taskbar shows two workbooks are currently open.

3   Click **File** once more and then click **New**, and click **Sample templates**.

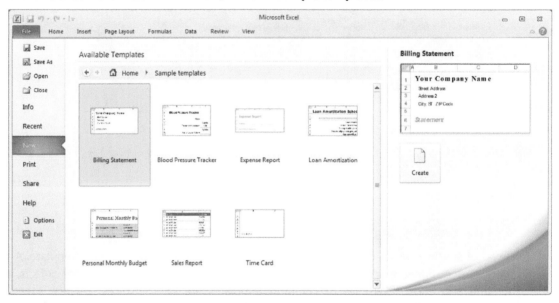

Note that a preview of the currently selected template is displayed in the right hand pane.

4   In the **Available Templates** pane, click **Loan Amortization**, and then click **Create**.

Excel now displays a blank loan amortization schedule.

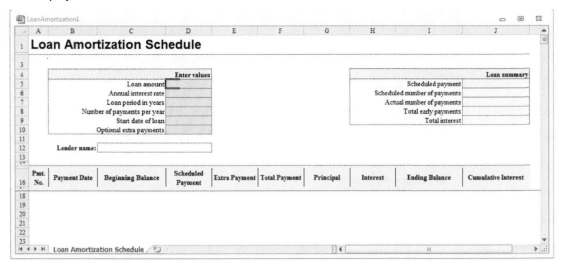

This is an example of how templates can save you time and effort when creating a workbook. Many of the elements you see in this document will be covered in more depth later in this courseware.

You can also select from your own templates, from Microsoft's Web site, or other Internet Web sites. To use templates from Microsoft's Web site, select one of the items from the list in the **Microsoft Office Online** section of the Templates pane.

5   Click **File** once more and then click **New**.

6   Type: budgets in the text box on the right side of the Office.com Templates bar, and press Enter.

7   Select one of the Event budget templates and click **Download**.

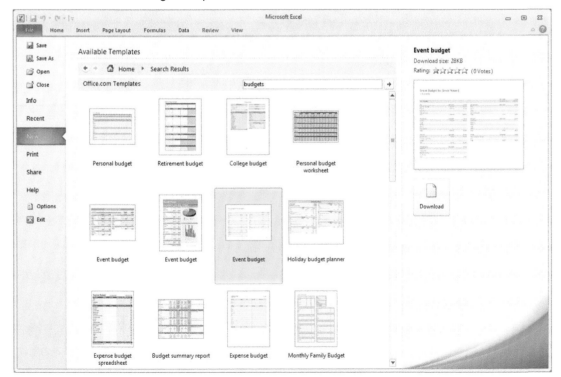

Switching Between Workbooks

4.3

When you have multiple workbooks open on the screen, you can switch between workbooks quickly and easily using one of the following methods:

- On the **View** tab, in the **Window** group, click **Switch Windows;** or

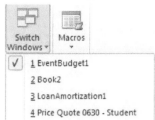

- if you are using Windows 7: click the **Excel** button on the taskbar to display a preview of each open workbook; or

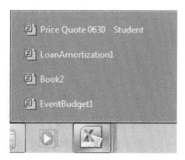

- if you are using Windows XP or Vista: click on the workbook icon in the taskbar; or

- if Excel is in Restore Down view, the open workbooks may display in a cascading layout; click the title bar for the appropriate workbook to pull it to the front.

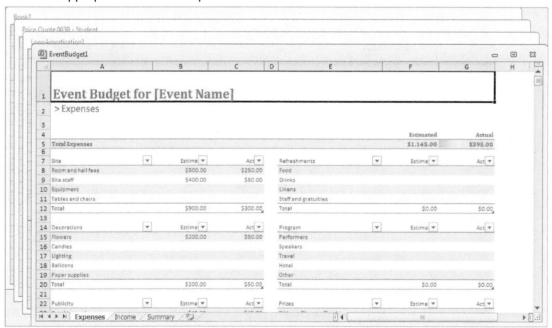

Learn the Skill

This exercise demonstrates how to switch between multiple workbooks that are open at the same time.

1 Click the **View** tab.

2 In the Windows group at the right, click **Switch Windows**.

3 Click *LoanAmortization1*.

This workbook should now be displayed on top of the other workbooks.

4 Point at the **Excel** button on the taskbar at the bottom of the screen.

5 Click *Price Quote 0630 - Student*.

Opening a Workbook

If you want to work with a previously created and saved workbook, you must first open it. You can open as many workbooks as needed; the only limitation is the amount of memory available on your system to handle multiple workbooks.

You may not always know or recall the name or location of the Excel workbook and you may have to use the Windows Explorer to try to find the workbook on the computer or on the network. Alternatively, Excel displays a list of the most recently opened workbooks, which you can use if you know that the workbook was recently used on the computer you are using.

Use one of the following methods to open a workbook:

- Click **File**, click **Recent**, and then click the file from the list of recently used workbooks; or

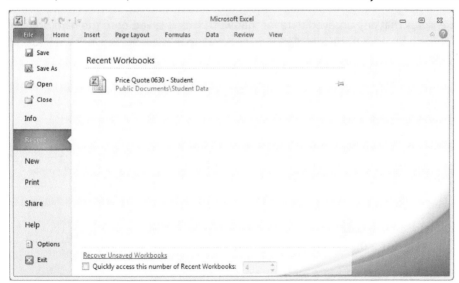

As you open workbooks, Excel displays the files in the same order as you opened them, with the most recent at the top of the list. As you reach the maximum number of files that show in this list, the oldest drops from the list. You can click the pin icon at the right of the file name to make this file always available in the list until it is unpinned. By default, you can see a list of up to 20 recent workbooks at a time; this number can be customized.

- click **File** and then click **Open**; or
- press $\boxed{\text{Ctrl}}$+$\boxed{\text{O}}$ or $\boxed{\text{Ctrl}}$+$\boxed{\text{F12}}$.

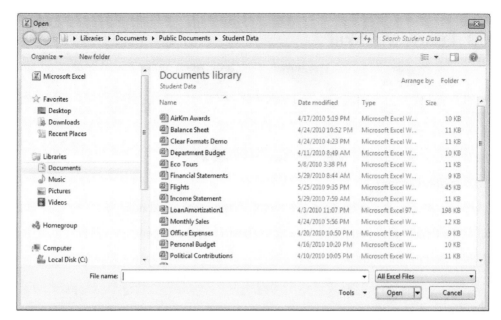

Once the Open dialog box displays, you can navigate using the mouse or keyboard to display the files or folders and then use one of the following methods to open a document:

- Double-click the file name; or

- click on the file name to select it, and then click **Open** or press (Enter); or

- if the file is stored in a different location, navigate to the location and then use one of the above methods to open a file.

Closing a Workbook

Once you have finished creating or updating a workbook, close it to clear the screen and free up computer memory. This ensures that any unsaved data for that workbook is saved onto the hard drive, and protects the workbook from unintended changes. Closing your workbook is much like closing a book and putting it back on the shelf before opening another book.

If you try to close a workbook containing unsaved changes, Excel displays a message to advise you of the unsaved changes. You can then choose to close the workbook without saving the changes, or save the changes and close the workbook.

You can use one of the following methods to close a workbook:

- Click **Close** for the Excel application (this action will close all open workbooks); or

- click **File** and then **Close;** or

- press (Ctrl)+(W) or (Ctrl)+(F4); or

- click the ⬚ button for the workbook.

Using the last two methods keeps Excel open after you close the last workbook on screen. The first method displays the Windows desktop because all workbooks and Excel are closed.

If you add or change something in a new or existing document, which has not yet been saved, Excel prompts you with the option of saving the workbook before closing it. If the workbook has been open for more than 10 minutes (this time interval can be changed), an additional note is added to the message box to indicate that it will still be available even if you accidentally discard the workbook without saving it.

 or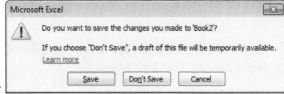

When you close all documents in Excel, the screen looks something like this:

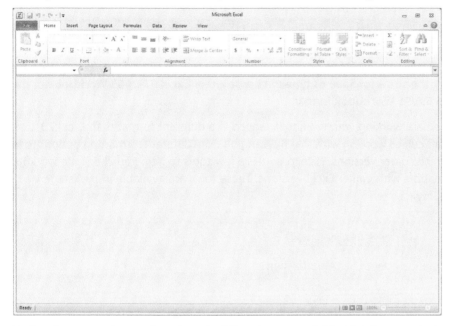

MMM
Opening,
Saving and
Closing
Online
Exercise

Notice that no options, other than the **File** tab, are available. This is to remind you that no workbooks are currently active in Excel, and you have to create a new workbook or open an existing one before the features become available.

Learn the Skill

In this exercise, you will use several different formats to save and then close multiple documents.

1   Click **File** and then **Open**.

2   Navigate to where the student data files are located, as directed by your instructor.

3   Click the *Popular Tours* file, and click **Open**.

Assume that you are now satisfied with viewing the contents of this workbook, and you no longer need to continue viewing it.

4   Click **File**, and then click **Close**.

The *Popular Tours* file is no longer on the screen.

5   On the **View** tab, in the Windows group, click **Switch Windows**.

6   Click LoanAmortization1.

7   Click the **Close** button in the upper right corner of this workbook.

8   When a message displays: "Do you want to save the changes you made to Loan Amortization1?" click **Don't Save**.

9   Click the Excel button in the taskbar, then click on the *Price Quote 0630 - Student* workbook to make it active, and press Ctrl+W.

10   Point at the Excel button in the taskbar, then point at the *EventBudget1* workbook, and click ☒ for that workbook. Click **Don't Save**.

11   Click **File** and then click **Exit** to close down Excel and discard the *Book2* workbook.

Working with the Compatibility Mode

Excel provides two different formats for saving your workbooks if you need to share it with other people who may be using an older version of Excel. These older Excel versions are not able to open workbooks that use the Excel 2010 (or Excel 2007) format. To save a workbook in an older Excel format, click **File**, click **Save As** and then click the arrow for **Save as type** to choose either **Excel 97-2003 Workbook** or the much older **Microsoft Excel 5.0/95 Workbook** format.

Occasionally, when you are working with workbooks saved in a different format than Excel 2010 (or Excel 2007), you may find difficulties working with that file, ranging from different formatting options to features that did not exist with the older versions. Excel provides a few tools to help you check the workbook and ensure that it is compatible with earlier Excel versions. These tools are available in Backstage via the **File** tab and the **Info** category.

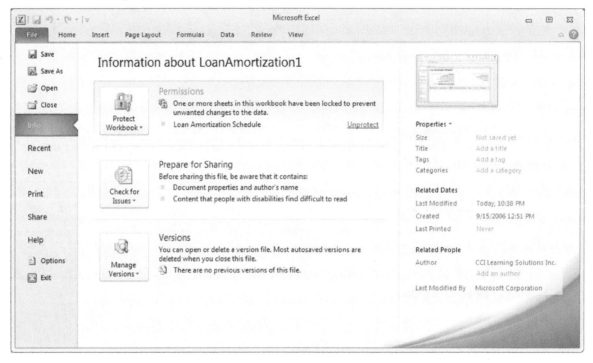

To check if there may be problems with converting your workbook to a different file format than Excel 2010, click **File**, click **Info**, click **Check for Issues**, and then **Check Compatibility**.

Any potential problems between the versions appear in the list. You then need to decide whether to continue saving the file in this file format or return to the document to make appropriate changes.

Learn the Skill

In this exercise, you will check a workbook for compatibility before saving it in the Excel 2003 format.

1 Start up Excel.

2 Click the **File** tab, then click **New,** and click **Sample templates**.

3 Click the **Loan Amortization** template, and click **Create**.

4 Click **File** and, on the left panel, ensure **Info** is selected.

5 Click **Check for Issues**.

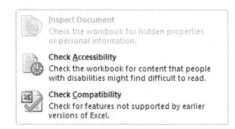

6 Click **Check Compatibility**.

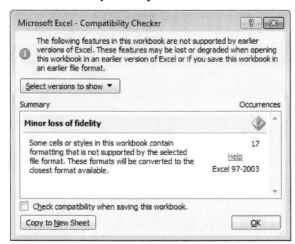

7   Read the findings, then click **OK**.

8   Click **File** and then click **Save As**.

9   Navigate to the folder where your student data files are located.

10   Click the arrow for the **Save as Type** list, and then click **Excel 97-2003 Workbook**.

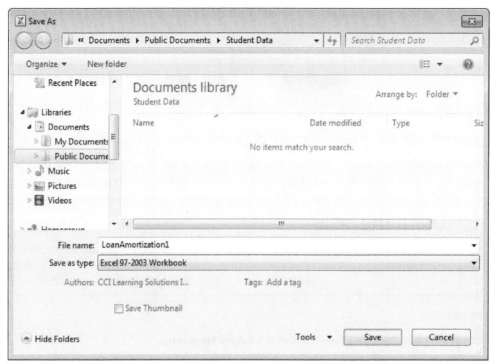

11   Leave the **File name** as displayed and click **Save**.

The Compatibility Checker dialog box is displayed again as a warning.

12   Click **Continue**.

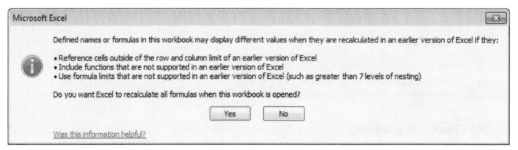

This message box contains a standard warning whenever you convert a workbook to an earlier version. The Compatibility Checker dialog box gave you the details of the differences; since only minor formatting issues were found, none of these problems with names or formulas will apply.

13   Click **Yes**.

14   Close the workbook.

15   Click **File** and then **Open**. Select the *LoanAmortization1* workbook and click **Open**.

The workbook name in the title bar now shows the label [Compatibility Mode] next to it. This indicates that this workbook uses the file format for an earlier version of Excel.

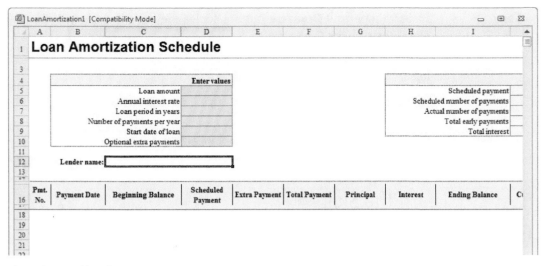

16 Close the workbook again.

Managing Files and Folders

1.3

If you wanted to save the file in a new location other than the default (i.e., generally \My Documents), you could either move to a different location or create a new folder. You should always save your documents— including Excel workbooks—in the *My Documents* folder or one of the folders underneath it. This will ensure all of your documents containing your data are in one place, thereby simplifying the process of finding all files to be backed up onto removable storage media such as CDs or DVDs.

You should use the Windows Explorer to perform most of your file management tasks, such as copying, moving, and deleting files and folders. However, you can also perform many of the basic file management functions from inside Excel using the Open, Save and Save As dialog boxes.

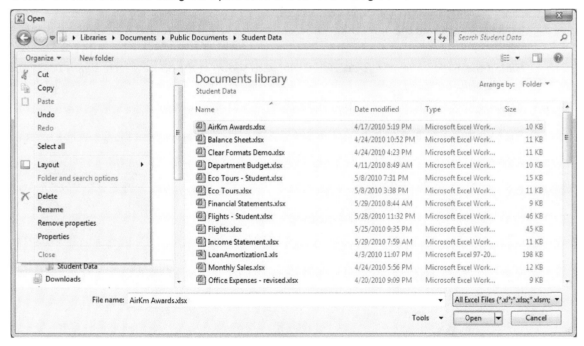

The file management features available in the Open, Save and Save As dialog boxes are:

New folder	This button is located near the top of the dialog box. It creates a new folder in the currently selected folder.
Cut	Located under the **Organize** button, removes the currently selected files or folders and places them on the Clipboard.

Copy	Located under the **Organize** button, copies the currently selected files or folders and places them on the Clipboard.
Paste	After you have used **Cut** or **Copy**, you can place the contents of the cut or copied files or folders into the new location.
Delete	Located under the **Organize** button, deletes the currently selected files or folders and moves them into the Recycle Bin.
Rename	Located under the **Organize** button, highlights the selected file or folder for you to enter the new name. The (F2) key performs the same function.

Learn the Skill

In this exercise, you will create, rename, and delete folders using the Save As and Open dialog boxes.

1   Open the *Popular Tours* workbook.

2   Click the **File** tab, then click **Save As**.

3   If necessary, navigate to the data folder as directed by your instructor.

4   Click **New folder** near the top of the Save As dialog box.

A new folder now appears at the top of the list of files. The initial default name of *New folder* should be highlighted, and you can change it by typing in a new name.

5   If necessary, click on the new folder name, and press the (F2) key so that it is highlighted and ready to be changed.

Hint: If the name in the new folder is highlighted as shown in the above screen, simply begin typing the new name for the folder.

6   Type: Draft as the new folder and press (Enter). Then click **OK**.

The Save As dialog box now shows the *Draft* folder as the location where the file will be saved.

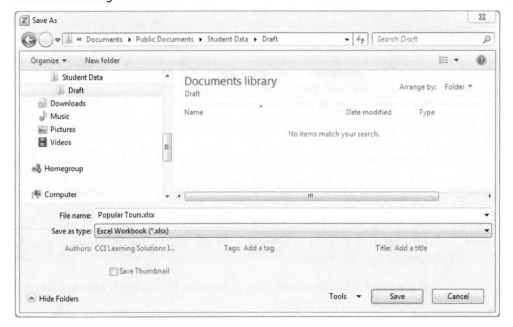

7 Leave the file name as is and click on the **Save** button.

You now have a copy of the same file in the default folder as well as the new folder just created.

If you need to change the name of the folder, you can do so from within the Save As dialog box. Before you can do so, you must ensure that none of the files in that folder are currently in use on your computer or any others in your local area network.

8 Close the *Popular Tours* workbook.

9 Click the **File** tab, then click **Open**.

Notice how Excel takes you to the last location you were at when you saved or opened a file.

10 In the Address Bar, click the folder name immediately to the left of *Draft* to return to the folder that contains the student files.

11 Click the *Draft* folder to select it and then press the F2 key.

12 Replace the current folder name of *Draft* by typing: Final and pressing the Enter key.

The name of the folder is now changed.

13 With the folder named *Final* selected, press Delete.

A Delete Folder message box appears with the question "Are you sure you want to move this folder to the Recycle Bin?"

14 Click **Yes**.

15 Click **Cancel** in the Open dialog box to close it.

Selecting Cells

The ability to select a range of cells is a fundamental skill in Excel. Prior to issuing a command or undertaking a procedure, you must indicate what part of the worksheet you wish to affect with the command. Range selection is the means to indicate this area.

A range selection can be as small as a single cell, or as large as the entire spreadsheet. Excel keeps the cell(s) highlighted until you change or remove the selection. Clicking a cell or using an arrow key will remove the selection.

In a worksheet, you can select:

- a single cell, i.e., the active cell
- a single range, e.g., a rectangular section of a worksheet containing two or more cells
- multiple ranges of cells

Excel displays the selected range by reversing the color of the cells. Within the selected range, one cell appears in a normal color. This is the active cell of the range.

You can use the mouse to select different ranges as follows:

A single cell	Click the cell.
Extend the selection	Click the cell, hold the mouse button down, drag to the end of the desired range, and then release the mouse button.
An entire row	Click the row heading.
An entire column	Click the column heading.
The entire worksheet	Click Select All in the top left corner of the worksheet (the button to the left of the column headings and above the row headings).

Make a selection	Click the beginning cell in the range, then point to the ending cell in the range and hold (Shift) down while clicking on the ending cell in the range.
Extend/shrink a selection	Hold (Shift) and click inside the previously selected range to shrink the selection, or click outside the range to extend the selection.

Other selection techniques include:

Non-adjacent columns, rows, or cells	Click the cell, column, or row. Move the pointer to the next cell, column, or row, hold (Ctrl) down, then click and drag.
Extend the row selection	Click the row number, hold the left mouse button down, and drag.
Extend the column selection	Click the column letter, hold down the left mouse button, and drag.

In some cases, you may want to use the keyboard to select cells by using (Shift) with the arrow keys. Generally, you have better control when selecting large cell ranges with the keyboard, especially when having to scroll to other parts of the worksheet at the same time. Note that you cannot select non-adjacent rows, columns or cells using the keyboard only.

MMM
Selecting Cells
Online
Exercise

Learn the Skill

This exercise demonstrates how to select ranges of cells using the mouse in a blank worksheet so you can quickly identify the ranges.

1   Create a new blank workbook.

2   Select a single cell by clicking cell **A9**.

3   Select a range of cells by holding down the mouse in cell **A9**, drag the mouse to cell **C5**, and then release the mouse button.

The screen should look similar to the following example:

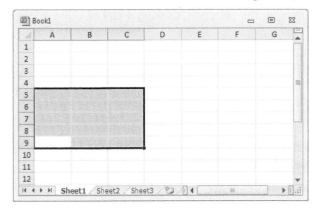

4   Select an entire column by clicking on the column **E** header at the top of the worksheet.

5   Select an entire row by clicking on the row **14** header on the left side of the worksheet.

6   Select the entire worksheet by clicking **Select All** in the top left corner of the worksheet (the gray button to the left of the column **A** header and above the row **1** header).

Now select more than one non-contiguous range of cells.

7   Select the range of cells **B4** to **B7**.

8   Hold (Ctrl) and select cells **D11** to **D18**.

9   Continue holding (Ctrl) and select cells **F1** to **F3**. Release (Ctrl).

The completed screen should appear similar to the following example:

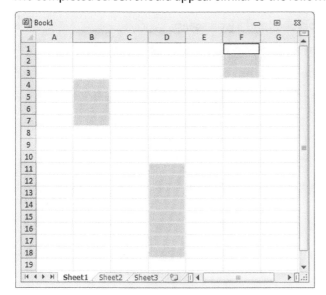

Now use the keyboard to select a range of cells.

10   Select cell **A9**.

11   While holding down (Shift), press the appropriate arrow keys to extend the range to cell **C5**. Release (Shift).

Now try selecting another range of cells using an alternate method with the keyboard.

12   Select cell **E10**.

13   While holding down (Shift), click in cell **G15.**

14   Close and discard the workbook.

Lesson Summary

The objectives of this lesson are to introduce the Excel program, learn how it works, and understand how to move in the program, create a workbook, enter data into a worksheet, and work with files. Upon completion of this lesson, you should be able to:

☑   understand what an electronic spreadsheet is

☑   understand what Excel is and what it can do

☑   identify elements on the Excel screen

☑   understand some basic terminology

☑   use the Quick Access Toolbar

☑   move around in Excel

☑   use keyboard shortcuts

☑   enter text, numbers, dates and times

☑   insert symbols or special characters

☑   move around a worksheet

☑   use Backstage to save, create new, open, and close a workbook

☑   switch between workbooks

☑   save in a previous version Excel format

☑   manage files and folders

☑   select cells

Review Questions

MMM
Go online for
Additional
Review and
Activities

1. List some benefits of using an electronic spreadsheet.

2. Explain the difference between a workbook and a worksheet.

3. Explain how commands are grouped on the Ribbon and how you access them

4. Explain how you can access the Ribbon using the keyboard and then how to access the commands.

5. Explain when it is better to create a blank workbook and when it is better to create a new workbook using a template.

6. Explain the difference between using the Save and Save As commands.

7. Provide examples of different types of data.

8. List different formats you can use to enter a date so that Excel will recognize it as a date value.

Microsoft®
Excel® 2010
Core Certification

Lesson 2: Constructing Cell Data

Lesson Objectives

In this lesson, you will learn how to select items to make changes to data in the worksheet, change the structure of the worksheet, and add and remove worksheets in the workbook. Upon successful completion of the lesson, you will know how to:

☐ edit cells and undo changes

☐ cut, copy, and paste data

☐ use Paste Special

☐ use the Office Clipboard

☐ change column widths

☐ change row heights

☐ use AutoFit with columns or rows

☐ hide and unhide rows and columns

☐ insert and delete rows and columns

☐ insert and delete cells

☐ find data in the worksheet

☐ replace data with different data in the worksheet

☐ use AutoFill to copy and fill series

☐ rename worksheets

☐ insert and delete worksheets

☐ move and copy worksheets

☐ hide and unhide worksheets

☐ add color to the worksheet tabs

Editing Cells and Undoing Changes

Once you have entered your data into a worksheet, you may want to rearrange the data or change it to suit your needs and preferences. If you were working with the manual method on columnar sheets, you would have to reconstruct the worksheet each time your requirements changed. Now, you can use Excel's tools to make quick changes to the display and arrangement of the data on the worksheet.

There are two ways to modify a cell containing data:

- Enter the new value into the cell and press (Enter) to replace the original contents with the new contents. This method is popular because it does not require the use of any special keys or modes.

- Activate Excel's editing mode by pressing the (F2) key, then use the (←), (→), (Backspace), (Delete), (Home) and (End) keys to move inside the cell and make the changes. Note that anything you type is added to existing content. You can also type over the cell contents by pressing (Insert) while you are in the editing mode. You may still have to delete any remaining characters from the previous text.

You can also activate the editing mode by double-clicking on the data in a cell.

If you are entering data into an empty cell (i.e., it does not have a value currently), you can only make corrections by pressing (Backspace) prior to pressing (Enter). Excel only allows you to use the cursor movement keys when you are in edit mode ((F2)).

Excel has an **Undo** function that enables you to undo commands that you have executed in your worksheet. You can undo a maximum of 100 most recently used commands.

This history of commands is listed in reverse order (the most recent action is listed at the top, followed by the next most recent) and can be accessed by clicking the arrow next to the **Undo** button. The list remains available to you even if you save the workbook, but will be lost once you close it.

To undo an action, use one of the following methods:

- On the Quick Access Toolbar, click **Undo** to reverse the last action. Alternatively, click the arrow next to **Undo** to display the history of the most recently used commands; or

- press (Ctrl)+(Z) to reverse the last action. Each time you press this key sequence, you will undo a previous action.

Some actions cannot be undone—specifically any **Backstage** actions such as saving, opening or printing a workbook.

In addition to undoing commands, Excel enables you to redo commands. If you reverse a command, then immediately want to undo your undo, you can redo the command to put it back in your worksheet. The **Redo** function is only available if one or more commands were undone.

To redo an action, use one of the following methods:

- On the Quick Access Toolbar, click **Redo** to reverse the last undo. Alternatively, click the down arrow next to **Redo** to display the list of all actions that can be reversed; or

- press (Ctrl)+(Y) to reverse the last action. Each time you press this key sequence, you will redo a previous action.

Learn the Skill

This exercise demonstrates how to edit the contents of cells containing text, numbers and dates.

1   Open the *World Travel Destinations* workbook.

2   Save the workbook as World Travel Destinations - Student.

First, you notice that Egypt and France have each other's capital city; you will switch them around by replacing the cells with the correct values.

3   Select cell **B8**, type: Cairo and press (Enter).

4   Select cell **B9** and type: Paris.

Now try using the editing mode to modify the contents of a cell.

5   Select cell **A2** and press (F2).

6   Press the (Backspace) key twice.

7   Type: na and press (Enter).

The contents of the cell should now be *Argentina*.

Next, make some corrections to numbers.

8   Select cell **C4** and type: 30,510.

9   Select cell **C3**, press (F2) and press (Home). Type: 768 and press (Enter) so the final value shows as 7,686,850.

You can also modify date values. Note that the month and day sequence on your computer will depend on your computer's region setting.

10   Select cell **B22**, press (F2) and press (Home) or (←) to position the cursor to the left of the month value of 1. Press (Delete) and type: 6 to change the month to June, then press (Enter).

Finally, make the corrections to the rest of the worksheet.

11   Use (F2), (←), (→), (Delete), (Backspace) and other keyboard keys as necessary to correct the indicated cells as follows:

Cell	Should Be
A5	Brazil
A10	Germany
A14	Italy
A20	United States of America
B14	Rome
B19	London
C13	3,287,590
C11	1,092

The screen should now look similar to the following example:

	A	B	C
1	Country	Destination	Size (sq km)
2	Argentina	Buenos Aires	2,766,890
3	Australia	Melbourne	7,686,850
4	Belgium	Brussels	30,510
5	Brazil	Rio de Janeiro	8,511,965
6	China	Shanghai	9,596,960
7	Cuba	Havana	110,860
8	Egypt	Cairo	1,001,450
9	France	Paris	547,030
10	Germany	Berlin	357,021
11	Hong Kong	Hong Kong	1,092
12	Iceland	Reyjkavik	103,000
13	India	Mumbai	3,287,590
14	Italy	Rome	301,230
15	Netherlands	Amsterdam	41,526
16	South Africa	Cape Town	1,219,912
17	Spain	Barcelona	504,782
18	Thailand	Bangkok	514,000
19	United Kingdom	London	244,820
20	United States of America	New York	9,629,091
21			
22	List updated on:	30-Jun-10	

12   Save the workbook but don't close it.

Suppose you change your mind at this point and need to reverse the last change made.

13   On the Quick Access Toolbar, click **Undo**.

The value in cell C11 has changed back to *101,092*.

If you then decide that the change was actually correct, you can redo or repeat the last change made.

14   On the Quick Access Toolbar, click **Redo**.

The value in cell C11 has changed back to *1,092*.

15   Save and close the workbook.

Copying and Moving Data

Cutting, Copying and Pasting Data

2.1

Excel enables you to copy or move cell contents and their formats to simplify editing tasks and streamline worksheet construction. There are very significant differences between copying the contents of a cell and moving the contents to another worksheet cell.

You can move the contents of a cell or range of cells to a different part of the worksheet, a different part of the workbook, or even a different workbook. The important concept here is that you remove the values from the original location and place them in the new location.

Alternatively, you can copy the contents of a cell and range of cells to a different location. The significant difference here is that by copying, you do not affect the original cells—the originating data remain in their current cells.

Cut	Remove the contents of a cell or a range of cells and place them on the Clipboard.
Copy	Copy the contents of a cell or a range of cells and place them on the Clipboard. The original cell contents remain in their current location.
Paste	After you have used **Cut** or **Copy**, you can place the contents of the cut or copied cells into a new cell location. If the new cell location already contains data or formatting, the pasted data will overwrite the existing data.
Paste Special	Modify the effects of the paste option (i.e., you can paste the contents or format only). In comparison, the **Paste** command is non-selective and pastes all features of the originating cells.

When you select either the **Cut** or **Copy** command, a marquee (a rectangle outlined with a moving, dotted line) appears around the selected cell range. This marquee identifies the cell range that you can paste to another part of the worksheet or to another worksheet. You can remove the marquee (cancelling the copying or moving action) by pressing (Esc). You can also cancel the copying or moving action by typing new data into a cell. When you enter new data, Excel interprets that you want to continue the editing process on your spreadsheet, and so the marquee disappears.

- You can copy or move any kind of data—text, numbers, dates, formulas, drawing objects and charts—that you have embedded in a worksheet.

- You can copy a range of cells more than once. On the **Home** tab, in the **Clipboard** group, click **Copy** and click **Paste** as many times as necessary in several cells.

- You can also cut or copy more than one cell range and retain up to 24 cell ranges on the Office Clipboard at one time. You can then paste any or all of these cell ranges from the Office Clipboard in any sequence you want.

To copy an item, select it and then use one of the following methods:

- On the **Home** tab, in the **Clipboard** group, click **Copy**; or
- press (Ctrl)+(C); or
- right-click the item, and then click **Copy** in the shortcut menu.

To cut or move an item, select it and then use one of the following methods:

- On the **Home** tab, in the **Clipboard** group, click **Cut**; or
- press (Ctrl)+(X); or
- right-click the item, and then click **Cut** in the shortcut menu.

To paste an item, move to the cell where you want to paste it, and then use one of the following methods:

- On the **Home** tab, in the **Clipboard** group, click **Paste**; or
- press (Ctrl)+(V); or
- right-click the destination cell, and then click **Paste** in the shortcut menu.

Using the Office Clipboard

The Microsoft Office suite maintains its own Office Clipboard separately from the Windows Clipboard. The differences between the two include the following:

Office Clipboard	Windows Clipboard
Able to hold up to 24 items (e.g. number, formula, range of cells, picture) at one time.	Only able to hold one item at a time. A new item copied into the Clipboard replaces the item that is currently there.
Any of the 24 items can be selected and pasted in any sequence.	Since there is only one item, it is the only value that can be pasted.
Contents can only be shared between Office programs, except the most recent item, which is copied to the Windows Clipboard and is available to be pasted to other Windows programs.	Contents can be shared with all programs running in Windows.
When all Office programs are closed, the Office Clipboard is closed and all items in it are lost except the most recent item, which is copied to the Windows Clipboard.	The one item in the Windows Clipboard remains until the computer is closed down or the item on the clipboard is replaced by another item. In Excel however, the Windows Clipboard is cleared when you press the (Esc) key or begin entering a new item of data.

The Office Clipboard shows you the contents of the item on the Clipboard task pane and an icon representing the software program it came from.

The Office Clipboard remains turned off by default, until you choose to display the Clipboard task pane. To display the Clipboard task pane, on the **Home** tab, in the **Clipboard** group, click the **Dialog box launcher**. You can set this task pane to display automatically whenever Excel starts by changing the options for the Clipboard.

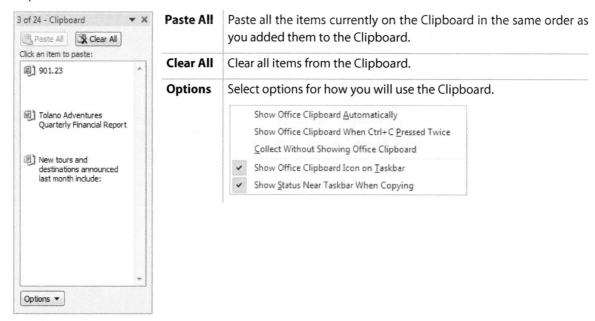

Paste All	Paste all the items currently on the Clipboard in the same order as you added them to the Clipboard.
Clear All	Clear all items from the Clipboard.
Options	Select options for how you will use the Clipboard.

For instance, you may be creating a report in which you want to include text from a Word document, some numbers from an Excel file, and some content from a PowerPoint presentation. You can collect items from all three programs up to a maximum of 24 items. Once you reach the maximum, the oldest item will be removed as each new item is added to the Clipboard.

To paste an item into the active cell in the worksheet, simply click the item on the Office Clipboard. Regardless of how many items are in the Office Clipboard, clicking the **Paste** button in the Ribbon or pressing Ctrl + V will always paste from the Windows Clipboard (the last item copied).

When you point to an item on the Clipboard with your pointer, an arrow appears on the right of the item. When you click the arrow, a menu appears with more options. Use the **Delete** command here when you want to delete the item from the Clipboard. If you want to paste the item in the active cell, you can either use the **Paste** command in this shortcut menu or simply click the item on the Clipboard.

Learn the Skill

This exercise demonstrates how to copy and move the contents of cells from one part of a worksheet to another. It also demonstrates the use of text labels as row and column titles.

1   Open the *Office Expenses* workbook and save it as Office Expenses - Student.

First, you will learn how to copy expenses that are the same for every month.

2   Click cell **B5** and drag the mouse down to select cell **B6**.

3   On the **Home** tab, in the **Clipboard** group, click **Copy**.

	A	B	C	D
1	Tolano Adventures			
2	Office Expenses			
3				
4		January	February	March
5	Rent	5000		
6	Telephone	150		
7	Internet	125		
8	Courier	300		
9	Postage	75		
10	Supplies	250		
11	Photocopier	80		
12	Travel			

Notice that the marquee appears around cells B5 and B6 to indicate that you have copied their contents onto the Clipboard.

4   Select cell **C5** and, in the **Clipboard** group, click **Paste**.

You can also press Enter to paste the entries into this location. However, this technique will only allow you to paste the entry once, and then will automatically turn off the marquee.

Notice how Excel has copied both cells from the original cell references into the correct place, even though you only chose one cell. Excel will automatically replace the contents of the existing cell(s) with the copied entries.

5   Select cell **D5** and click **Paste** again.

6   Select cells **B7** to **B8** and click **Copy**.

7   Select cells **C7** to **D8** and click **Paste**.

Alternatively, you can paste these two values to all four cells at the same time.

Next, see how the Office Clipboard works.

8   On the **Home** tab, in the **Clipboard** group, click the **Dialog box launcher** to display the Clipboard task pane.

*Hint: If you want this pane to open automatically whenever you copy data to the Clipboard twice consecutively, click the **Options** button at the bottom of the Clipboard task pane and select that option.*

9   Click **Clear All** at the top of the Clipboard.

10   Select cell **B9** and click **Copy**.

11   Select cell **C9** and then click **75** on the Clipboard.

12   Select cell **B10** and then click **Copy** once more.

Notice that the Clipboard has two items on it.

13   Click cell **C10**.

14   Point to the **250** entry on the Clipboard and then click the arrow.

15   Click **Paste**.

16   Select cell **D9**.

17   Click Paste All.

18   Click **Clear All** and then close the Clipboard.

The completed worksheet should look similar to the following example:

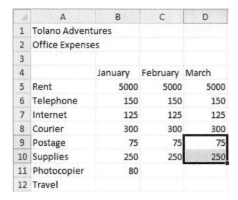

19 Save the workbook.

Using Paste Special

2.1

3.1

The standard **Paste** command will paste the entire contents of the Windows Clipboard into the target cell(s), including data, formatting, and any comments. In some cases, you may not want to do this. The **Paste Special** command enables you to selectively choose how the data will be pasted.

To activate the **Paste Special** command, on the **Home** tab, in the **Clipboard** group, click the arrow for **Paste**, then click **Paste Special**.

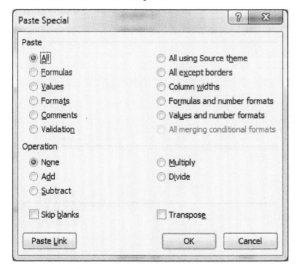

Paste	Specifies what components of the data in the Clipboard are pasted to the target cells. For example, if **Formulas** is specified, then only the formulas are selected and other components such as cell formatting will not be pasted.
Operation	Specifies how any data in the target cells will be treated. For example, if **Multiply** is selected then any existing data will be multiplied by the data pasted into the target cells.
Skip blanks	If selected, will avoid overwriting any existing data in the target cells if there is no data from the clipboard to be put into that cell.
Transpose	If specified, will rotate the data. Therefore data in the clipboard listed down a column will now be listed across a row in the target cells. Similarly, data listed across cells in a row become listed down cells in a column.

Learn the Skill

This exercise demonstrates how to use the Paste Special feature using a specialized workbook that highlights its capabilities.

1   Open the *Paste Special* workbook and save as Paste Special - Student.

▲	A	B	C	D
1	Values	Formulas	Values	
2	10.1	20.2	60.6	
3	20.20	40.40	70.7	
4	*$30.30*	*$60.60*	80.8	
5	4.04E+01	8.08E+01	90.9	
6	FRED	fred	JOE	
7				

Columns A and C contain data values in the cells. Column B contains formulas that reference cells in column A. First, try pasting just values from columns A and B to a set of target cells.

2   Select cells **A2:B6**, and on the **Home** tab, in the **Clipboard** group, click **Copy**.

3   Select cell **G3**. On the **Home** tab, in the **Clipboard** group, click the arrow for **Paste**.

A drop down menu is displayed.

4   Click **Paste Special** at the bottom of the drop down menu.

5   In the Paste Special dialog box, click **Values** and click **OK**.

▲	A	B	C	D	E	F	G	H	I
1	Values	Formulas	Values						
2	10.1	20.2	60.6						
3	20.20	40.40	70.7				10.1	20.2	
4	*$30.30*	*$60.60*	80.8				20.2	40.4	
5	4.04E+01	8.08E+01	90.9				30.3	60.6	
6	FRED	fred	JOE				40.4	80.8	
7							FRED	fred	
8									📋 (Ctrl) ▾
9									

*Alternatively, you can also select the left-most icon in the **Paste Values** section of the drop down menu. This is a faster method of accessing the feature instead of using the Paste Special dialog box.*

Now compare the contents of each of these two sets of cells—all of the data in the selected source cells were pasted into the target cells. Because you had selected **Values**, the formulas in column B were evaluated, and the results were pasted into the target cells. Note that none of the cell formatting was pasted into the target cells.

6   Select cells **B2:B6**, and on the **Home** tab, in the **Clipboard** group, click **Copy**.

7   Select cell **H3**. On the **Home** tab, in the **Clipboard** group, click the arrow for **Paste**, and point at the left-most icon in the **Other Paste Options** section of the drop down menu.

Notice that the cells in H3:H7 are displayed using the formats that are about to be pasted, even though you have not actually clicked the paste icon yet. This is a demonstration of the *Live Preview* capability of Excel—you can preview the effects of a formatting change as it will appear on the worksheet. If you then move your mouse cursor away without clicking, the formatting reverts back. The Live Preview capability is available for most of the formatting options on the Ribbon. It is not available from any of the formatting dialog boxes.

8   Click the left-most icon in the **Other Paste Options** section of the drop down menu to make the change permanent.

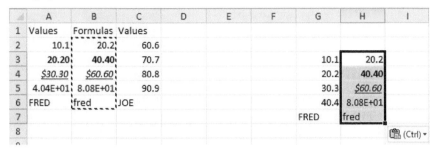

Now see what happens when you paste just the formulas to the target cells.

9   With cells **B2:B6** still selected, select cell **D2**.

10   On the **Home** tab, in the **Clipboard** group, click the arrow for **Paste**, click **Paste Special**, click **Formulas** and then click **OK**.

11   Point at different icons (but do not click on any of them) in the **Paste** drop down menu to see how the worksheet is affected.

12   Click on the **Formulas** icon (top row, second from the left in the **Paste** section) in the drop down menu.

	A	B	C	D	E	F	G	H
1	Values	Formulas	Values					
2	10.1	20.2	60.6	121.2				
3	20.20	40.40	70.7	141.4			10.1	20.2
4	$30.30	$60.60	80.8	161.6			20.2	40.40
5	4.04E+01	8.08E+01	90.9	181.8			30.3	$60.60
6	FRED	fred	JOE	joe			40.4	8.08E+01
7							FRED	fred

The formulas in column B are now copied into column D, referencing the values in column C. This is an example of relative addressing, which is explained in more detail in a later lesson in this courseware. Notice that this option did not copy the formatting from column B.

> Alternatively, you can also select the **Formulas** option from the Paste Special dialog box.

Now try the **Transpose** option.

13   Select cells **A2:B6**, and on the **Home** tab, in the **Clipboard** group, click **Copy**.

14   Select cell **B9**. On the **Home** tab, in the **Clipboard** group, click the arrow for **Paste**, and click the last icon (second row, far right) in the **Paste** section of the drop down menu.

> Alternatively, you can also select **Transpose** from the **Paste Special** dialog box.

The completed worksheet should now look similar to the following:

	A	B	C	D	E	F	G	H
1	Values	Formulas	Values					
2	10.1	20.2	60.6	121.2				
3	20.20	40.40	70.7	141.4			10.1	20.2
4	$30.30	$60.60	80.8	161.6			20.2	40.40
5	4.04E+01	8.08E+01	90.9	181.8			30.3	$60.60
6	FRED	fred	JOE	joe			40.4	8.08E+01
7							FRED	fred
8								
9		10.1	20.20	$30.30	4.04E+01	FRED		
10		20.2	40.40	$60.60	8.08E+01	fred		
11						(Ctrl) ▾		

15 Save and close the workbook.

Copying and Moving Cells Using the Mouse

Instead of cutting and pasting cell contents, you can simply move the cell(s) directly to the new location using the drag-and-drop method. This method requires the use of the mouse. As with the cut and paste method, the target cell(s) will lose all existing data or formatting.

You can also use the drag-and-drop method to copy a cell or range of the cells by pressing Ctrl at the same time. Using the drag-and-drop method does not involve either the Windows or Office Clipboards.

Learn the Skill

This exercise demonstrates how to copy and move the contents of cells from one part of a worksheet to another.

1 If necessary, open the *Office Expenses - Student* workbook.

Move the contents of one cell to another empty cell.

2 Select cell **A12**.

3 Position the cursor over any of the four edges of cell **A12**.

The cursor should change to a white pointer with a four-headed arrow at its tip (⇱).

	A	B	C	D
1	Tolano Adventures			
2	Office Expenses			
3				
4		January	February	March
5	Rent	5000	5000	5000
6	Telephone	150	150	150
7	Internet	125	125	125
8	Courier	300	300	300
9	Postage	75	75	75
10	Supplies	250	250	250
11	Photocopier	80		
12	Travel			
13				

4 Click and hold down the left mouse button and drag the cell down to cell **C13**. Release the left mouse button.

Notice that, as you drag the data around the worksheet, a gray outline of the selected cell moves along.

Now move the contents of this cell to another cell that contains data.

5 Repeat steps 3 and 4 to drag cell **C13** to **A6**.

A message box appears with the question: *Do you want to replace the contents of the destination cells?* If you accidentally selected the wrong cell, you can cancel this operation. Otherwise, you can proceed with the move.

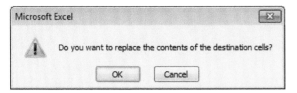

6 In the message box, click **OK**.

Next, try moving a group of cells to another location.

7 Select cells **C4** to **D10**.

8 Click and drag these cells down so that the upper left corner of the range of cells is in **D9**. Release the left mouse button.

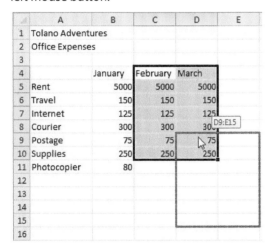

Now use the drag-and-drop method for copying cells.

9 With the cell range **D9** to **E15** selected, move the cursor to one of the four edges.

10 Press and hold down Ctrl, then click and hold down the left mouse button.

11 Drag the selected range to cells **B7** to **C13**.

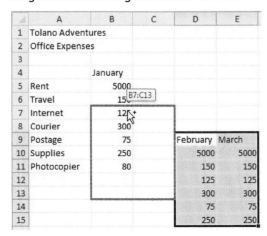

Notice the + symbol next to the arrow while you are holding down (Ctrl). You can actually press or release (Ctrl) at any time while you are dragging the mouse; this enables you to change your mind between moving and copying, and back again.

12 Release the mouse button and (Ctrl).

The completed worksheet should look similar to the following example:

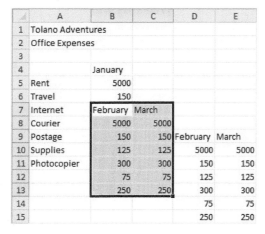

13 Close the workbook without saving the changes.

Inserting and Deleting Rows and Columns

Inserting Rows and Columns

2.2

Excel can insert new rows and columns, even between rows or columns containing data. This feature enables you to add information to a previously created spreadsheet, or to separate parts of your spreadsheet with blank rows or columns.

Worksheet columns start at **A** and end at column **XFD** (16,384 columns). For every new column inserted between **A** and **XFD**, one column is pushed off the far right side of the worksheet and deleted. Similarly, new rows inserted between rows **1** and **1,048,576** will result in the same number of rows being pushed off the bottom of the worksheet and deleted.

New rows or columns are added at the current cell position. That is, rows are always inserted directly above and columns are inserted to the left of the cell that you select before issuing the insert command. If you want to insert a row below the current active cell, simply move down one row to the next row and then use the Insert command. Similarly, to insert a column to the right of the active cell, shift to the right by one column before using the Insert command.

You can insert one or more rows or columns at the same time by selecting that number of rows or columns before using the Insert command. The rows or columns do not have to be next to each other.

To insert a row or column, use one of the following methods:

- On the **Home** tab, in the **Cells** group, click the arrow for **Insert**, and click **Insert Sheet Rows** or **Insert Sheet Columns**; or

- select the row heading or column heading where the new row or column is to be inserted, and then press (Ctrl)+(+) on the numeric keypad or the keyboard; or

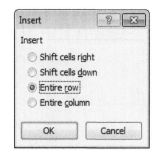

- select the row heading or column heading where the new row or column is to be inserted, and then on the **Home** tab, in the **Cells** group, click **Insert**; or

- right-click a row or column heading and click **Insert** from the shortcut menu; or

- right-click a cell in the row or column where the new row or column is to be inserted, click **Insert**, select **Entire row** or **Entire column** and click **OK**.

Be careful when using these commands, as they affect the entire spreadsheet and therefore may affect areas of the spreadsheet that are not visible on the screen.

Deleting Rows and Columns

Just as Excel enables you to insert new rows and column, you can also delete unnecessary rows and columns.

Before deleting entire rows or columns, take some time to verify that these rows or columns do not contain any valuable data elsewhere in the worksheet that is not visible on the screen.

To delete a row or column, use one of the following methods:

- On the **Home** tab, in the **Cells** group, click the arrow for **Delete**, and then click **Delete Sheet Rows** or **Delete Sheet Columns**; or

- select the row heading or column heading for the row or column to be deleted, and then press ⌈Ctrl⌉+⌈-⌋ on the numeric keypad or on the keyboard; or

- select the row heading or column heading for the row or column to be deleted, and then on the **Home** tab, in the **Cells** group, click **Delete**; or

- right-click a cell in the row or column to be deleted, click **Delete** and then click **Entire row** or **Entire column**; or

- right-click a row or column heading and click **Delete** from the shortcut menu.

You can delete more than one row or column at a time. The selected rows or columns do not have to be next to each other.

Inserting and Deleting Cells

You may also choose to insert or delete one or several cells. When you insert new cells, Excel shifts the existing cells to the right or down to make space for the new cell(s). When you delete existing cells, Excel shifts the remaining cells over from the right or below to take the place of the deleted cell(s). When you delete cells, any formulas that reference the cell(s) will display an error (the topic of formulas is discussed in more detail later in this courseware).

Alternatively, you may delete the contents of one or more cells by simply pressing ⌈Delete⌋. Unlike deleting the cell itself, using ⌈Delete⌋ will leave the structure of the worksheet intact, and formulas that reference the cell will assume the cell value is zero.

Learn the Skill

This exercise demonstrates how to add and delete rows, columns and cells in a workbook.

1   Open the *Office Expenses - Student* workbook.

Insert a new row above a row of data.

2   Select any cell in row **5**.

3   On the **Home** tab, in the **Cells** group, click the arrow for **Insert** and click **Insert Sheet Rows**.

Note that if you had clicked the **Insert** button instead of the arrow below it, all the data below the active cell in the same column would have shifted down by one row, and the data in the surrounding columns would not have moved. When you click **Insert**, Excel interprets that you mean to insert cells only and not entire rows.

Now insert two rows in the middle of the data.

4   Click the gray row headers for rows **7** and **8**.

Notice the row heading symbol that appears (➡) to show you that the entire row will be selected.

5   On the **Home** tab, in the **Cells** group, click **Insert**.

Because you selected entire rows (two of them in this case), Excel inserts rows rather than cells.

The combination of steps 4 and 5 is a popular method of adding a new row to a worksheet. Another method is using the Shortcut Menu – at step 5, right-click anywhere in the selected area, then click **Insert**. This method is popular because the Shortcut Menu only shows the most relevant commands for the selected cell(s) at the time of the right-click.

Now insert one column on the left side of the data.

6   Click the heading for column **B**.

Notice the column heading symbol that appears (⬇) shows you that the entire column will be selected.

7   On the **Home** tab, in the **Cells** group, click **Insert**.

8   Enter the following values:

Cell	Value
A7	Janitorial
A8	Long Distance
C7	100
C8	50

*Alternatively, on the **Home** tab, in the **Cells** group, click the arrow for **Insert** and click **Insert Sheet Columns**.*

9   Type or copy the values in cell **C7** to **C8** across to cell **D7** to **E8**.

The worksheet should now look similar to the following example:

	A	B	C	D	E
1	Tolano Adventures				
2	Office Expenses				
3					
4			January	February	March
5					
6	Rent		5000	5000	5000
7	Janitorial		100	100	100
8	Long Distance		50	50	50
9	Telephone		150	150	150
10	Internet		125	125	125
11	Courier		300	300	300
12	Postage		75	75	75
13	Supplies		250	250	250
14	Photocopier		80		
15	Travel				

Now delete a row of data, using the Shortcut Menu method.

10   Click the light blue row selector button for row **8**.

11   Right-click anywhere in row 8, then click **Delete**.

Notice that when an entire row is selected, Excel will remove the entire row without waiting for further commands. You can do the same thing for an entire column.

12   Select any cell in column **B**.

13   On the **Home** tab, in the **Cells** group, click the arrow for **Delete** and click **Delete Sheet Columns**.

The worksheet should now look similar to the following example:

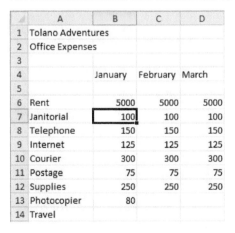

	A	B	C	D
1	Tolano Adventures			
2	Office Expenses			
3				
4		January	February	March
5				
6	Rent	5000	5000	5000
7	Janitorial	100	100	100
8	Telephone	150	150	150
9	Internet	125	125	125
10	Courier	300	300	300
11	Postage	75	75	75
12	Supplies	250	250	250
13	Photocopier	80		
14	Travel			

Now delete the contents of one cell.

14   Select cell **C8**.

15   Press (Delete).

Note that this key removes the contents of the cell, but not the cell formatting (this will be demonstrated in a different lesson in this courseware). The structure of the spreadsheet is also unaffected. Now try to delete the entire cell.

16   On the Quick Access Toolbar, click **Undo** to reverse the deletion.

17   On the **Home** tab, in the **Cells** group, click **Delete**.

The worksheet now looks similar to the following example:

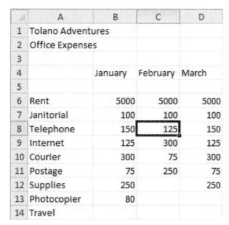

⊿	A	B	C	D
1	Tolano Adventures			
2	Office Expenses			
3				
4		January	February	March
5				
6	Rent	5000	5000	5000
7	Janitorial	100	100	100
8	Telephone	150	125	150
9	Internet	125	300	125
10	Courier	300	75	300
11	Postage	75	250	75
12	Supplies	250		250
13	Photocopier	80		
14	Travel			

Because you have selected only one cell, Excel removes only that cell and all data in the column below shifts up.

18   Click **Undo** to reverse the deletion.

19   With cell **C7** still selected, on the **Home** tab, in the **Cells** group, click the arrow for **Delete** and click **Delete Cells**.

20   With the **Shift cells up** option selected, click **OK**.

21   Click **Undo** to reverse the deletion.

22   Select cells **C7** to **C8**, and on the **Home** tab, in the **Cells** group, click **Delete**.

23   Click **Undo** to reverse the deletion.

24   Save and close the workbook.

Adjusting the Columns and Rows

As you work with data in Excel, you may want to improve the readability of your worksheets by adjusting the column width and row height so that you can see more or fewer characters in that column or row.

Changing the Column Widths

2.2

The standard column width in a new worksheet may not be enough to accommodate some of the entries you make in the cells. If the adjacent cells are empty, Excel will display your entire text label by overflowing into those cells. If the adjoining cells have entries, the text labels will appear truncated at the cell boundary.

You can select between zero and 255 for the width of your column. When you change a column width, the stored contents of the cells do not change; only the number of the characters displayed changes.

Numbers represent a special problem when there is insufficient space to display the whole number; Excel cannot simply truncate numbers as it does with text labels. If it did, the number would be misleading. For example, you would not want 1,000,000 to be displayed as 1,000 if there is not enough space to display the whole number. Excel uses several different rules to determine how to display a numeric value in a cell:

- If you enter a numeric value that is slightly larger than the current column width, Excel will automatically widen the column width to show the number with the current cell format.

- If you enter a numeric value that is much larger than the current column width, Excel automatically changes the cell format to scientific notation.

- If you reduce the width of a column that already contains numeric data, Excel may be unable to display the number. In this case, a series of pound signs (######) will be displayed in the affected cell(s). Excel will redisplay the number when you increase the column width to accommodate the number in its current format.

- A quick way of checking the width of the column is to click the vertical bar between the column headers. Excel displays the width in a screen tip located above and to the right of the mouse pointer.

To change the width for a column manually, use one of the following methods:

- On the **Home** tab, in the **Cells** group, click **Format** and click **Column Width**; or

- place the mouse cursor on the vertical line on the right of the column heading for the column to be adjusted. When the cursor changes to the ✛ symbol, click and drag to the appropriate width; or

- right-click the column heading for the column to be adjusted, and then click **Column Width**.

Adjusting the Row Height

Similar to column widths, the height of a row can be changed. This capability is not used as frequently as adjusting the width of columns, but there will be occasions when you need to over-ride the default row height setting used by Excel when you re-format the data in cells.

To adjust the height for a row, use one of the following methods:

- On the **Home** tab, in the **Cells** group, click **Format** and click **Row Height**; or

- place the mouse cursor at the bottom of the row heading to be adjusted. The cursor will change to a ╪ symbol and you can then drag to the desired new height.

Using AutoFit

AutoFit is a time-saving feature of Excel that will automatically adjust column width for you.

To fit the contents to the column's width automatically, use one of the following methods:

- On the **Home** tab, in the **Cells** group, click **Format** and click **AutoFit Column Width**; or

- use the mouse to double-click the vertical line on the right of the heading for the column you wish to adjust. The cursor will change to a double-headed arrow (✛).

These two methods can produce different results. When you use the AutoFit feature from the Ribbon, Excel will change (either widen or reduce) the column width to fully display the contents of the **selected cell(s)**. When you use the mouse method, Excel will automatically adjust the width so that it is just wide enough for the widest value in the **entire column**.

You can also select multiple columns and use either of these two methods. The result will be same as if you apply AutoFit to each of the columns.

Similarly, you can set row height to fit the height of the contents in the cells in that row automatically using one of the following methods:

- On the **Home** tab, in the **Cells** group, click **Format** and click **AutoFit Row Height**; or

- use the mouse to double-click at the bottom of the row heading to be adjusted.

Learn the Skill

This exercise demonstrates how to modify column widths, and the impact this has on how cell contents display.

1   Open the *Price Quote 0703* workbook and save it as Price Quote 0703 - Student.

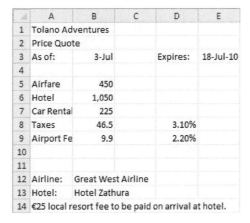

	A	B	C	D	E
1	Tolano Adventures				
2	Price Quote				
3	As of:	3-Jul		Expires:	18-Jul-10
4					
5	Airfare	450			
6	Hotel	1,050			
7	Car Rental	225			
8	Taxes	46.5		3.10%	
9	Airport Fe	9.9		2.20%	
10					
11					
12	Airline:	Great West Airline			
13	Hotel:	Hotel Zathura			
14	€25 local resort fee to be paid on arrival at hotel.				

2   Select any cell in column **A**.

3   On the **Home** tab, in the **Cells** group, click **Format** and click **Column Width**.

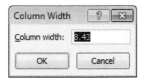

4   In the **Column Width** box, type: 14 and press ⌊Enter⌋.

5   Repeat steps 2 to 4 for column **C** with a width of 6.

Now try using the AutoFit option for column **B**. You will choose cell **B13** because it is wider than the current column width, but will not make the entire column too wide for many of the cells.

6   Select cell **B13**.

7   On the **Home** tab, in the **Cells** group, click **Format** and click **AutoFit Column Width**.

You can also use the mouse to AutoFit a column. It is a faster method than using the menu because it chooses the widest cell in the selected column.

8   Move the mouse pointer to the right edge of the column **A** header. The mouse pointer will change to a double-headed pointer.

9   Double-click that position.

Column A is now too wide to be visually appealing. Use the mouse to adjust the width.

10   Move the mouse pointer to point to the vertical line to the right of the column heading (i.e., the line separating columns **A** and **B**).

The pointer will change to a vertical bar with arrows on each side (↔).

11   Click and drag to the left to reduce the width.

Notice that a screen tip appears as you drag the column width, giving you the current column width as a visual reference.

You can expect to repeat steps 10 to 12 several times to determine an appropriate column width.

12 Release the mouse button when the column width is just right for displaying the full contents of cell **A9** (Airport Fees).

The screen should look similar to the following example:

	A	B	C	D	E
1	Tolano Adventures				
2	Price Quote				
3	As of:	3-Jul		Expires:	18-Jul-10
4					
5	Airfare	450			
6	Hotel	1,050			
7	Car Rental	225			
8	Taxes	46.5		3.10%	
9	Airport Fees	9.9		2.20%	
10					
11					
12	Airline:	Great West Airline			
13	Hotel:	Hotel Zathura			
14	€25 local resort fee to be paid on arrival at hotel.				

Use the mouse to adjust the height of some of the rows.

13 Move the mouse pointer to the bottom edge of the row **1** header.

The mouse pointer will change to a double-headed pointer.

14 Click and drag the row **1** header down until it is twice the current height—about **30.00 (40 pixels)**.

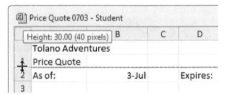

15 Click and drag the row **4** header up to a height of about **9.00 (12 pixels)**.

The completed worksheet should look similar to the following example:

	A	B	C	D	E
1	Tolano Adventures				
2	Price Quote				
3	As of:	3-Jul		Expires:	18-Jul-10
4					
5	Airfare	450			
6	Hotel	1,050			
7	Car Rental	225			
8	Taxes	46.5		3.10%	
9	Airport Fees	9.9		2.20%	
10					
11					
12	Airline:	Great West Airline			
13	Hotel:	Hotel Zathura			
14	€25 local resort fee to be paid on arrival at hotel.				

16 Save and close the worksheet.

Hiding/Unhiding Rows & Columns

3.4

On occasion, you may need to hide one or more rows or columns in your worksheet. You may want to do this for different reasons. For example:

- You may be printing a worksheet with more columns or rows than the page width allows. If you print all of the data, you will have to either break it up across multiple pages or reduce the scale—and therefore reduce the readability—of the data.

- The columns or rows may contain formulas used for intermediate calculations only. In some cases, you may be developing complex calculations that you cannot perform in one formula, or you may want to view how Excel is calculating the data across multiple cells containing simpler formulas. An example of a complex formula is converting a text field containing numeric data, which needs to be extracted and converted into numeric values. This kind of complex formula will be difficult to read on its own—and therefore difficult to correct if there is an error in it.

- You may want to prevent other users from viewing these hidden rows or columns, or the formulas used in these hidden cells. Note that you will have to prevent users from unhiding the data by activating the workbook protection feature.

You can easily identify hidden rows or columns by the gaps in the row or column headers. They remain hidden until you unhide them again. Excel will continue to correctly calculate any formulas in hidden cells, or formulas in visible cells that reference hidden cells.

Hidden rows and columns will not appear, even if you print the worksheet, until you unhide them again.

To hide a row or column, select the row or column headings first, and then use one of the following methods:

- On the **Home** tab, in the **Cells** group, click **Format**, click **Hide & Unhide**, and then **Hide Columns** or **Hide Rows**; or

- right-click the selected rows or columns and then click **Hide**; or

- drag the right edge of the column to the left or the bottom edge of the row upwards until it is hidden.

To unhide a row or column, select the appropriate headings on both sides of the hidden row(s) or column(s), and then use one of the following methods:

- On the **Home** tab, in the **Cells** group, click **Format**, click **Hide & Unhide**, and then **Unhide Columns** or **Unhide Rows**; or

- right-click the selected rows or columns and then click **Unhide**; or

- drag the right edge of the hidden column to the right or the bottom edge of the hidden row downwards until the desired width or height is attained.

Learn the Skill

This exercise demonstrates how to hide and unhide rows and columns.

1   Open the *Political Contributions* workbook and save it as Political Contributions - Student.

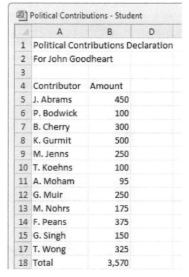

	A	B	D
1	Political Contributions Declaration		
2	For John Goodheart		
3			
4	Contributor	Amount	
5	J. Abrams	450	
6	P. Bodwick	100	
7	B. Cherry	300	
8	K. Gurmit	500	
9	M. Jenns	250	
10	T. Koehns	100	
11	A. Moham	95	
12	G. Muir	250	
13	M. Nohrs	175	
14	F. Peans	375	
15	G. Singh	150	
17	T. Wong	325	
18	Total	3,570	

Political Contributions - Student

Notice that there appears to be a gap between columns B and D, and between rows 15 and 16.

2 Select columns **B** to **D**.

Hint: *Alternatively, you can select any range of cells that include both columns B and D to indicate that you are selecting the hidden column between these two columns.*

3 On the **Home** tab, in the **Cells** group, click **Format**, click **Hide & Unhide** and then click **Unhide Columns**.

A column header now appears with an intriguing description.

4 Select rows **15** to **17**.

5 Right-click the **15** or **17** row header and then click **Unhide**.

The worksheet should now look similar to the following:

	A	B	C
1	Political Contributions Declaration		
2	For John Goodheart		
3			
4	Contributor	Amount	Add'l Amt
5	J. Abrams	450	
6	P. Bodwick	100	
7	B. Cherry	300	
8	K. Gurmit	500	
9	M. Jenns	250	
10	T. Koehns	100	
11	A. Moham	95	
12	G. Muir	250	
13	M. Nohrs	175	
14	F. Peans	375	
15	G. Singh	150	
16	S. Sleazy	500	350,000
17	T. Wong	325	
18	Total	3,570	

Now hide the row and column again to cover your tracks.

6 Select column **C**.

7 On the **Home** tab, in the **Cells** group, click **Format**, click **Hide & Unhide** and then click **Hide Columns**.

Use the mouse to hide a row.

8 Move the mouse pointer to the bottom edge of the row **16** header.

The mouse pointer will change to a double-headed pointer.

9 Click and drag the row **16** header upwards until the height is 0.00 (touching the bottom edge of row 15).

10 Save and close the workbook.

Finding and Replacing Data

Finding Data

You can search a worksheet for every occurrence of a value (text label or number), function name or cell reference. In the event you need to find every cell that contains this search item, the **Find** feature is invaluable.

To activate the Find feature, use one of the following methods:

- On the **Home** tab, in the **Editing** group, click **Find & Select** and then click **Find**; or
- press (Ctrl)+(F).

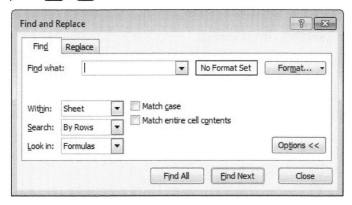

MMM
Find and
Delete a Line
Online
Exercise

You will have to click the **Options** button to display all of the options shown in the diagram above.

Find what	Define the value to search.
Within	Search only within the current worksheet or the entire workbook.
Search	Indicate which direction to search by: **By Rows**: Search from left to right across each row in the worksheet or workbook starting from the top row. **By Columns:** Search down each column starting from the leftmost column.
Look in	Specify whether to look only at the value, the underlying formula or any comment in each cell. The **Formulas** option is generally more flexible even if the cell contains just a value.
Match case	Specify whether to match the upper and lower case of alphabetic characters in the cell.
Match entire cell contents	Specify whether the **Find what** value must form the entire contents of the searched cell.

Replacing Data

You can also replace the search item with a new value, on an individual basis by using Replace, or for all cells that contain that value by using **Replace All**. The **Replace** function simplifies and speeds up the job of replacing one word or value with another. This automated process virtually eliminates any typing errors you would have made if you had done it manually.

To activate the Replace feature, use one of the following methods:

- On the **Home** tab, in the **Editing** group, click **Find & Select**, and click **Replace**; or
- press (Ctrl)+(H); or
- if the Find dialog box is displayed, click the **Replace** tab.

You may want to use **Replace** to control and verify that each replacement should be made. An alternative is to use the **Find** tab before using the replace function to search through the worksheet and verify that your search value and options have been set correctly. Once you are certain that your search value and options are correct, you can proceed with using **Replace All**.

Learn the Skill

This exercise demonstrates how to find all cells that contain a specific data value, and then replace that data value with a new value.

1   Open the *World Capitals* workbook.

First try looking for a word.

2   On the **Home** tab, in the **Editing** group, click **Find & Select** and then click **Find**.

3   In the **Find what** text box, type: united and click **Find Next**.

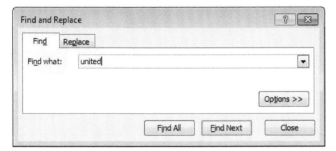

4   Click **Find Next** several more times, and observe which cells are selected.

Now try different find options.

5   In the Find and Replace dialog box, click **Options** to display all find options.

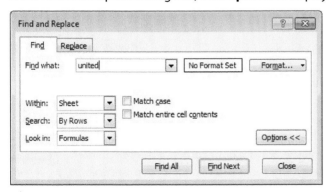

6   Click **Match case** to turn it on and then click **Find Next**.

A message box displays with the message "Microsoft Office Excel cannot find the data you're searching for." Even though Excel had no problem earlier looking for the word *united*, none of the cells contains the word *united* in all lower case characters.

7   Click **OK** to close the message box.

8   Click **Find what**, and change the value to search for to: United (be sure to use upper case for the first letter).

9   Click **Find Next** several times.

10   In the **Find what** text box, delete United and replace it with spain.

11   Click **Match case** to turn it off, and then click **Find Next** several times.

12 Click **Match entire cell contents** to turn it on, and then click **Find Next** several times.

Now only one row is found with the word Spain as the full name.

13 Click Match entire cell contents to turn it off.

Now try the Replace feature.

14 In **Find what**, type: x and click **Find Next** several times to find all words containing the letter *x*.

15 Click the **Replace** tab.

16 In **Replace with** type: zh and click **Find Next**.

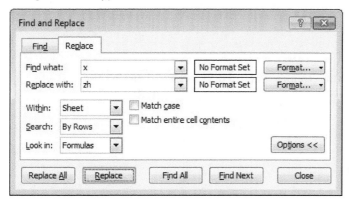

*Instead of using **Find Next**, you could click **Replace All** to replace all occurrences in the worksheet at one time.*

Excel has now found the first word with an *x* in it.

17 Click **Replace**.

18 Click **Replace All** to replace every instance of the letter *x*.

Excel has completed replacing all specific text occurrences when a message box appears with "Excel has completed its search and has made 3 replacements."

19 Click **OK** to close the message box.

20 Click **Close**.

21 Close the workbook and discard all changes.

MMM
Find and
Replace Online
Exercise

Using AutoFill

2.2

The AutoFill feature is very useful when you want to copy data or formulas to one or more consecutive, adjacent cells. You simply select the cells you want to copy and then drag the AutoFill handle (the small black square at the bottom right corner of the cell pointer) across the target cells. When you release the mouse, an AutoFill icon appears. A menu appears when you click the icon.

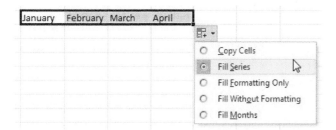

The contents of this menu vary depending on the type of data you are copying or filling. Some of the more common options include:

Copy Cells	Copy text, values or formulas with their formatting; does not create a series.
Fill Series	Create a simple linear series and copy the formatting of the source cell. A series is a sequentially incrementing or decrementing set of values, such as 1 2 3 4, E F G H, Sun Mon Tues, -5 -10 -15 -20, Jun Jul Aug Sep.
Fill Formatting Only	Copy formatting from the source cell but leave the contents of the target cells unchanged.
Fill Without Formatting	Create a simple linear series without copying the formatting of the source cell.
Fill Months	This option appears when AutoFill recognizes the data value is the name of a month (e.g., Jan or January) and, by default, it assumes that the next value is the next month.

Depending on the type of data you are copying, AutoFill selects the **Copy Cells** or **Fill Series** option for you. In most cases, it correctly guesses which option you want in a particular situation without requiring you to use the AutoFill icon. Usually, when Excel cannot determine what the series is, you can resolve the problem by inserting another cell in the source to help identify the series (e.g., where 1 3 6 identifies a pattern of increasing by two first, then by three, and so on. If you did not enter the 6, Excel would guess that the pattern would be to increase by two for every subsequent cell.

Learn the Skill

This exercise demonstrates how the AutoFill feature works.

1. Open the *Department Budget* workbook and save as Department Budget - Student.

	A	B	C	D
1	Tolano Adventures			
2	Department Budget			
3				
4				
5	Revenues:			
6		Sales	6500	
7		Other Revenues	35	
8		Total:		
9				
10	Expenses:			
11		Rent	5000	
12		Telephone	150	
13		Internet	125	
14		Courier	300	
15		Postage	75	
16		Supplies	250	
17		Photocopier	80	
18		Travel		
19		Total:		

First, enter the initial values of the series.

2. Select cell **C4** and type: Jan.

3. Select cell **C4** again and position the mouse pointer on the AutoFill handle at the bottom right corner of the cell.

The mouse cursor will change to a **+**.

4   Select and drag the mouse across to cell **E4**.

Excel also displays the last AutoFill value as a screen tip while you drag the mouse across the cells. Now observe the effects of using AutoFill on cells containing numeric values.

5   Select cells **C6** to **C17** and use the mouse to drag the AutoFill handle across to column **E**.

Repeat for the other two worksheets.

6   Select **Sheet2**.

7   Select cell **C4** and type: Apr. Select cells **C4** to **C17** and use the mouse to drag the AutoFill handle across to column **E**.

8   Select **Sheet3**.

9   Select cell **C4** and type: Jul. Select cells **C4** to **C17** and use the mouse to drag the AutoFill handle across to column **E**.

10 Select **Sheet1** again.

The worksheet should look similar to the following:

	A	B	C	D	E	F
1	Tolano Adventures					
2	Department Budget					
3						
4			Jan	Feb	Mar	
5	Revenues:					
6		Sales	6500	6500	6500	
7		Other Revenues	35	35	35	
8		Total:				
9						
10	Expenses:					
11		Rent	5000	5000	5000	
12		Telephone	150	150	150	
13		Internet	125	125	125	
14		Courier	300	300	300	
15		Postage	75	75	75	
16		Supplies	250	250	250	
17		Photocopier	80	80	80	
18		Travel				
19		Total:				
20						
21						

Sheet1 / Sheet2 / Sheet3

11 Save the workbook.

Learn the Skill

This exercise demonstrates how to use the Auto Fill Options feature.

1   Open the *AutoFill Series* workbook and save as AutoFill Series - Student.

	A	B	C	D	E	F	G
1	*Monday*	10	1-Jan-10	text	Harry	11:00 AM	$15.45
2	*Monday*	10	1-Jan-10	text	Harry	11:00 AM	$15.45
3	*Monday*	10	1-Jan-10	text	Harry	11:00 AM	$15.45
4	*Monday*	10	1-Jan-10	text	Harry	11:00 AM	$15.45
5	*Monday*	10	1-Jan-10	text	Harry	11:00 AM	$15.45
6	*Monday*	10	1-Jan-10	text	Harry	11:00 AM	$15.45

First, enter the initial values of the series.

2   Select cell **A1** and position the mouse pointer on the AutoFill handle at the bottom right corner of the cell.

3   Select and drag the mouse across to cell **G1**.

4   Click **Auto Fill Options** to look at which options are selected.

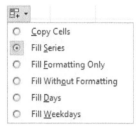

5   Select the **Copy Cells** option.

The **Copy Cells** option changes the AutoFill feature to a copy and paste.

Repeat these steps using the remaining rows to demonstrate the other **Auto Fill Options**.

6   Select cell **A2**, drag the AutoFill handle across to cell **G2**, and select **Fill Series** from the **Auto Fill Options** menu.

The **Fill Series** option is the default for AutoFill, where the next consecutive value is automatically generated for each successive cell in the series.

7   Select cell **A3**, drag the AutoFill handle across to cell **G3**, and select **Fill Formatting Only** from the **Auto Fill Options** menu.

This option copies only the formatting from the originating cell to the target cells, but the data is not changed.

8   Select cell **A4**, drag the AutoFill handle across to cell **G4**, and select **Fill Without Formatting** from the **Auto Fill Options** menu.

This option creates the series, except the formatting in the target cells is not changed.

9   Select cell **A5**, drag the AutoFill handle across to cell **G5**, and select **Fill Days** from the **Auto Fill Options** menu.

This option only appears when AutoFill recognizes the data as a day of week value. The target cells then become the next day of week value in the series.

10 Select cell **A6**, drag the AutoFill handle across to cell **G6**, and select **Fill Weekdays** from the **Auto Fill Options** menu.

This option is also only valid when the originating cell is a day of week value. Notice that the days of week value in the series are only Monday to Friday values.

The completed worksheet should appear similar to the following:

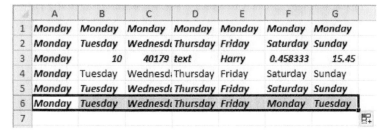

11 Save and close the workbook.

Managing Worksheets

An Excel workbook is actually a collection of several worksheets. Each of these worksheets can be treated as being independent from one another although typically, they are related to one another. For example, one worksheet may contain the list of expenses for a company, another worksheet may contain the revenues for each product sold, and a third worksheet may have the summary of both the revenues and expenses. Formulas can be used to refer to any cell in any worksheet, to bring data together into one worksheet and to perform calculations.

You can rename worksheets, as well as adding, deleting, copying or moving them around in a workbook. You move from one worksheet to another by using worksheet tabs.

To navigate between the worksheets, use the tab scrolling buttons at the bottom left of each workbook's window. If your workbook has many worksheets (e.g. more than 10) or the worksheet names are very long, your screen may not display all of the worksheet tabs at the same time and some may become hidden behind the horizontal scroll bar. Use these buttons to shift the hidden worksheet tabs to the left or right. Alternatively, you can view more worksheet tabs by shrinking the horizontal scroll bar.

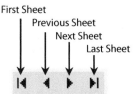

Most workbooks typically make use of only one worksheet although, by default, Excel creates every new workbook with three worksheets (named *Sheet1*, *Sheet2*, and *Sheet3*).

On the opposite extreme, you should avoid using a single workbook to store all of your information. The workbook would become unwieldy to manage, would take too long to load and save, and would consume too many computer resources when it is open. Instead, put unrelated information—such as the list of employees for the company—in a different workbook from the one containing a list of sales office addresses.

Renaming Worksheets

Excel's use of *Sheet1, Sheet2, Sheet3,* and so on is useful to identify the different sheets when you first access your workbook. However, it is not very descriptive after you have entered information on several worksheets. Assigning more descriptive names to the tabs will make navigating your worksheets much easier, particularly when you have used several sheets to enter the information.

As you rename your worksheets, Excel will adjust the size of the tabs based on the number of characters in the name. Even though Excel permits up to 31 characters per tab, it is best to keep the tab names short. If you have several worksheets with long sheet tab names, you will not be able to see very many of the worksheet tabs on the screen at one time, which will make navigating between them more difficult.

To rename a worksheet tab, use one of the following methods:

- Double-click the sheet tab to put it in editing mode for renaming; or
- right-click the sheet tab and click **Rename**.

Learn the Skill

The following exercise involves placing sheet tab names in a workbook.

1   If necessary, open the *Department Budget - Student* workbook.

2   Double-click the *Sheet1* tab.

   The tab label for this sheet is now highlighted.

3   Type: Quarter 1 to rename the tab and press (Enter).

4   Right-click the *Sheet2* tab.

5   Click **Rename**.

6   Type: Quarter 2 to rename the tab and press (Enter).

7   Right-click the *Sheet3* tab.

8   Click **Rename**.

9   Type: Quarter 3 to rename the tab and press (Enter).

10 Click the *Quarter 1* sheet tab.

   The worksheet should now appear as shown in the following example:

	A	B	C	D	E	F
1	Tolano Adventures					
2	Department Budget					
3						
4			Jan	Feb	Mar	
5	Revenues:					
6		Sales	6500	6500	6500	
7		Other Revenues	35	35	35	
8		Total:				
9						
10	Expenses:					
11		Rent	5000	5000	5000	
12		Telephone	150	150	150	
13		Internet	125	125	125	
14		Courier	300	300	300	
15		Postage	75	75	75	
16		Supplies	250	250	250	
17		Photocopier	80	80	80	
18		Travel				
19		Total:				
20						
21						

   ◄ ◄ ► ► **Quarter 1** / Quarter 2 / Quarter 3 / 💬 /

11 Save the workbook.

Inserting or Deleting Worksheets

4.1

When you create a new workbook, Excel includes three worksheets by default. You can change this default setting any time. You can also manually add more worksheets to a workbook at any time.

If there are more worksheet tabs than the status bar can display at one time, you can use the tab scrolling buttons to display the other worksheet tabs.

When you no longer need worksheets, you can remove them from the workbook. You should save your workbook before deleting a worksheet because, once deleted, you cannot retrieve a worksheet with the **Undo** command. You should also check every worksheet for error messages after deleting it—there may have been formulas in the deleted worksheet that will affect the values in the rest of the worksheets.

To insert a new blank worksheet into a workbook, use one of the following methods:

- On the **Home** tab, in the **Cells** group, click the arrow for **Insert**, and click **Insert Sheet**; or
- click the **Insert Worksheet** tab; or

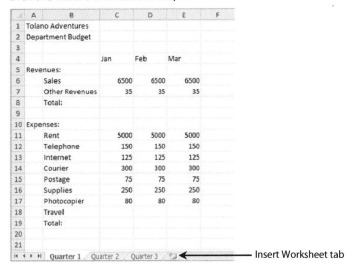

right-click the sheet tab where the worksheet is to be inserted and click **Insert**. In the Insert dialog box, click the **Worksheet** template and then click **OK**.

- If you use the **Insert Worksheet** method, Excel will add the tab for the new worksheet to the far right of all existing worksheets. If you use either of the other two methods, Excel will add the new worksheet to the left of the active worksheet.

To delete a worksheet, use one of the following methods:

- On the **Home** tab, in the **Cells** group, click the arrow for **Delete**, and then click **Delete Sheet**; or
- right-click the sheet tab to be deleted and click **Delete**.

Moving or Copying Worksheets

4.1

You may occasionally want to change the sequence of the worksheets in a workbook, although you are actually simply changing the sequence in which the tabs appear. This feature is useful in organizing multi-worksheet workbooks. For example, placing related worksheets close together enables you to switch between them without the additional step of using the tab scrolling buttons.

It is also easy to make an exact copy of an existing worksheet. This is a useful feature for creating different scenarios when performing a what-if analysis.

To move or copy a worksheet within a workbook, use one of the following methods:

- Right-click the sheet tab to be moved or copied and click **Move or Copy**; or
- to quickly move a worksheet, click the sheet tab for the sheet to be moved and then drag the sheet tab to the new location; or
- to quickly copy a worksheet, click the sheet tab for the sheet to be copied, press Ctrl and then drag the sheet tab to the new location.

You can also move or copy a worksheet from one workbook to a new workbook by dragging the worksheet tab. If you drag the worksheet tab and drop it in an empty part of the Excel application window, Excel will automatically create a new workbook with that worksheet.

Learn the Skill

The following exercise involves adding a new worksheet to a workbook.

1 Select the *Department Budget - Student* workbook.

2 Click the **Insert Worksheet** tab next to the *Quarter 3* worksheet tab to add a new worksheet.

Note that the new worksheet is added to the right of the existing worksheet tabs.

3 Right-click on the new worksheet tab and click **Rename**.

4 Type: Company to rename the tab and press ⎣Enter⎤.

5 On the **Home** tab, in the **Cells** group, click the arrow under **Insert** and click **Insert Sheet**.

Notice that this procedure adds the new worksheet to the left of the current worksheet instead of the far right. The worksheet should now look similar to the following example:

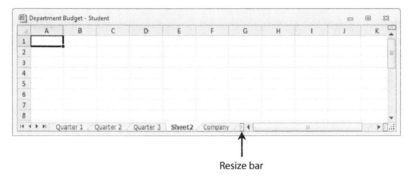

Resize bar

With the addition of this second worksheet, the number of tabs may now exceed the space available to display them all, resulting in some worksheet tabs or the **Insert Worksheet** tab being hidden from view.

6 Position the cursor over the **Resize bar** located at the left side of the horizontal scroll bar so that the mouse cursor changes to ╫.

7 Click and drag the **Resize bar** to the right or left as desired.

Now enter data into this new worksheet and try deleting it.

8 Select the *Sheet2* worksheet and type your first name in cell **A1**.

9 On the **Home** tab, in the **Cells** group, click the arrow for **Delete** and then click **Delete Sheet**.

If nothing has been entered into the worksheet, Excel deletes it without any further prompting. However, if the worksheet contains data, Excel issues a warning message regarding data contents that might affect other data in the workbook.

10 Click **Delete**.

The worksheet has been deleted from the workbook.

11 Right-click the *Quarter 1* worksheet tab and click **Move or Copy**.

The Move or Copy dialog box now appears. By default, Excel moves the current active worksheet to a new position. Selecting the **Create a copy** check box creates a copy of the current active worksheet at the new position.

12   Select the **Create a copy** check box.

13   Click **Company** in the **Before sheet** list and click **OK**.

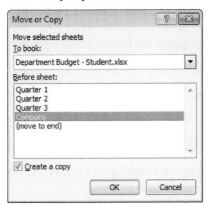

Excel has now created a copy of the current worksheet, including the worksheet name. Because no two worksheets can have the exactly the same name, Excel has appended a number at the end of the new worksheet name.

14   Double-click the *Quarter 1 (2)* worksheet tab and change it to Quarter 4.

15   Select cell **C4**. Type: Oct and select cell **C4** again. Use the mouse to drag the AutoFill handle across to column **E**.

Now move one of the worksheets to a different location.

16   Click the *Company* tab and drag it to a new position to the left of the *Quarter 1* sheet tab, but do not release the mouse button yet.

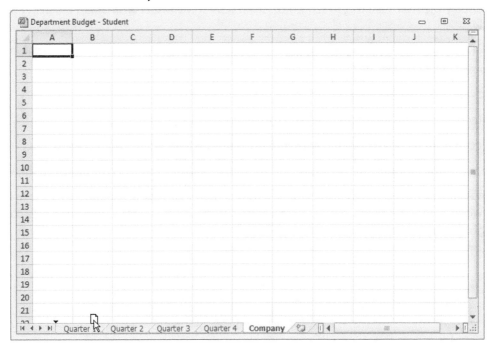

Notice the icon and arrow indicating that you are moving a sheet into this location.

17   At the new location, release the mouse button.

18   Save and close the workbook.

Hiding/Unhiding Worksheets

4.1

Similar to hiding and unhiding a column or row, you can also hide or unhide an entire worksheet. The main reason for hiding a worksheet is to prevent other users from viewing the data or formulas used there.

You can hide as many worksheets in a workbook as you want, in any sequence. However, you must have at least one unhidden worksheet in a workbook. If you need to hide all worksheets, then you likely need to apply protection to the workbook instead.

When unhiding worksheets, you will be presented with a dialog box displaying all hidden worksheets for this workbook. From this list, you can select the worksheets to unhide.

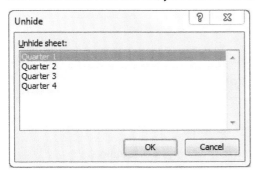

Learn the Skill

This exercise demonstrates how to hide and unhide a worksheet.

1   Select the *Department Budget - Student* workbook.

2   Select the *Quarter 1* worksheet.

3   On the **Home** tab, in the **Cells** group, click **Format**, point at **Hide & Unhide**, and then click **Hide Sheet**.

   The *Quarter 1* worksheet is now hidden. Hide another worksheet using the right-click menu.

4   Right-click on the *Quarter 2* worksheet tab, and click **Hide** in the pop-up menu.

Hide all of the remaining worksheets.

5   Repeat step 4 with the *Quarter 3* and *Quarter 4* worksheets.

6   Attempt to repeat step 4 with the *Company* worksheet.

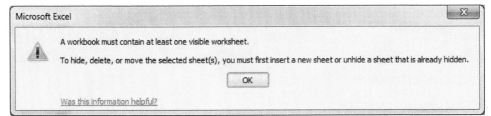

7   Click **OK** to close the message box.

Unhide each of the hidden worksheets. Excel does not allow you to unhide more than one worksheet at a time.

8   On the **Home** tab, in the **Cells** group, click **Format**, point at **Hide & Unhide**, and then click **Unhide Sheet**.

> *If a workbook does not have any hidden worksheets, the **Unhide Sheet** menu item is grayed out.*

The Unhide dialog box displays, showing a list of all worksheets currently hidden in this workbook.

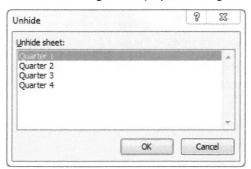

9   Select the *Quarter 1* worksheet and click **OK**.

Use the right-click menu to display the Unhide dialog box.

10   Right-click on the *Quarter 1* worksheet tab and click **Unhide**.

11   Select the *Quarter 4* worksheet and click **OK**.

12   Repeat steps 10 and 11 for the *Quarter 2* and *Quarter 3* worksheets.

The workbook is now restored with all sheets showing in their original sequence.

13   Save the workbook.

Adding Color to the Worksheet Tabs

You can add color to the worksheet tabs to help identify your worksheets. The color will appear as a line below the worksheet name when the worksheet is active on the screen and it will have a colored background when the worksheet is not active (similar to a divider tab). This can be handy if, for example, you are creating a budget for multiple departments in your company; you can use different colors for each department and then color code the budget in each worksheet tab for the corresponding departments.

Similar to background colors for worksheet cells, you can choose from standard or theme colors for worksheet tabs.

To display the color palette for a worksheet tab, click the worksheet tab and then use one of the following methods:

*   On the **Home** tab, in the **Cells** group, click **Format** and click **Tab Color**, or
*   right-click the worksheet tab and click **Tab Color**.

Learn the Skill

This exercise demonstrates how adding color to worksheet tabs can help to identify the worksheets.

---

1   Select the *Department Budget - Student* workbook.

2   Select the *Quarter 1* worksheet.

3   On the **Home** tab, in the **Cells** group, click **Format** and point at **Tab Color** to display the color palette.

4   Click **Blue** in the Standard Colors section (third from the right) of the color palette.

Notice how the worksheet tab now shows a blue line below it.

The color palette can also be displayed by right-clicking the worksheet tab.

5   Click the *Quarter 2* tab.

Notice how Excel now displays the full color for the *Sheet1* tab.

6   Repeat steps 2 to 4 for the *Quarter 2* , *Quarter 3*, and *Quarter 4* tabs, picking different colors for each tab.

7   When complete, click the *Company* tab.

Your worksheet tabs should look similar to the following example:

Company   Quarter 1   Quarter 2   Quarter 3   Quarter 4

8   Save the workbook.

Lesson Summary

In this lesson, you looked at how to select items to make changes to data in the worksheet, change the structure of the worksheet, and add and remove worksheets in the workbook. You should now know how to:

☑ edit cells and undo changes

☑ cut, copy, and paste data

☑ use Paste Special

☑ use the Office Clipboard

☑ change column widths

☑ change row heights

☑ use AutoFit with columns or rows

☑ hide and unhide rows and columns

☑ insert and delete rows and columns

☑ insert and delete cells

☑ find data in the worksheet

☑ replace data with different data in the worksheet

☑ use AutoFill to copy and fill series

☑ rename worksheets

☑ insert and delete worksheets

☑ move and copy worksheets

☑ hide and unhide worksheets

☑ add color to the worksheet tabs

Review Questions

MMM
Go online for
Additional
Review and
Activities

1. Provide examples of when you might want to add several items to the Office Clipboard.

2. Provide examples of when using the AutoFit command would be the best option.

3. Explain how pressing **Delete** to delete the contents of a cell differs from using the **Delete Cells** command.

4. Provide examples of when you may want to hide rows or columns.

5. What items can Excel search for in a worksheet?

6. Give an example of when you would use **Replace** rather than **Replace All** in a worksheet.

7. Explain the difference between using the **Copy** and AutoFill features.

8. How would you set up the values if the AutoFill series is not a common series, such as weekdays, months or years?

9. Provide examples of when you might want to duplicate a worksheet.

10. What is the maximum length of a worksheet tab name?

11. How many new worksheets can you add to an Excel workbook?

12. When you insert a new worksheet using the **Insert Worksheet** tab, the new worksheet tab appears:

    a. To the left of the current worksheet tab

    b. To the far left of all worksheet tabs

    c. To the far right of all worksheet tabs

    d. In a random position, depending on which worksheet is active

    e. To the right of the current worksheet tab

Microsoft®
Excel® 2010
Core Certification

Lesson 3: Using Formulas

Lesson Objectives

In this lesson, you will learn about formulas—what they are, how they work, how to insert simple formulas and use built-in functions to create some formulas. Upon successful completion of this lesson, you will be familiar with:

- □ what formulas are

- □ how to create and edit simple formulas

- □ how to use math operators and understand the precedent order of calculations

- □ how to reference other worksheets

- □ how to use common functions

- □ how to use a conditional function

- □ how to use absolute and relative cell references

- □ how to use mixed absolute and relative cell addresses

- □ how to display and print formulas

Using Formulas
Creating and Editing Formulas

5.1
5.2
5.3

In Excel, every worksheet cell is capable of using a formula. A formula is simply a calculation involving values, cell references, and/or built-in functions. This seemingly simple concept is actually a very powerful feature for worksheets, which makes it possible to

- automatically calculate sum totals horizontally and vertically, quickly and without any calculation errors

- perform "what-if" analyses by having the worksheet recalculate a large number of formulas simultaneously to display the end result; this can save a tremendous amount of manual work, avoid calculation errors, and facilitate an almost endless cycle of trial-and-error use of base numbers in formulas that can be analyzed quickly

- create a workbook as a template for future use by removing the data values, leaving only the structure and formulas, and create new workbooks from the template much faster by entering only the new data

Worksheets can contain formulas that refer to other worksheet cells. It is to your advantage to use as many cell references in your formulas as possible; then, when these values or amounts change, changes to the dependent cells (the cells containing the formulas) are not forgotten.

A formula can have a maximum of 8,192 characters. Enter your formula in the cell where you want the results to appear. To prepare Excel for a formula, start by typing the equal sign (=).

A formula can be as simple as a single cell reference, or as complex as many cell references in addition to functions from one or multiple worksheets. For example, if the cursor is in cell **C8** and you enter a formula of *=B6*, cell **C8** will then display the same contents as in cell **B6**. If you change the value in cell **B6**, the contents in cell **C8** will also reflect the change.

If you manually enter the contents in cell **C8**, when you change cell **B6**, you also have to change cell **C8** to keep them the same.

There are two ways to enter a cell reference into a formula:

- type the cell reference (or cell address) directly; or

- point to the cells.

Excel does not display the formula you type into a cell in the worksheet, only the result of the formula. To view the formula, select the cell and you will see the formula and cell references in the formula bar. If the formula uses any cells from another worksheet, Excel will display the name of the worksheet, giving you a reference point to where the data was obtained.

You can also copy formulas to other cells. Excel will make a copy of the formula and the format while automatically adjusting cell references for the offset distance and direction. This may appear illogical at first, but it is actually a desirable feature in worksheets because the copied formulas are usually supposed to refer to different sets of input values.

When you are entering formulas in a worksheet, Excel helpfully prompts you when it detects an error or inconsistency in your formula, with a suggestion for how to correct it.

Excel displays a ⅂ symbol for easy identification whenever a formula has changed from a trend in the worksheet. This can be very handy if you have to review the worksheet for differences or discrepancies.

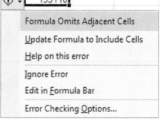

Mathematical Operators

The following show the symbols used in Excel to represent the standard mathematical operators:

* * Multiplication
* / Division
* + Addition
* − Subtraction

You generally use formulas to perform calculations, such as ordinary arithmetic. Excel calculates formulas using the standard precedence rule used in mathematics, as follows:

1. Exponents and roots
2. Multiplication and division
3. Addition and subtraction

You can alter this standard order of operation by placing components of the formula within parentheses. Excel will then calculate the portion of the formula in parentheses before defaulting to calculations in the order listed above. Thus, you can control the order of calculations in your formulas with careful use of parentheses.

Learn the Skill

This exercise demonstrates some of Excel's formula capabilities.

1 Open the *Quarterly Income Statement* workbook and save it as Quarterly Income Statement - Student. Be sure that the *Quarter 1* worksheet is selected.

2 Select cell **C8** and type: =c6+c7 (but do not press Enter yet).

Excel now shows which cell(s) you selected as part of the formula. You can use this visual tool to see what is happening on the screen when you set up a formula.

3 Press Enter to complete the formula.

4 Select cell **C8** again.

In cell **C8,** Excel displays the number *6535*, which is the sum of the numbers in cells C6 and C7. Note the formula displayed in the formula bar.

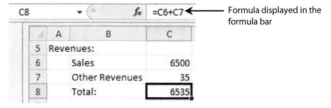

5 In cell **C7**, type: 125 and press Enter.

Excel has automatically recalculated the displayed value in cell **C8** because it contains a formula that refers to the values in cells **C6** and **C7,** and a change in either (or both) cells will cause Excel to update the total in cell **C8**. This demonstrates the advantage of using formulas in a worksheet and using a cell reference rather than the cell contents.

6   In cell **D6**, type: 6000 and press (Enter).

This time, the displayed value in cell **C8** does not change when you change the value in cell **D6**. Remember that the formula in cell **C8** has the cell reference to cell **C6**, not **D6**.

Once you enter a formula into the worksheet, you can copy the formula to another location, if the formula operation for the new location is the same. For instance, you can use the same formula to calculate the total revenues for each of the next two months, except that you must use the respective cells for each of those two months. Rather than entering the formula in each of the two cells twice, you can simply copy the formula.

7   Select cell **C8** and, on the **Home** tab, in the **Clipboard** group, click **Copy**.

8   Select cells **D8** to **E8** and, on the **Home** tab, in the **Clipboard** group, click **Paste**.

If you change a value in a referenced cell, all cells that depend on that value will also change.

9   Select each of the cells in the range **C8** to **E8**.

Notice that Excel has adjusted the formula in each of these cells. This is called *relative addressing*.

Now enter a similar formula, this time adding across three columns.

10   Select cell **F4** and enter: Total.

11   Select cell **F6** and enter: =C6+D6+E6.

12   Select cell **F6** again and copy this formula down to cells **F7** to **F8**.

If a value is changed in one cell, Excel will recalculate all formulas that directly or indirectly reference this cell automatically.

13   In cell **E7**, type: 80 and press (Enter).

14   On the Quick Access Toolbar, click **Undo** to see that the displayed values in cells E7, **E8**, **F7** and **F8** change back to their previous values.

15   On the Quick Access Toolbar, click **Redo** to re-apply the change in cell **E7**.

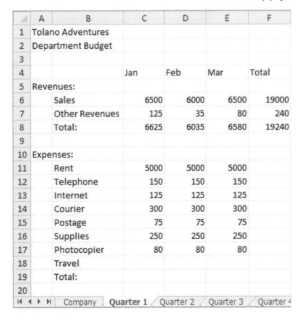

	A	B	C	D	E	F
1	Tolano Adventures					
2	Department Budget					
3						
4			Jan	Feb	Mar	Total
5	Revenues:					
6		Sales	6500	6000	6500	19000
7		Other Revenues	125	35	80	240
8		Total:	6625	6035	6580	19240
9						
10	Expenses:					
11		Rent	5000	5000	5000	
12		Telephone	150	150	150	
13		Internet	125	125	125	
14		Courier	300	300	300	
15		Postage	75	75	75	
16		Supplies	250	250	250	
17		Photocopier	80	80	80	
18		Travel				
19		Total:				
20						

Company   **Quarter 1**   Quarter 2   Quarter 3   Quarter 4

Repeat these same formulas in the other quarterly worksheets.

16   Select cell **C8** and, on the **Home** tab, in the **Clipboard** group, click **Copy.**

17   Select the *Quarter 2* worksheet, then select cells **C8** to **E8** and, on the **Home** tab, in the **Clipboard** group, click **Paste**.

18   Select the *Quarter 1* worksheet, then select cells **F4** to **F8** and, on the **Home** tab, in the **Clipboard** group, click **Copy.**

19   Select the *Quarter 2* worksheet, then select cell **F4** and, on the **Home** tab, in the **Clipboard** group, click **Paste.**

20   Repeat steps 16 to 19 for the two remaining quarterly worksheets: *Quarter 3* and *Quarter 4*.

The series of steps from 16 to 20 demonstrates one way of copying formulas from one worksheet to others. The same end result can be achieved using fewer mouse clicks by doing step 16 first, then repeating step 17 for all three quarterly worksheets. Then do step 18, and repeat step 19 for the same three worksheets. You can then do step 20. This may be faster because all you have to do is copy once and paste three times (once for each worksheet). With more experience in copying and pasting, you will find your own shortcuts to make tasks easier.

21   Save and close the workbook.

Learn the Skill

This exercise demonstrates Excel's formula capabilities.

Imagine that you are a prospective, first-time home-buyer; this worksheet will help you determine how large a mortgage you can assume given your current income and personal expenses. Many financial institutions rely on two calculations when deciding whether to approve a mortgage application: the gross debt service and the total debt service. The gross debt service is the percentage of gross income required to cover the basic costs of house, including mortgage payments (principal and interest), property taxes, heating and condo fees. The total of this cannot exceed 32% of the buyer's gross income. The total debt service is the percentage of gross income required to cover house and all other debts, such as credit card payments and car loans. This percentage cannot exceed 40% of the buyer's gross income.

1   Open the *Personal Budget* workbook and save it as `Personal Budget - Student`.

	A	B	C	D
1	Personal Budget			
2				Gross Debt Service:
3	Monthly Gross Salary	4000		
4	Monthly Take Home Pay			
5				
6	Expenses:			
7	Rent	1300		
8	Property taxes	0		
9	Condo monthly fee	0		
10	Food	250		
11	Car payments	300		Total Debt Service:
12	Car insurance	150		
13	Parking	130		Other debts:
14	Clothing	150		
15	Heat & electricty	50		
16	Phone	60		
17	Entertainment	250		
18	Student loan payments	150		
19	Credit card payments	200		
20	Total Expenses	2990		
21				
22	Savings/Withdrawals			

First, calculate your monthly take-home pay by reducing the monthly gross salary by 25%. This calculation assumes that income taxes and other payroll deductions add up to 25% of your gross pay. You need both your gross pay and take-home pay amounts for these calculations.

2   Select cell **B4**, type: =b3*0.75 and press (Enter).

Now calculate the excess of your take-home pay over your expenses, which you accumulate as savings in a bank account.

3   Select cell **B22**, type: =b4-b20 and press (Enter).

At first glance, you appear to be ready to apply for a mortgage to buy your very first home! Now assume that the current rent payments will become the new monthly mortgage payment.

4   Select cell **A7**, type: Mortgage payments and press (Enter).

After looking at some homes, you can now estimate your property taxes and monthly condominium fees.

5   Select cell **B8**, type: 125 and press (Enter).

6   Select cell **B9**, type: 100 and press (Enter).

Your income can no longer cover all of your expenses. You will have to cut back.

7   Select cell **B17**, type: 100 and press (Enter).

8   Select cell **B14**, type: 100 and press (Enter).

Your cost cutting will have to include getting a smaller mortgage.

9   Select cell **B7**, type: 1285 and press (Enter).

With your monthly expenses now under control, calculate the mortgage qualification ratios.

10 Select cell **D3**, type: =A7 and press (Enter).

Notice that you can make a cell reference to a cell containing a text value, as demonstrated here.

11 Select cell **E3**, type: =B7 and press (Enter).

Alternatively, you can copy the formula from cell **D3** to cell **E3**; Excel will automatically adjust the formula to reference the next cell to the right.

12 Enter the following formulas in the specified cells:

D4	=A8
D5	=A9
D6	=A15
D7	Total housing costs
D8	Ratio (max 32%)

13 Select cells **D4** to **D6** and, on the **Home** tab, in the **Clipboard** group, click **Copy**.

14 Select cell **E4** and, on the **Home** tab, in the **Clipboard** group, click **Paste**.

15 Enter the following formulas in the specified cells:

E7	=E3+E4+E5+E6
E8	=E7/B3

You calculate the gross debt service as 39% (0.39), which is higher than the maximum allowable 32%. Now calculate the total debt service ratio.

16   Enter the following formulas in the specified cells:

       D12   =D7
       D14   =A11
       D15   =A18
       D16   =A19
       D17   Total debt costs
       D18   Ratio (max 40%)

17   Copy the contents of cell **D12** to cell **E12**.

18   Select cells **D14** to **D16**, then click the AutoFill handle (✛) in the bottom right corner of this block and drag it across to column **E**.

19   Enter the following formulas in the specified cells:

       E17   =E12+E14+E15+E16
       E18   =E17/B3

You have calculated the total debt ratio as 55.25% (0.5525)—much higher than the maximum allowable 40%. You have too many debt (and other mandatory) payments to make every month to qualify for this mortgage. You will need to make more adjustments in your lifestyle to qualify for a mortgage, such as reducing or paying off your credit card debt, student loans, and car payments. You should also consider looking for a better-paying job.

20   Enter the following values in the specified cells:

       B19   100
       B18   0
       B7   1000
       B3   4100

This income level is still not enough.

21   Change the contents of cell **B3** again to: 4200.

This demonstrates how you can use cell references very effectively in what-if analyses. The completed worksheet should look similar to the following example:

	A	B	C	D	E
1	Personal Budget				
2				Gross Debt Service:	
3	Monthly Gross Salary	4200		Mortgage payments	1000
4	Monthly Take Home Pay	3150		Property taxes	125
5				Condo monthly fee	100
6	Expenses:			Heat & electricty	50
7	Mortgage payments	1000		Total housing costs	1275
8	Property taxes	125		Ratio (max 32%)	0.303571
9	Condo monthly fee	100			
10	Food	250			
11	Car payments	300		Total Debt Service:	
12	Car insurance	150		Total housing costs	1275
13	Parking	130		Other debts:	
14	Clothing	100		Car payments	300
15	Heat & electricty	50		Student loan payments	0
16	Phone	60		Credit card payments	100
17	Entertainment	100		Total debt costs	1675
18	Student loan payments	0		Ratio (max 40%)	0.39881
19	Credit card payments	100			
20	Total Expenses	2465			
21					
22	Savings/Withdrawals	685			

22   Save and close the workbook.

Referencing Other Worksheets

In addition to referencing other cells within the same worksheet, formulas can reference cells in other worksheets within the same workbook. The general format of this kind of reference is: '<worksheet name>'!<cell reference>

Excel uses the ! symbol to indicate that this cell is located in a different worksheet. The single quotes are required if the worksheet name has blank spaces in it.

Learn the Skill

This exercise demonstrates how to create formulas that reference cells in other worksheets.

1   Open the *Quarterly Income Statement - Student* workbook.

2   Click the *Company* worksheet tab to make it the active worksheet.

	A	B	C	D	E
1	Tolano Adventures				
2	Quarterly Income Statement				
3					
4					
5	Revenues:				
6		Sales			
7		Other Revenues			
8		Total:			
9					
10	Expenses:				
11		Rent			
12		Telephone			
13		Internet			
14		Courier			
15		Postage			
16		Supplies			
17		Photocopier			
18		Travel			
19		Total:			

3   In cell **C4**, type: Qtr 1 and press (Enter).

4   In cell **C6**, type: = (but do not press (Enter) yet).

5   Click the *Quarter 1* worksheet and select cell **F6**.

Notice that a marquee now appears around cell **F6** and the formula bar shows =*'Quarter 1'!F6* with single quotes around the worksheet name.

6   Press (Enter).

7   Copy the contents of cell **C6** (in the *Company* worksheet) to cells **C7** to **C8** using your preferred method.

Notice that Excel automatically adjusts only the cell reference part, while keeping the worksheet reference component unchanged.

8   Select cell **C4.** Then click the AutoFill handle (**+**) in the bottom right corner and drag it across the worksheet to column **F**.

9   Repeat steps 4 to 7 for the other three quarters in columns **D** to **F**.

The completed workbook should look similar to the following example:

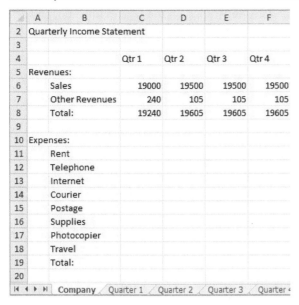

	A	B	C	D	E	F
2	Quarterly Income Statement					
3						
4			Qtr 1	Qtr 2	Qtr 3	Qtr 4
5	Revenues:					
6		Sales	19000	19500	19500	19500
7		Other Revenues	240	105	105	105
8		Total:	19240	19605	19605	19605
9						
10	Expenses:					
11		Rent				
12		Telephone				
13		Internet				
14		Courier				
15		Postage				
16		Supplies				
17		Photocopier				
18		Travel				
19		Total:				
20						

Company / Quarter 1 / Quarter 2 / Quarter 3 / Quarter 4

10 Save the workbook.

Using Functions
Common Excel Functions

5.4
5.6

Typing cell addresses and plus signs is a good method when you are adding the contents of a small number of cells. However, if you need to sum up a column of 50 numbers, this method is time-consuming and will soon exceed the maximum limits on cell contents. It would be very inefficient to enter something like "=B1+B2+B3+B4+…B50" for each cell you want to include.

Excel provides a large library of pre-built functions to facilitate this and other types of mathematical and data operations. More details are available later in the courseware and in Microsoft Excel Help. In this courseware, you will learn the most commonly used functions.

An Excel function follows this general format:

=FUNCTION(arguments)

At first, it may appear that the number and variety of Excel functions is intimidating. The most commonly used ones are similar to each other, and very easy to use. The functions you will learn in this lesson are:

=SUM	Sum the range of specified cells.
=AVERAGE	Average the specified cells (total the range and divide the total by the number of entries).
=MIN	Display the minimum value of specified cells.
=MAX	Display the maximum value of specified cells.
=COUNT	Count the number of cells in the specified range that contain numbers.

The Excel Expert courseware examines many of the other functions available.

There are some general rules to understand regarding the arguments used in the functions:

- Functions accept values (numeric, text or date, depending on the type of function) and cell references as arguments within parentheses. Each function has specifications for its arguments, but the most common type of argument is a cell range. The format of the cell range is as follows:

    <first cell address>:<last cell address>
    Examples:
    A10:B15
    D25:B5
    C5:C25

- Many functions allow you to enter a variable number of arguments. For example:

    =SUM(C6:C18) – calculates the sum of the numbers in all cells from C6 to C18

    =SUM(C6:C18,D6:D18,F6:F18) – calculates the sum of the numbers in all cells from C6 to C18, and D6 to D18, and F6 to F18

    =SUM(C6:C18,C20) – calculates the sum of the numbers in all cells from C6 to C18, and cell C20

You can enter a cell range either by typing the cell reference(s) directly, or by using the pointing method. To use the pointing method, simply use the mouse to click and drag to select the cell range. The latter method has the advantage of visually identifying the cell range, which reduces the possibility of entering incorrect cell references.

An alternative to entering the SUM function into a cell is to use the AutoSum button in the Ribbon. Because the SUM function is so commonly used, Excel provides three ways of activating it:

If the Excel window is in Maximize view, this command appears as AutoSum. If the window is in Restore view, this appears as just an icon.

- On the **Formulas** tab, in the **Function Library** group, click **AutoSum;** or
- on the **Home** tab, in the **Editing** group, click **AutoSum.**
- You can also click **Insert Function** on the left of the formula bar.

When using AutoSum, be sure to verify that you have selected the correct cell range. Excel will automatically select the range of cells immediately above or to the left of the selected cell, and display it for you to accept or change.

Notice that there is an arrow next to AutoSum. When you click the arrow, it will display other common functions that you can use in your formulas.

Learn the Skill

This exercise demonstrates how to calculate the sum total of a row or column of numbers.

1　Open the *Quarterly Income Statement - Student* workbook.

2　Click the *Quarter 1* worksheet tab and select cell **C19**.

3　On the **Home** tab, in the **Editing** group, click **AutoSum**.

Notice that the cell now shows *=SUM(C11:C18)*, with the cell range **C11:C18** highlighted, and a marquee showing around that cell range. Excel also reminds you of other ways to enter this formula using individual data values.

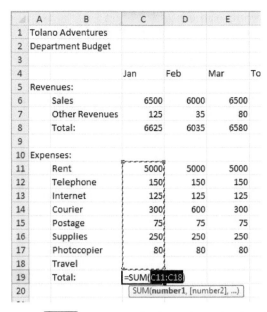

	A	B	C	D	E	
1	Tolano Adventures					
2	Department Budget					
3						
4			Jan	Feb	Mar	To
5	Revenues:					
6		Sales	6500	6000	6500	
7		Other Revenues	125	35	80	
8		Total:	6625	6035	6580	
9						
10	Expenses:					
11		Rent	5000	5000	5000	
12		Telephone	150	150	150	
13		Internet	125	125	125	
14		Courier	300	600	300	
15		Postage	75	75	75	
16		Supplies	250	250	250	
17		Photocopier	80	80	80	
18		Travel				
19		Total:	=SUM(C11:C18)			
20			SUM(**number1**, [number2], ...)			

4   Press (Enter) to accept the formula as displayed.

Excel always includes the cell immediately above the active cell, even if it is blank, and extends up the current column until it finds a blank cell. There are still numbers in the cells above the selected range, but they are not automatically included because there is at least one blank cell between them. You can manually extend the range to include additional cells.

5   Select cell **C19** again and copy it to cells **D19** to **E19**.

6   Select cell **F11** and type: =SUM(but do not press (Enter) yet.

7   Use the mouse to select the cell range **C11** to **E11.** Then type:) and press (Enter).

You may enter cell references and the function name in lower or upper case characters. Excel will convert them all to upper case.

In this case, Excel permits you to omit entering the last parenthesis for this function. However, Excel does not always permit this, and it is poor practice.

8   Select cell **F11** again and copy it to cells **F12** to **F19**.

Other arithmetic operations can be performed in a formula, such as multiplication. If a cell contains a formula that is different from the cells around it (if any), Excel displays a marker symbol.

9   Select cell **F14**.

10   Type: =C14+D14+E14 and press (Enter).

The worksheet should look similar to the following example:

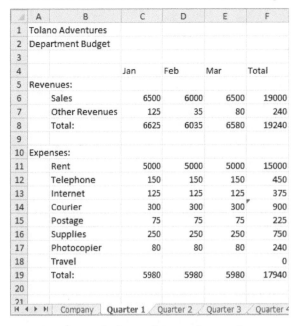

▲	A	B	C	D	E	F
1	Tolano Adventures					
2	Department Budget					
3						
4			Jan	Feb	Mar	Total
5	Revenues:					
6		Sales	6500	6000	6500	19000
7		Other Revenues	125	35	80	240
8		Total:	6625	6035	6580	19240
9						
10	Expenses:					
11		Rent	5000	5000	5000	15000
12		Telephone	150	150	150	450
13		Internet	125	125	125	375
14		Courier	300	300	300	900
15		Postage	75	75	75	225
16		Supplies	250	250	250	750
17		Photocopier	80	80	80	240
18		Travel				0
19		Total:	5980	5980	5980	17940
20						
21						

◄ ◄ ► ►   Company   **Quarter 1**   Quarter 2   Quarter 3   Quarter 4

Note the ⊤ symbol in cell **F14**. This marker is a reminder that this cell contains a formula that is different from the cells around it. It is not an error symbol because the different formula may be intentional. To remove the symbol, click on the smart tag.

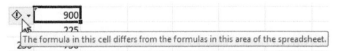

The formula in this cell differs from the formulas in this area of the spreadsheet.

11 Select cell **F14** again, position the mouse over the smart tag, click the arrow and select **Ignore Error**.

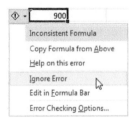

900

Inconsistent Formula

Copy Formula from Above
Help on this error

Ignore Error
Edit in Formula Bar
Error Checking Options...

12 Select cell **C19** again and copy it to cells **C19** to **E19** in worksheets *Quarter 2*, *Quarter 3*, and *Quarter 4*.

13 Select cell **F11** in the *Quarter 1* worksheet again and copy it to cells **F11** to **F19** in worksheets *Quarter 2*, *Quarter 3* and *Quarter 4*.

14 Save and close the workbook.

There is no need to be concerned about the look of your worksheet. At this point, it is important to make sure the data is accurate. Enhancing the look of the worksheet can take place later. We will look at formatting in the next lesson.

3243-1 v1.00 © CCI Learning Solutions Inc.

Learn the Skill

This exercise demonstrates some of the other commonly used functions. You will use an alternative way of inserting functions into the worksheet.

1   Open the *Rainfall* workbook and save it as Rainfall - Student.

	A	B	C	D	E	F	G
1	Rainfall at Weather Stations						
2							
3		Station 1	Station 2	Station 3	Station 4	Station 5	Total
4	Monday	9.2	3.5	2.6	9.1	1	
5	Tuesday	8.5	7	4.2	10	5	
6	Wednesday	8.1	1.4	9.6	9.3	3.9	
7	Thursday	9.6	7.2	2	7	0.5	
8	Friday	7.4	9.4	9		8.9	
9	Saturday	7.2	1.1	5.4	6.9	8.5	
10	Sunday		1.3	3	4.4	5.9	
11	Total Rainfall for Week						
12							
13	Average Rainfall						
14	Lowest Rainfall						
15	Highest Rainfall						
16	# of Days of Rain						

Now use the **Sum** button to generate the SUM function for each row.

2   Select cell **B11**.

3   On the **Formulas** tab, in the **Function Library** group, click **AutoSum** and press (Enter).

> *The AutoSum button is commonly used; Excel has put this button in two locations in the Ribbon.*

Copy the SUM function to the remaining cells.

4   Select cell **B11** again and copy that formula across to the cell range **C11** to **F11**.

You can also manually select the range of cells before activating the AutoSum.

5   Select the cell range **B4** to **F4**, then on the **Formulas** tab, in the **Function Library** group, click **AutoSum** .

6   Select cell **G4** again and copy that formula down to the cell range **G5** to **G11**.

Now use some other common functions.

7   Select cell **B13**.

8   Click **Insert Function** to the left of the formula bar.

> *You can also activate the Insert Function by clicking the arrow for AutoSum and clicking More Functions.*

This dialog box will display the functions most recently used on this computer.

9   Under **Select a function**, click **AVERAGE**. If it does not appear there, click the arrow for **Or select a category**, click **Statistical** and then click **AVERAGE**. Click **OK**.

The **Number1** and **Number2** text boxes are the arguments that you will include in the **Average** formula. As the **Average** function is capable of evaluating multiple cell ranges, Excel displays more than one text box. In this case, you have only to enter the one cell range in the **Number1** box. If the cell range is not correct, you must enter the correct range. You can either type in the range in the appropriate area or point to the cell range in the worksheet. If Function Arguments dialog box is hiding the desired cell range, you can move it out of the way, or click the **Collapse** button to the right of the cell area. The dialog box will disappear temporarily while you point to the range.

10 If necessary, click **Collapse** to the right of the **Number1** box.

Hint: You do not have to collapse the Function Arguments dialog box to select the cell range; you can leave the dialog box as full size and simply move it out of the way. The collapse button is useful if you have limited viewing area such as when viewing multiple documents at once, or when using a small monitor.

11 If necessary, drag the collapsed Function Arguments dialog box out of the way and, on the worksheet, select cells **B4** to **B10** and press ⟨ Enter ⟩.

The Function Arguments dialog box now appears similar to the following example:

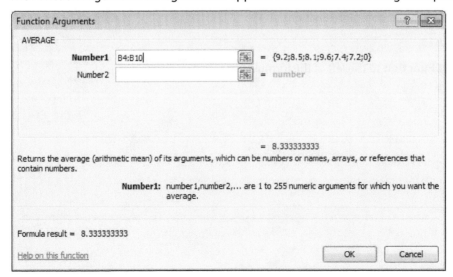

12 Click **OK** to complete the **Average** formula.

The Insert Function dialog box is the tool of choice for many Excel users. It not only gives you full access to all available functions in Excel, but also provides full context-sensitive help on each argument in each function. This extensive capability helps users correctly set up any function, no matter how complex it is. However, once you have mastered a particular function, the dialog box method can become tedious. Now insert the other formulas using the Ribbon, which is the faster method.

13 Select cell **B14**.

14 On the **Home** tab, in the **Editing** group, click the arrow for **AutoSum** and click **Min**. Select cells **B4** to **B10** and press ⏎ Enter .

15 Repeat steps 13 to 14 to calculate the maximum (Max) value and the number of rainy days (Count Numbers) for each station.

Note that the AVERAGE, MIN, MAX and COUNT functions ignore cells that do not contain numeric values. Depending on the purpose of the calculation, this may or may not be desirable. Copy these formulas to the other station readings.

16 Copy cells **B13** to **B16** over to cells **C13** to **F16**.

Add another formula to calculate an average value manually.

17 In cell **A18**, type: `Avg Station 2 and 3`.

18 In cell **C18**, type: `=(C11+D11)/2`.

This formula demonstrates how to over-ride the natural precedence of mathematical operators. If the parentheses were not used, the resulting value would be 48.8 (the value of cell **C11** plus half of cell **D11**) because the division operator normally takes precedence over the addition operator.

The completed worksheet should look similar to the following example:

	A	B	C	D	E	F	G
1	Rainfall at Weather Stations						
2							
3		Station 1	Station 2	Station 3	Station 4	Station 5	Total
4	Monday	9.2	3.5	2.6	9.1	1	25.4
5	Tuesday	8.5	7	4.2	10	5	34.7
6	Wednesday	8.1	1.4	9.6	9.3	3.9	32.3
7	Thursday	9.6	7.2	2	7	0.5	26.3
8	Friday	7.4	9.4	9		8.9	34.7
9	Saturday	7.2	1.1	5.4	6.9	8.5	29.1
10	Sunday		1.3	3	4.4	5.9	14.6
11	Total Rainfall for Week	50	30.9	35.8	46.7	33.7	197.1
12							
13	Average Rainfall	8.33333333	4.41428571	5.11428571	7.78333333	4.81428571	
14	Lowest Rainfall	7.2	1.1	2	4.4	0.5	
15	Highest Rainfall	9.6	9.4	9.6	10	8.9	
16	# of Days of Rain	6	7	7	6	7	
17							
18	Avg Station 2 and 3		33.35				

19 Save the workbook.

Now change the value in one cell from blank to the number *0*.

20 Select cell **B10**, type: `0` and press ⏎ Enter .

Note that although the total rainfall value does not change, the average and lowest rainfall calculations change, as does the # of days calculation. These results demonstrate that a cell containing the value of zero is not the same as an empty cell.

11	Total Rainfall for Week	50
12		
13	Average Rainfall	7.14285714
14	Lowest Rainfall	0
15	Highest Rainfall	9.6
16	# of Days of Rain	7

21   On the Quick Access Toolbar, click **Undo**.

Now add three rows to the data and observe the results.

22   Click the gray header for row **11** to select the entire row and, on the **Home** tab, in the **Cells** group, click **Insert**.

23   Insert a new row at row **7**.

24   Insert a new row at row **4**.

25   Select any of the cells in the range **B14** to **F14**.

The cell range in the SUM function now only includes rows 5 to 12—it does not include the rows added at the very top or the very bottom of the original cell range, but rows added anywhere *inside* the range are included. You will obtain similar results if you add new columns.

When you add new rows or columns to a worksheet, be sure to verify any formulas that reference the cells in that area of the worksheet.

26   On the Quick Access Toolbar, click the **Undo** button three times to remove the three added rows.

27   Close the workbook and discard any changes made since step 19.

Conditional Functions

The ability to perform different calculations based on changing values is one of the most powerful and useful features of spreadsheets. The primary function used for this is the **IF** function. This function makes an evaluation or logical test and performs one of two different calculations based on the result. This automatic evaluation provides "on the fly" worksheet calculations.

The format of the IF function is as follows:

=IF(logical test,value if true,value if false)

Logical Test	Specify what the IF statement will evaluate.
Value if True	If the Logical Test is found to be true, then the result of the IF function will be whatever is in this section of the formula.
Value if False	If the Logical Test is found to be false, then the result of the IF function will be whatever is in this section of the formula.

The Logical Test section of the function often uses comparison operators that will help you obtain the desired result. Qualifiers are punctuation marks used to identify or define different types of data; for example, text used in a formula requires double quotes as qualifiers.

Some of the comparison operators you can use are:

- =   Equal to (or the same as)
- >   Greater than
- <   Less than
- >=   Greater than or equal to
- <=   Less than or equal to
- <>   Not equal to

The Value if True/False sections can contain a text string, values or other functions. In fact, you can nest or embed up to seven IF functions within one IF statement. An example of a nested IF function would appear as follows:

=IF(A1=10, "text A",IF(A1=20, "text B", "text C"))

In this example, Excel will display the following values when the conditions are met:

If A1 contains	Then this will display
10	text A
20	text B
Any other value	text C

Learn the Skill

This exercise demonstrates how to use the **IF** function.

You will use a worksheet that will calculate the number of travel points given to customers based on the amount they spend. For every dollar a customer spends, the program awards 100 AirKm points. In addition, the program awards customers an additional 20 points for every dollar if the total amount is over $500.

1   Open the *AirKm Awards* workbook and save it as *AirKm Awards - Student*.

	A	B	C	D
1	Tolano Adventures			
2	AirKm Points Awarded			
3				
4	Passenger Name	Amount	Points	Bonus Pts
5	Chan, A	968.48		
6	Chan, H	968.48		
7	Cox, T	315.58		
8	Cox, W	315.58		
9	Dali, P	548.27		
10	Dali, S	548.27		
11	Koehn, J	370.82		
12	Koehn, P	370.82		
13	Moore, M	366.03		
14	Noire, N	464.78		
15	Singh, G	835.69		
16	Smith, A	528.28		
17	Smith, B	492.44		
18	Smith, T	528.28		
19	Williams, M	441.44		
20	Wong, K	578.28		

First, calculate the number of points per dollar.

2   Select cell **C5**, type: =B5*100 and press ⌐Enter⌐.

3   Select cell **C5** again and copy it down to cells C6 to C20.

Now calculate the bonus points per dollar, but only do this where the amount is greater than 500.

4   Select cell **D5**, and click **Insert Function**.

5   In the **Or select a category** list, click **Logical**.

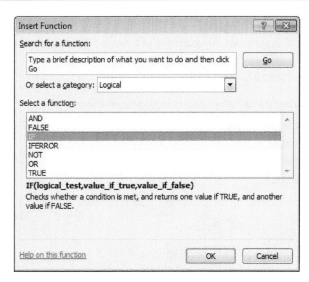

6   In the **Select a function** list, click **IF** and click **OK**.

Excel displays the Function Arguments dialog box to help you enter the correct arguments for this function. You will base the conditional on the cost of travel, which is in cell B5, and must be over 500.

7   In the **Logical_test** field, type: B5>500.

The next section is the Value_if_true section. If the result of the conditional test (B5 > 500 in this case) is true, Excel will return the value in this box to the worksheet cell. In this case, the value has to be calculated.

8   In the **Value_if_true** field, type: B5*20.

The last part of the function is the Value_if_false section. If the result of the conditional test is false, Excel will return this value. In this case, the value would be zero.

9   In the **Value_if_false** field, type: 0.

The Function Arguments dialog box appears as follows:

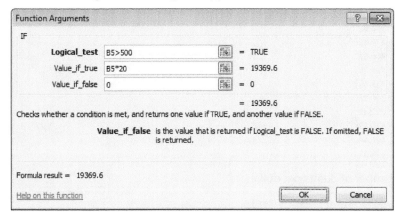

10   Click **OK**.

Note that the resulting formula is =IF(B5>500,B5*20,0).

Since the calculated value could result in a decimal value, you can use an additional rounding function to round the value up or down to the nearest whole number. You can accomplish this by embedding the IF function inside the ROUND function.

11   In cell D5, press (F2).

12   Move the cursor inside the cell to the left, to a position between the = and IF, and type: ROUND(

13 Press the (End) key, type: ,0) and press (Enter).

=ROUND(IF(B5>500,B5*20,0),0)

14 Copy the formula from cell **C5** to cells **C6:C20**.

Bonus points are now calculated only if the amount in column B is greater than $500.

The worksheet should now look similar to the following:

	A	B	C	D
1	Tolano Adventures			
2	AirKm Points Awarded			
3				
4	Passenger Name	Amount	Points	Bonus Pts
5	Chan, A	968.48	96848	19370
6	Chan, H	968.48	96848	19370
7	Cox, T	315.58	31558	0
8	Cox, W	315.58	31558	0
9	Dali, P	548.27	54827	10965
10	Dali, S	548.27	54827	10965
11	Koehn, J	370.82	37082	0
12	Koehn, P	370.82	37082	0
13	Moore, M	366.03	36603	0
14	Noire, N	464.78	46478	0
15	Singh, G	835.69	83569	16714
16	Smith, A	528.28	52828	10566
17	Smith, B	492.44	49244	0
18	Smith, T	528.28	52828	10566
19	Williams, M	441.44	44144	0
20	Wong, K	578.28	57828	11566

15 Save and close the workbook.

You can modify your IF function if you want a more presentable worksheet. For example, if you want the IF formula to show a blank cell instead of zeros or dashes when the amount is $500 or less, modify the formula to appear as follows:

=IF(B5>500,B5*20,"")

The set of double quotes will cause Excel to insert a blank in any cell that proves FALSE based on the argument in the **Logical_test**.

To have either example work properly, remember to copy the changed formula to the other cells on the worksheet.

When using the Insert Function, Excel will insert the quotes for you when entering text in the Value if True/False fields. When you want either of these fields to be blank, you must type both quotation marks or the word True or False will appear in the cell.

Using Absolute and Relative Cell References

Using Absolute Cell References

5.3

Most formulas in an Excel worksheet are relative. If you copy a formula that contains a relative cell address and paste it to another cell, Excel automatically adjusts it for the new location. For example, suppose you have a formula that adds three rows together within one column. You can copy this formula to another column to add the adjusted set of three rows in the new column. The formula is relative to the column in which you place it.

This automatic adjustment feature is advantageous when you are creating sheets, such as budget sheets, which require the same formula to repeat across many months or line items. However, in some cases you may not want this automatic adjustment feature.

Fortunately, Excel enables you to make cell addresses absolute or fixed. An absolute cell address refers to a fixed (non-moving) location on the worksheet.

To change a relative cell address to an absolute (fixed) cell address in a formula or function, enter a dollar sign before the row number and/or column letter (e.g. *$E$5*). This ensures that when you copy a formula, Excel will not adjust the absolute cell addresses for the new location.

Another method to obtain the absolute signs in cell addresses is to press (F4) once you have typed the cell address. You can also go back to formulas you have typed previously, edit them, position the insertion point in the cell address you wish to make absolute and press (F4).

The number of times you press (F4) determines which references become absolute:

- Press once to make both the column and row reference absolute.
- Press twice to make only row references absolute.
- Press three times to make only the column reference absolute.
- Press four times to remove the absolute references on both column and row.

Using Mixed Absolute and Relative Cell References

Cell addresses do not have to have both absolute column and row references. You can have mixed cell references. The column reference can be absolute and the row reference relative (e.g. $E5). If a formula including this reference is copied to a new location, only the column reference ($E) is constant, and the row reference is adjusted for the new location.

Conversely, if you copy a formula including a cell reference with an absolute row reference and a relative column reference (e.g. E$5) to a new location, Excel will adjust only the column reference for the new location. This adds flexibility for creating cell formulas, which will become increasingly important as your worksheets become more complex.

As a general rule of thumb: if you intend to copy the formula to other cells in the same row and keep the column reference locked, place the $ in front of the column letter; if you intend to copy the formula to other cells in the same column and keep the row reference locked, place the $ in front of the row number.

Learn the Skill

This exercise demonstrates the use of absolute cell references.

1   Open the *Quarterly Income Statement - Student* workbook. If necessary, click the *Company* worksheet tab.

First create a new column of totals.

2   Select cell **G4** and type: Total.

3   Select cells **C6** to **G8** and on the **Home** tab, in the **Editing** group, click **AutoSum**.

4   In cell **C11**, type: = then click the *Quarter 1* worksheet and select cell **F11** and press (Enter)..

5   Repeat step 4 for other cells in this row:

      D11   Quarter 2 worksheet cell F11

      E11   Quarter 3 worksheet cell F11

      F11   Quarter 4 worksheet cell F11

6   Select cells **C11** to **G11** and on the **Home** tab, in the **Editing** group, click **AutoSum**.

7   Copy the contents of the cell range **C11** to **G11** down to cells **C12** to **G19**.

The relative addressing feature in Excel has saved you a lot of time in setting up these formulas.

8   Select cell **A21** and type: Profit.

9   Select cell **C21** and type: =C8-C19.

10   Copy cell **C21** across to cells **D21** to **G21**.

11   Select cell **A22** and type: Quarterly Margin.

12   Select cell **C22** and enter: =C21/G8.

13   Copy cell **C22** across to cells **D22** to **G22**.

At first, it appears as if you can copy the formula into the other cells in row **22**. However, the result is as shown in the following example:

	A	B	C	D	E	F	G
1	Tolano Adventures						
2	Quarterly Income Statement						
3							
4			Qtr 1	Qtr 2	Qtr 3	Qtr 4	Total
5	Revenues:						
6		Sales	19000	19500	19500	19500	77500
7		Other Revenues	240	105	105	105	555
8		Total:	19240	19605	19605	19605	78055
9							
10	Expenses:						
11		Rent	15000	15000	15000	15000	60000
12		Telephone	450	450	450	450	1800
13		Internet	375	375	375	375	1500
14		Courier	900	900	900	900	3600
15		Postage	225	225	225	225	900
16		Supplies	750	750	750	750	3000
17		Photocopier	240	240	240	240	960
18		Travel	0	0	0	0	0
19		Total:	17940	17940	17940	17940	71760
20							
21	Profit		1300	1665	1665	1665	6295
22	Quarterly Margin		0.016655	#DIV/0!	#DIV/0!	#DIV/0!	#DIV/0!

Clearly, the answers provided are incorrect—Excel displays a *#DIV/0!* (division by zero) error message in the other cells. Now examine the formulas you had copied in column **C**.

14   Select cell **D22** and examine the formula bar.

As you can see, Excel has adjusted the cell address using relative addressing for each cell where you copied the formula. This adjustment process, which was so useful when you were creating and copying other formulas, is now causing a problem. You can resolve this problem by returning to cell **C22** and editing the formula. The formula must have an absolute value for the **G8** cell reference. Thus, the formula in cell **C22** should be =C21/$G$8.

15   Select cell **C22** and press (F2) to activate the editing mode.

16   Press (F4) to put the absolute value signs around the nearest cell reference in the formula (G8).

17   Press (Enter) to accept this formula.

Note that the amount in cell **C22** does not change.

18   Copy the formula from cell **C22** to cells **D22** through to **G22**.

Your worksheet should now look like the following example:

	A	B	C	D	E	F	G
1	Tolano Adventures						
2	Quarterly Income Statement						
3							
4			Qtr 1	Qtr 2	Qtr 3	Qtr 4	Total
5	Revenues:						
6		Sales	19000	19500	19500	19500	77500
7		Other Revenues	240	105	105	105	555
8		Total:	19240	19605	19605	19605	78055
9							
10	Expenses:						
11		Rent	15000	15000	15000	15000	60000
12		Telephone	450	450	450	450	1800
13		Internet	375	375	375	375	1500
14		Courier	900	900	900	900	3600
15		Postage	225	225	225	225	900
16		Supplies	750	750	750	750	3000
17		Photocopier	240	240	240	240	960
18		Travel	0	0	0	0	0
19		Total:	17940	17940	17940	17940	71760
20							
21	Profit		1300	1665	1665	1665	6295
22	Quarterly Margin		0.016655	0.021331	0.021331	0.021331	0.080648

Check the formulas now entered in column **C**:

C22   contains   =C21*$G$8

D22   contains   =D21*$G$8

E22   contains   =E21*$G$8

F22   contains   =F21*$G$8

G22   contains   =G21*$G$8

When the reference to cell **G8** is absolute, it is anchored to the total revenues cell.

19   Save the workbook.

Displaying and Printing Formulas

To see the formula in a cell, you must select that cell and examine the formula displayed in the formula bar, or press (F2) to see the formula in the cell. In some circumstances, you may want to see all the formulas in all the cells at the same time, especially when you are verifying the accuracy of the spreadsheet. Excel has an option available to display all formulas at the same time. Cells that contain numeric or other values will simply display those data values.

Excel enables you to print the worksheet with the formulas displayed. This is an excellent technique for verifying that you have entered all the formulas correctly.

Learn the Skill

This exercise demonstrates how to display the formulas in worksheet cells, or to display the formula results.

1   If necessary, open the *Quarterly Income Statement - Student* workbook.

2   Click the **File** tab, then click **Options**.

3   Click **Advanced** in the left pane of the Excel Options dialog box.

4   Scroll down to the **Display options for this worksheet** group of options.

5   Verify that you have set the display options box to **Company**, and then click the **Show formulas in cells instead of their calculated results** check box.

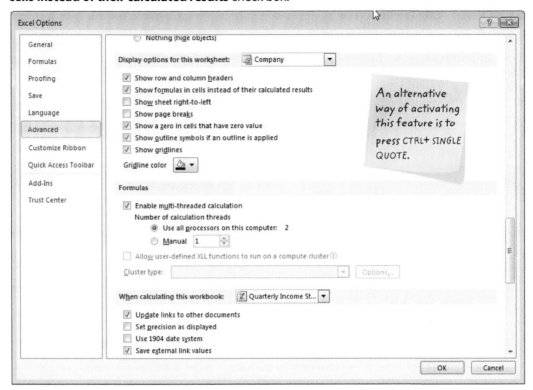

6   Click **OK**.

7   If necessary, increase the size of the workbook window.

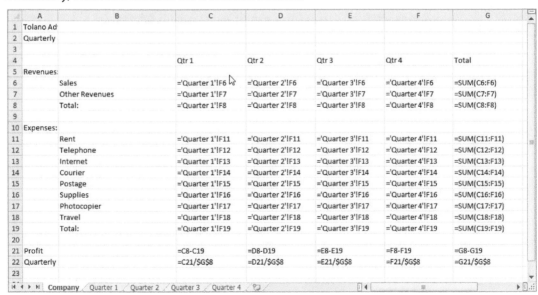

To turn off the display of the formulas, repeat the same steps but clear the check box.

8   Click the **File** tab, then click **Options**.

9   Click **Advanced** in the left pane of the Excel Options dialog box.

10   Scroll down to the **Display options for this worksheet** group of options and clear the **Show formulas in cells instead of their calculated results** check box. Click **OK**.

You can also print the worksheet with the formulas displayed.

11   Close the workbook and discard any changes.

Lesson Summary

In this lesson, you learned about formulas—what they are, how they work, how to insert simple formulas and how to use built-in functions to create some formulas. You should now be familiar with:

☑ what formulas are

☑ how to create and edit simple formulas

☑ how to use math operators and understand the precedent order of calculations

☑ how to reference other worksheets

☑ how to use common functions

☑ how to use a conditional function

☑ how to use absolute and relative cell references

☑ how to use mixed absolute and relative cell addresses

☑ how to display and print formulas

Review Questions

MMM
Go online for
Additional
Review and
Activities

1. List which standard math operators Excel uses and what is their order of precedence.

2. Give examples of how using formulas to perform a what-if analysis is beneficial to you.

3. Which of the following are invalid?

   a) =MAX(B5:B15)

   b) =MAX(B5,B6,B7,B8,B9,B10,B11,B12,B13,B14)=MAX(B5:B15,C7:C17)

   c) =MAX(B5:B7,B8:B10,B11:B15)=MAX(B5,C7)

   d) =MAX(B1,B5:B8,B9:B15)

   e) All of the above

   f) None – all are valid formulas

   g) c

   h) b, c, and d

4. Define the different parts of a reference to other worksheets using the reference Tours!B4 as an example.

5. What is the main difference between a conditional function and the other functions discussed in this lesson?

6. Explain the difference between absolute and relative cell references.

7. Provide examples of when or why it may be beneficial to print the formulas in the worksheet.

Microsoft®

Excel® 2010
Core Certification

Lesson 4: **Formatting the Worksheet**

Lesson Objectives

In this lesson, you will look at how to use a variety of methods to format cells in a worksheet to emphasize different worksheet areas. Upon successful completion, you should be able to:

☐ format numbers and decimal places

☐ change the alignment of cell contents

☐ change fonts and font size

☐ apply borders around cell(s)

☐ apply background colors and patterns to cell(s)

☐ use the Format Painter

☐ clear cell contents and formatting

☐ apply and modify themes

☐ apply and modify cell styles

☐ apply conditional formatting

Formatting a Cell

3.1
3.2

How you present your worksheet is almost as important as the data it contains. Formatting is all about changing the appearance of the data. You are using the various features of Excel to draw attention to parts of the worksheet, or to make the data presented easier to understand. When you change the format of a cell, you do not alter its underlying value.

You should note the following important points:

- You can format a cell, or a range of cells, either before or after you enter the data. You can even format an entire row or column at one time.

- A cell remains formatted even after you clear the contents of the cell, unless you also clear the format or reformat a cell. When you enter new data in the cell, Excel displays the data in the existing format.

- When you paste or fill a cell from another cell, you copy the format and the contents of the originating cell. This feature enables you to save time, provided you apply the formatting before copying.

Some of the formatting features provided to change the appearance of your document include different fonts or sizes, bold and italic styles, borders around a cell or group of cells, and shading of cells. You will find the most commonly used formatting features displayed on the **Home** tab as well as on the Mini toolbar.

Certain types of formatting may not be compatible with the data values, and Excel will simply ignore that formatting until you enter the appropriate data type into that cell. For example, you may format a cell as numeric with commas and two decimal digits, but if the cell contains a word (such as "Total"), then Excel will apply only the cell formatting that pertain to text values.

Excel has a feature called **Live Preview** that temporarily changes the appearance of the selected cell(s) to the format that your mouse is currently pointing at on the Ribbon. If you click on that button on the Ribbon, Excel applies the formatting change. However, if you move your mouse away, the selected cell(s) revert to their current format. This useful feature allows you to preview a formatting change without having to click the Undo button if it turns out to be unsuitable. Be aware that only some formatting buttons on the Ribbon include Live Preview capability. Note that Live Preview does not function when you have a formatting dialog box in front of the worksheet.

Formatting Numbers and Decimal Digits

3.1

The formatting of numbers is undoubtedly the predominant activity on most spreadsheets. To meet a wide variety of needs, Excel provides a rich set of standard formats with changeable options. Except where you see it noted in each of the following sample screens, the underlying number in the cell is 123.4. As you select the formatting options, the sample box at the top of the dialog box shows what the number will look like with the selected options.

To format a cell, select the cell, and then use one of the following methods:

- On the **Home** tab, in the **Font**, **Alignment** or **Number** groups, click the appropriate button; or

- press (Ctrl)+(1); or

- right-click and click **Format Cells** on the shortcut menu; or

- right-click and click the appropriate number formatting from the Mini toolbar; or

- on the **Home** tab, in the **Font**, **Alignment** or **Number** groups, click the **Dialog box launcher** for the appropriate group.

General

The General category is the default format for all cells. When you enter numbers into an unformatted cell, Excel displays them exactly as you entered them, except that it does not display trailing zeros after the decimal point. The difficulty with this is that, if the values in a column have different numbers of decimal places, the decimal points will not be lined up. This can make the worksheet quite difficult to read. In addition, when you enter a number that is much larger than the width of the cell, Excel automatically changes the format to Scientific notation, adding another display format that is inconsistent with the other cells.

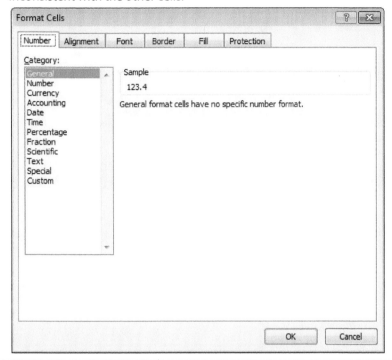

Number

The Number category is a standard format for numbers, with the option to show the comma (period in European countries) separator for values of 1,000 and higher. The number of digits after the decimal point must also be specified (the default is 2); if there are insufficient digits, the number will be right-filled with zeroes. Excel can show negative numbers with different options: in red, with a minus sign, or with parentheses.

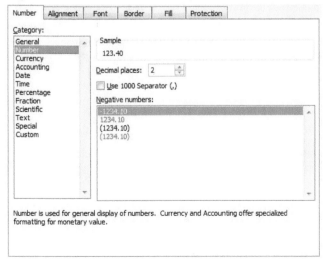

Currency
The Currency format is similar to the Number format, except that a currency symbol (e.g., $ symbol) is shown, and the comma separator is automatically displayed.

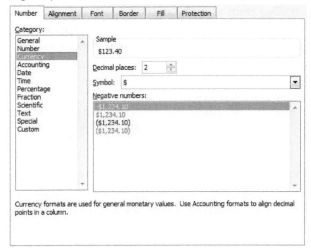

Accounting
The Accounting format is similar to the Currency format, except that negative numbers appear in parentheses (you cannot change this) and the currency symbol appears at the far left side of the cell.

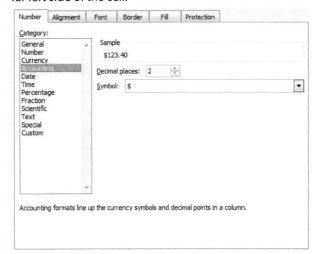

Percentage
The underlying cell value in this screen sample is 0.1234—Excel always shows percentage values as 100 times the number value. This format shows a percentage sign at the right side of the cell. You must also specify the number of decimal places (the default is 2).

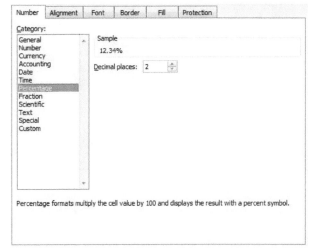

Fraction   The Fraction format converts decimal digits to fractional values based on the fraction type that you select.

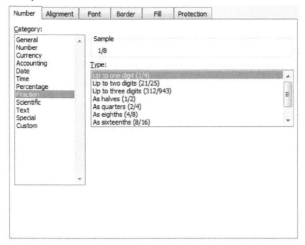

Scientific   You will usually use this format in scientific applications for very large and very small numbers. Excel shows only one digit to the left of the decimal point, and you control the number of significant digits by specifying the number of decimal places.

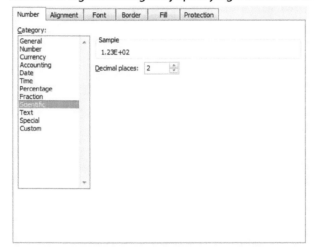

Date   The Date format category displays date values in various ways. The default format is a custom date format of d-mmm-yy where mmm indicates the first three characters of the month's name. The d indicates that Excel will display single-digit day values as one digit—without filling in the left with a zero.

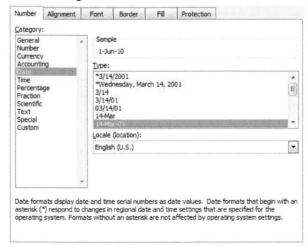

Special   Use the Special format category for miscellaneous items, such as phone numbers and zip codes.

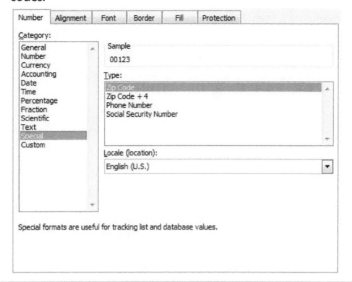

Special formats are useful for tracking list and database values.

Custom   If you cannot find the exact format you want in the other categories, you can create a format of your own with the Custom category.

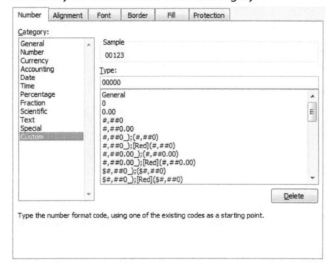

Type the number format code, using one of the existing codes as a starting point.

Learn the Skill

In this exercise, you will examine some of the numeric formats available in Excel.

1   Open the *Travel Itinerary* workbook and save it as Travel Itinerary - Student.

Now format some of the cells containing numbers.

2   Select the cell range **B18** to **B21**.

3   On the **Home** tab, in the **Number** group, click the arrow for **Number Format**.

A list appears showing the most commonly used numeric formats for a cell. Below the title of each numeric format, Excel displays the number from the selected cell (or the top-left cell, if you select a range) using that format. For example, the value of 3298 in cell B18 displays as 3298.00 under the Number format, and as $3,298.00 under the Currency format.

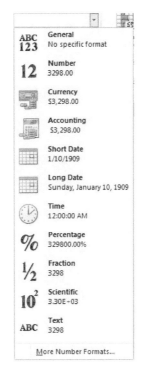

	General
ABC 123	No specific format
12	Number 3298.00
	Currency $3,298.00
	Accounting $3,298.00
	Short Date 1/10/1909
	Long Date Sunday, January 10, 1909
	Time 12:00:00 AM
%	Percentage 329800.00%
½	Fraction 3298
10²	Scientific 3.30E-03
ABC	Text 3298

More Number Formats...

4   Click **Number** on the list.

18	Airfare:	3298.00
19	Hotel:	2750.00
20	Taxes & Fees:	750.52
21	Total:	6798.52

Excel has applied a uniform format—two decimal digits—to all of the numbers. You can also quickly format numeric cells using Comma Style. However, Excel interprets this formatting choice as the Accounting format with no currency symbol displayed. Note that, in Comma format, negative numbers appear with parentheses instead of the minus sign, and positive numbers appear with a slight indent to the left.

If any number has more than two decimal digits, applying this format will cause rounding to the nearest second decimal digit. As with all formatting, this is for display purposes only—the actual number stored in the cell does not change.

However, you can see that these numbers do not have the comma separator.

5   On the **Home** tab, in the **Number** group, click the **Dialog box launcher**.

In the Format Cells dialog box, the **Category** is already set to **Number** and 2 decimal places are specified. You only need to add the comma separator.

6   Turn on the **Use 1000 Separator (,)** check box and click **OK**.

Now try the currency format.

7   Select cell **B18**.

8   On the **Home** tab, in the **Number** group, click the arrow for **Number Format** and then click **Currency**.

9   Select cell **B21** and change this number format to **Currency** as well.

Using the Ribbon, you can also quickly change the number of digits appearing after the decimal point.

10   With cells **B21** still selected, on the **Home** tab, in the **Number** group, click **Decrease Decimal** twice to remove all decimal digits.

Notice that Excel has rounded the number up. You can also increase the number of decimal digits.

11   On the **Home** tab, in the **Number** group, click **Increase Decimal** twice to show two decimal digits again.

You can also format cells containing date values.

You can also right-click and then click Increase Decimal or Decrease Decimal on the Mini toolbar.

12 Select cell **B5**.

13 On the **Home** tab, in the **Number** group, click the arrow for **Number Format** and click **Long Date**.

The long date format is much too wide for this cell.

14 On the Quick Access Toolbar, click the **Undo** button.

The cells containing the flight numbers are also numeric, but the General format is acceptable for them.

The completed worksheet should look similar to the following example:

	A	B	C	D	E	F	G	H
1	Tolano Adventures							
2	Travel Itinerary							
3	Prepared For:	Williams, R						
4								
5	Date:	8-Sep-10						
6	Depart From:	Toronto YYZ	Time:	6:55 PM	Airline:	British Air	Flight #	2409
7	Arrive:	London LHR	Time:	6:55 AM				
8								
9	Date:	15-Sep-10						
10	Depart From:	London LHR	Time:	3:25 PM	Airline:	Lufthansa	Flight #	75
11	Arrive:	Toronto YYZ	Time:	6:25 PM				
12								
13	Hotel:	Times Plaza	Address:	Stratton Street, London, England				
14	Check in Date:	8-Sep-10						
15	Check out:	15-Sep-10						
16								
17	Invoice							
18	Airfare:	$3,298.00						
19	Hotel:	2,750.00						
20	Taxes & Fees:	750.52						
21	Total:	$6,798.52						

15 Save the workbook.

Changing Cell Alignment

3.1

Alignment refers to the position or placement of data within the cell. In Excel, you can align the cell contents horizontally as well as vertically, although you will most commonly see horizontal alignment. By default, Excel assigns General alignment to new values entered into a worksheet. This means that Excel aligns numbers, including dates, to the right, while it aligns text labels to the left. In most cases, you will not change the alignment of numbers and dates. It is very common to change the alignment of text labels using two features: wrapping text and merging.

Wrapping text means forcing any text label in a cell to stay within the vertical boundaries of the cell. Excel increases the height of that row to accommodate the full length of the text (in some cases, you may have to do this manually). If you turn off the wrap text feature for a cell, the text will stay on one line and continue into the cell(s) to the right unless those cells contain data.

	A	B	C	D	E
1	This is a very long text label that is too wide for one cell.				
2	This is also very long and wraps around in this cell.				

Merging cells is a feature commonly used on text labels to identify a group of cells together, such as in the following example.

	A	B	C	D	E	F	G
1	Sales Office	Quarter 1			Quarter 2		
2		Jan	Feb	Mar	Apr	May	Jun
3	New York	$7,395	$8,525	$5,805	$7,022	$8,787	$7,936

The months of January to March belong to Quarter 1; the months of April to June belong to Quarter 2. When you merge cells, Excel removes the walls separating the selected cells and treats the group as a single cell. It then becomes very easy to center text across these merged cells, as demonstrated in this example. Excel offers a merge and center button on the Ribbon, which first merges the selected cells and then centers the text across these cells. A less common technique is to merge cells vertically, but there are occasional uses as demonstrated in the example above. Merged cells can also contain numeric and date values.

If merged cells need to be split apart again into their separate cells, simply turn off the **Merge cells** check box in the Format Cells dialog box or click **Merge & Center** again in the Ribbon.

As with the number formatting features, the most commonly used alignment options are readily available on the **Home** tab.

To change the alignment for the contents of a cell, after selecting the cells, use one of the following methods:

- On the **Home** tab, in the **Alignment** group, click the appropriate alignment button; or

- press Ctrl + 1 and then click the **Alignment** tab; or

- right-click, click **Format Cells**, and then click the **Alignment** tab; or

- on the **Home** tab, in the **Alignment** group, click the **Dialog box launcher**.

MMM
Create an
Invoice Online
Exercise

Learn the Skill

This exercise demonstrates the most commonly used alignment options.

1   Make sure the *Travel Itinerary - Student* workbook is active on the screen.

At the top of the worksheet are two rows of text that you need to center across the width of the invoice document. To accomplish this, you will use the merge and center function.

2   Select cells **A1** to **H1**.

3   On the **Home** tab, in the **Alignment** group, click **Merge & Center**.

Notice that Excel has now merged the eight cells together and centered the title across these cells.

The merge and center function can only work on one row at a time; you will have to repeat the previous step for the next row.

4   Select cells **A2** to **H2** and on the **Home** tab, in the **Alignment** group, click **Merge & Center**.

Remember that, although you have merged cells together and therefore centered the data contents across these cells, you entered the data in the original cell; therefore, to make changes to those contents, you must go back to the original cell (A1 or A2).

Now align the text in some of the cells to the right.

5   Select cells **C6** to **C7** and, on the **Home** tab, in the **Alignment** group, click **Align Text Right**.

6   Select cells **C10** to **C11** and, on the **Home** tab, in the **Alignment** group, click **Align Text Right** again.

7   Select cell **E6** and hold down the Ctrl key. Then select cell **E10** and release the Ctrl key to select both cells.

8   On the **Home** tab, in the **Alignment** group, click **Align Text Right** again.

9   Select cells **G6** and **G10** using the Ⓒⓣⓡⓛ key and, on the **Home** tab, in the **Alignment** group, click **Align Text Right** again.

Earlier, you tried to use the Long Date format, but there was not enough space in the cell to display it. You can now use it by merging across adjacent cells.

10   Select cells **B5** to **D5** and, on the **Home** tab, in the **Alignment** group, click the arrow next to **Merge & Center.** Then click **Merge Across.**

11   On the **Home** tab, in the **Number** group, click the arrow for **Number Format** and click **Long Date**.

12   On the **Home** tab, in the **Alignment** group, click **Align Text Left**.

13   Repeat steps 10 to 12 with cells **B9** to **D9**.

Your completed worksheet should look similar to the following example:

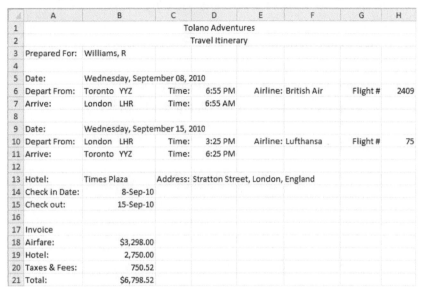

	A	B	C	D	E	F	G	H
1				Tolano Adventures				
2				Travel Itinerary				
3	Prepared For:	Williams, R						
4								
5	Date:	Wednesday, September 08, 2010						
6	Depart From:	Toronto YYZ	Time:	6:55 PM	Airline:	British Air	Flight #	2409
7	Arrive:	London LHR	Time:	6:55 AM				
8								
9	Date:	Wednesday, September 15, 2010						
10	Depart From:	London LHR	Time:	3:25 PM	Airline:	Lufthansa	Flight #	75
11	Arrive:	Toronto YYZ	Time:	6:25 PM				
12								
13	Hotel:	Times Plaza	Address:	Stratton Street, London, England				
14	Check in Date:	8-Sep-10						
15	Check out:	15-Sep-10						
16								
17	Invoice							
18	Airfare:	$3,298.00						
19	Hotel:	2,750.00						
20	Taxes & Fees:	750.52						
21	Total:	$6,798.52						

14   Save the worksheet again.

Changing Fonts and Sizes

3.1

A font is a style of text. Changing fonts will alter how the text and numbers appear in the worksheet. As a rule, it is best if you do not use more than three different fonts in a worksheet, as too many fonts on the worksheet can be distracting. You can apply font changes to any type of data displayed in the worksheet, including numbers, text, dates and so on.

Generally, when you make changes to the font or size, Excel applies these changes to the entire cell or range of cells that you have selected. You can also select individual characters and numbers inside a cell and change the font or size.

Excel also enables you to change other font style options, such as bold, italics and underline, as well as font colors.

To display the **Font** tab on the Format Cells dialog box, on the **Home** tab, in the **Font** group, click the **Dialog box launcher**.

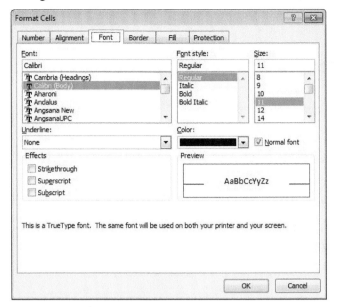

Font	This refers to the typeface of the text characters Excel displays. A set of characters in the same typeface is a font. A large selection of fonts is included with Microsoft Office.
Font style	Most fonts can be formatted bold, italicized or both.
Size	Size refers to the height of a character, with a proportionate width. Most of the fonts are scalable; that is, they have a variety of sizes. A point is equal to a seventy-second of an inch. Thus, twelve-point type is twelve seventy-seconds of an inch high, or 1/6th of an inch high.
Underline	You can select various underline styles, such as single, double, single accounting or double accounting. Note that an underline is not the same as a cell border—if selected, the underline appears inside the cell, whereas borderlines appear along the selected edge(s) of the cell.
Color	You can select and change the color of the characters.
Effects	You can use special character effects, such as **Strikethrough**, **Superscript** and **Subscript**. Note that the latter two are mutually exclusive—you can use either one, but not both at the same time on the same cell.

As you select different options in this dialog box, the Preview box shows sample text with the options displayed.

Note that the most commonly changed font options (i.e., font, point size, bold, italics, underline and font color) can be changed directly on the **Home** tab, in the **Font** group. You can also select the text in editing mode to display the Mini toolbar and then click the appropriate option.

Learn the Skill

In this exercise, you will practice changing font options.

1   Make sure the *Travel Itinerary - Student* workbook is active on the screen.

First, change the font size and style for the document heading.

2   Select cell **A1**.

3   On the **Home** tab, in the **Font** group, click the arrow next to **Font Size** and click **24**.

4   On the **Home** tab, in the **Font** group, click **Bold**.

5   Select cell **A2** and, on the **Home** tab, in the **Font** group, click the arrow next to **Font Size** to display the list of font sizes available.

6   Move the cursor down to point at various font sizes, but do not click on any of them yet.

Notice that the Live Preview feature temporarily changes the look of the active cell using the font size at which you are pointing.

7   Click on font size **14**.

8   On the **Home** tab, in the **Font** group, click **Bold**.

Live Preview does not work with the Bold, Italics, or Underline buttons.

Now bold all of the cell titles.

9   Select the cell range **A3** to **A21** and then, on the **Home** tab, in the **Font** group, click **Bold**.

10   Select all of the rest of the cell titles together by holding down the (Ctrl) key until you have selected the last cell:

C6 to C7	Time (x 2)
C10 to C11	Time (x 2)
E6 to E10	Airline
G6 to G10	Flight #
C13	Address
A17 to A21	Invoice, Airfare, Hotel, Taxes & Fees, Total

11   On the **Home** tab, in the **Font** group, click **Bold** to bold all of these cells at the same time.

If you miss one or more cell(s) or accidentally bold an incorrect cell, just select those cells and click the **Bold** button again to reverse the setting.

Now select a different font for a cell.

12   Select cell **A17** and, on the **Home** tab, in the **Font** group, click the arrow next to **Font**. Select **Arial Black**.

13   With cell **A17** selected, on the **Home** tab, in the **Font** group, click the arrow next to **Font Size** and select **14**.

Now select another font for all of the data cells.

14   Hold down the (Ctrl) key and click on the gray column headers for columns B, D, F, and H. Release the (Ctrl) key.

You can actually select anywhere between A1 and H1 to select cell A1, as this whole range of cells has been merged.

When you click the arrow and point at the new size (but do not click on it yet) Live Preview changes the appearance of the text.

Enable Live Preview by clicking Font on the Ribbon.

15 With these columns selected, on the **Home** tab, in the **Font** group, click the arrow next to **Font** and select **Arial**.

The completed worksheet should look similar to the following example:

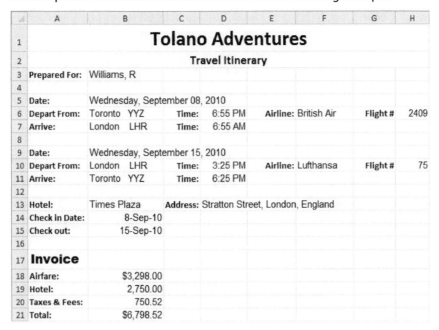

16 Save the workbook.

Applying Cell Borders

3.1

Borders separate groups of data from each other to improve the readability of a worksheet, especially when it includes a large volume of numbers.

The border feature enables you to draw lines around any or all of the four edges of a cell or range of cells. The dialog box displays several presets, line thicknesses, color and style options, and allows you to specify where the lines will appear.

The **Border** tab in the Format Cells dialog box displays the various options and settings borders:

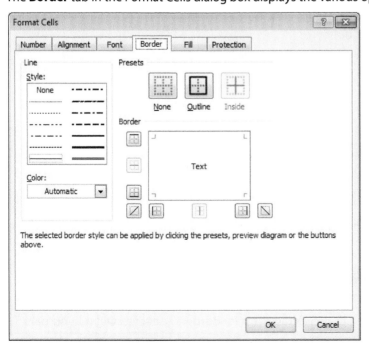

Line	Choose a line style or color for the border(s). If you want different lines or colors for specific borders, you have to select the style or color and then click in the Border area for the appropriate border.
Presets	Remove all borders, apply borders on all four outside edges or apply borders on all inside edges (only applicable when a range of cells is selected) for the selected cell or range of cells using the three preset configuration settings.
Border	Use the buttons to apply or remove borders on specific edges of the selected cell or range of cells. The graphics within each button help you see which borders you are applying or removing.

To apply a border, select the cell or range of cells and then use one of the following methods:

- On the **Home** tab, in the **Cells** group, click **Format**, click **Format Cells**, and click the **Border** tab; or
- On the **Home** tab, in the **Font** group, click the **Dialog box launcher** and click the **Border** tab; or
- On the **Home** tab, in the **Font** group, click the arrow for **Borders** and click **More Borders;** or
- Right-click and then click **Format Cells** in the pop-up menu, and click the **Border** tab; or
- Press (Ctrl)+(1) and click the **Border** tab.

These methods display the full borders options in the Format Cells dialog box.

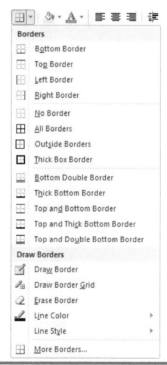

Using the **Borders** button on the Ribbon is a faster method of applying borders to the selected cell(s): you can click on the button to apply the border using the current border settings for this button, or you can click the arrow for it to display a drop down menu with commonly combined borders for a cell.

By default, when you start up Excel, the **Borders** button on the Ribbon is set to **Bottom Border**. As you select different border options from the drop down menu, the icon for the Borders button changes to show that new setting. This convenient feature allows you to minimize mouse clicks while applying borders to multiple cells throughout a worksheet.

To apply a border from the Ribbon, select the cell or range of cells and then use one of the following methods:

- On the **Home** tab, in the **Font** group, click **Border** to apply the current border settings for this button; or
- Right-click and then click **Border** on the Mini toolbar to apply the current border settings.

Learn the Skill

This exercise demonstrates how to apply borders to cells.

1   Make sure the *Travel Itinerary - Student* workbook is active on the screen.

First, place a border on all four outside edges of a range of cells.

2   Select cells **A5** to **H7**.

3   On the **Home** tab, in the **Font** group, click the arrow for **Borders** and select **Outside Borders**.

The **Borders** button in the Ribbon is now set to **Outside Borders**. Draw borders around the other two itinerary items.

4   Select cells **A9** to **H11**. On the **Home** tab, in the **Font** group, click **Outside Borders** directly from the Ribbon.

5   Select cells **A13** to **H15**. On the **Home** tab, in the **Font** group, click **Outside Borders** directly from the Ribbon.

Select a different border for the invoice section of the worksheet.

6   Select cells **A17** to **C22**.

7   On the **Home** tab, in the **Font** group, click the arrow for **Borders**.

8   Point to the **Line Color** option in the **Borders** menu, then click the **Dark Blue** color in the **Standard Colors** section of the menu.

9   On the **Home** tab, in the **Font** group, click the arrow for **Borders** again.

10   Point to **Line Style**, and then click the medium solid line style (sixth from the bottom).

Notice that when you select either of these two border options, the cursor changes to a pencil icon. This indicates that you can manually draw the border around any cell of your choosing. For this exercise, you want borders only around the currently selected cells. Note that with the cursor changed to a pencil icon, it appears that no cells are currently selected; however, the cells selected at step 6 are actually still selected.

11   On the **Home** tab, in the **Font** group, click the arrow for **Borders** once more and click **Outside Borders**.

12   Click in any other cell in the worksheet to see the results.

Now draw borders inside a range of cells, using the current line style and color.

13   Select cells **A17** to **C17**.

14   On the **Home** tab, in the **Font** group, click the arrow for **Borders** and select **Bottom Borders**.

15   Select cells **A18** to **A22** and, on the **Home** tab, in the **Font** group, click the arrow for **Borders** and click **Right Border**.

The completed worksheet should look similar to the following example:

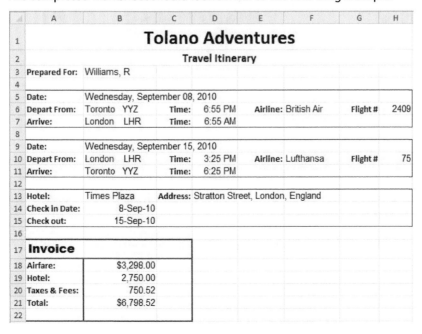

The Borders button is now set to a new style, color and position, which will continue to apply to all worksheets and workbooks until you exit Excel. Excel then resets these options back to the default settings.

16   On the **Home** tab, in the **Font** group, click the arrow for **Borders**.

17   Point to the **Line Color** option in the **Borders** menu and then click **Automatic**.

18   On the **Home** tab, in the **Font** group, click the arrow for **Borders** again.

19   Click **Line Style**, and then click the thin solid line style (second from the top).

20   Press ⎋ Esc to deactivate the pencil.

21   Save the worksheet again.

Using Colors and Patterns

3.1

You can also fill cells and ranges of cells with background colors to increase the visual appeal of the overall worksheet. Patterns and color can help draw a viewer's attention to particular parts of your worksheet, or serve to divide it off visually from the balance of the information. This can prove useful when trying to highlight the sum totals row or differentiate heading information from data.

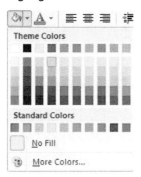

Like the **Borders** button, the **Fill Color** button in the Ribbon has a default color, and assumes new colors as you choose different options. The icon also displays the current color setting. If you click the arrow next to the Fill Color button, Excel presents a color palette, which includes a **No Fill** option.

You can choose from two sets of colors on the color palette: the bottom row of colors comprises the Standard Colors, while the Theme Colors section offers a wider range of tones, based on the current selected document theme. You can also click **More Colors** to access an even wider range of colors and tones, up to the full color spectrum.

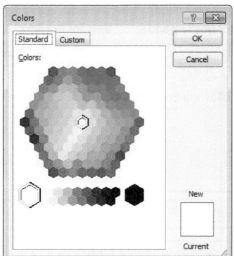

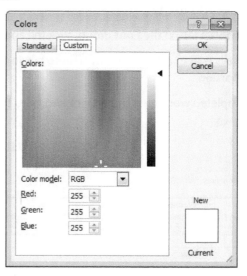

To select a fill color, select the cell or range of cells and then use one of the following methods:

•   On the **Home** tab, in the **Font** group, click the arrow for **Fill Color;** or

•   right-click the selection and, in the Mini toolbar, click the arrow for **Fill Color.**

If you click on the **Fill Color** button, Excel applies the currently selected color to the range of cells currently selected.

In addition to filling a cell using color, you can also select different fill patterns. Excel offers several background patterns for cells; however, you should use them sparingly because the formatting can overwhelm the appearance of the worksheet. You need to open the Format Cells dialog box to access these settings. To display the full set of options for filling a cell, select the cell or range of cells and then use one of the following methods:

- On the **Home** tab, in the **Cells** group, click **Format**, click **Format Cells**, and then click the **Fill** tab; or
- On the **Home** tab, in the **Font** group, click the **Dialog box launcher**, and then click the **Fill** tab; or
- right-click the selection, click **Format Cells**, and then click the **Fill** tab.

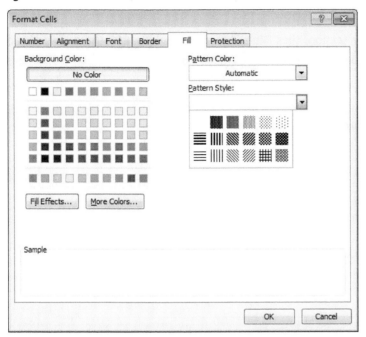

Patterns and background colors are distinctly different features; you can use either or both of them at the same time.

Dark colors and dense patterns may obscure the information in the cells; it is best to avoid them.

Learn the Skill

This exercise demonstrates how to apply patterns and background color to cells on a worksheet.

1   Make sure the *Travel Itinerary - Student* workbook is active on the screen.

Add a background color to the worksheet titles.

2   Select cells **A1** to **A2**.

3   On the **Home** tab, in the **Font** group, click the arrow for **Fill Color**.

Live Preview works with the fill colors; that is, the background of the selected cells temporarily changes to display that color until you move on to another color.

4   Point to various colors to see the different effects.

5   Click **Light Green** (fifth from the left) in the **Standard Colors** section of the palette.

Now add a pattern and a background color to a range of cells.

6   Select cells **A17** to **C22**.

7   On the **Home** tab, in the **Cells** group, click **Format** and then click **Format Cells**.

8   In the Format Cells dialog box, click the **Fill** tab and then click the **Pattern Style** arrow.

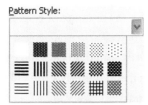

Pattern Style:

9   Click **6.25% Gray** (far right in the top row).

10   In the **Background Color** section, click **Blue, Accent 1, Lighter 80%** (fifth column from the left, second row from the top). Click **OK**.

Add a background color to the hotel section of the itinerary.

11   Select cells **A13** to **H15** and, on the **Home** tab, in the **Font** group, click the arrow for **Fill Color** and select **Yellow** from the **Standard Colors** section.

Now remove the fill color.

12   With cells **A13** to **H15** selected, on the **Home** tab, in the **Font** group, click the arrow for **Fill Color** and then click **No Fill**.

The completed worksheet should look similar to the following example:

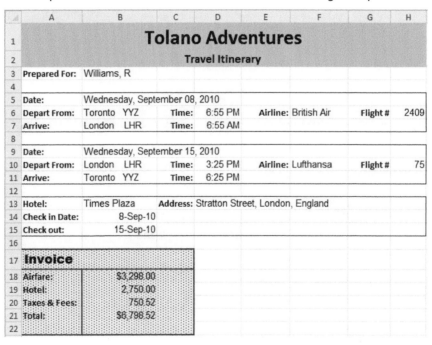

13   Save the workbook.

Paste With Live Preview

3.1

One aspect of the Live Preview capability is the ability to preview the cells before they are pasted into the worksheet. This is a new feature in the Excel 2010 that will assist you with choosing the right paste option without having to make the additional effort of pasting and then undoing several times.

The Paste With Live Preview has several paste options, such as data only, data with the original formatting, without borders, and others.

Learn the Skill

This exercise demonstrates how to use the Paste with Live Preview feature, using data with formatting.

1 Make sure the *Travel Itinerary - Student* workbook is active on the screen.

Copy the original data into the Clipboard, and then select Paste.

2 Select cells **A17** to **C22**.

3 On the **Home** tab, in the **Clipboard** group, click **Copy**.

4 Select cell **E17**.

5 On the **Home** tab, in the **Clipboard** group, click the arrow under **Paste**.

The Paste menu appears below the Ribbon.

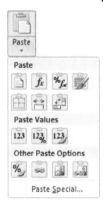

6 Position the cursor over each of the icons in the **Paste** menu. Shortly afterwards, the data will be displayed in Live Preview mode.

The worksheet should look similar to the following example with one of the paste options selected:

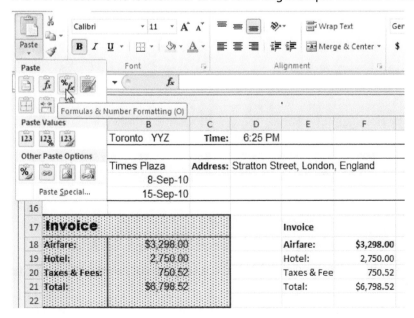

7 Click in a blank area of the workbook to close the **Paste** menu.

8 Close the workbook and discard the changes made.

Using the Format Painter

3.1

Once you have formatted a cell or range of cells, you may want to duplicate its formatting to the remaining parts of your worksheet. Excel provides a tool called the **Format Painter** that enables you to copy formats quickly from one area on the worksheet to another.

Before using the Format Painter, you must select the cell or range of cells that display the formatting you wish to copy. To activate the Format Painter, use either the one-click or the double-click method:

- On the **Home** tab, in the **Clipboard** group, click **Format Painter** once, and then click the target cell you wish to format with the same features; the Format Painter turns off as soon as you click the target cell; or

- On the **Home** tab, in the **Clipboard** group, double-click **Format Painter** to keep the tool on while you click several cells; when you are finished formatting the cell, turn off the Format Painter by clicking the button again or pressing (Esc).

MMM
Format Painter
Online
Exercise

Learn the Skill

In this exercise, you will learn how to use the Format Painter feature.

1   Open the *RV Booking* workbook and save it as RV Booking - Student.

	A	B	C	D	E	F	G	H
1		**Tolano Adventures**						
2		**Recreational Vehicle Booking**						
3	Prepared For:	Pursers, J						
4								
5	Vehicle:	26 ft Coachmen	Unit #:	5381				
6	Sleep Capacity:	6						
7								
8	Pick Up:							
9	Location:	George's RV Center	Address:	1250 Main Street, Seattle, Washington				
10	Date:	15-Jul-10	Time:	12:00 PM				
11								
12	Drop Off:							
13	Location:	Arrow RV Rentals	Address:	9644 Memorial Drive SE, Atlanta, Georgia				
14	Date:	22-Jul-10	Time:	10:00 AM				
15								
16	**Invoice**							
17	RV rental:	1085						
18	Deluxe package:	275						
19	Taxes:	115.6						
20	Total:	1475.6						

Format the Invoice section first.

2   **Select cells B17 to B20** and, on the **Home** tab, in the **Number** group, click the **Dialog box launcher**.

3   In the **Number** tab, select **Number** under **Category**, increase the **Decimal places** to 2, click the **Use 1000 Separator (,)** check box to turn it on and click **OK**.

4   On the **Home** tab, in the **Font** group, click the arrow next to **Font** and click **Arial**.

Change the first number to the currency format, and then use the Format Painter to copy the format down to the bottom number.

5   **Select cell B17** so that it is the only cell selected and, on the **Home** tab, in the **Number** group, click the **Dialog box launcher**.

6   In the **Number** tab, under **Category,** select **Currency** and click **OK**.

7   With cell **B17** still selected, on the **Home** tab, in the **Clipboard** group, click the **Format Painter** once.

8   Select cell **B20** to apply the same formatting to that cell.

Add a border for the bottom number.

9   Select cell **B20** and, on the **Home** tab, in the **Font** group, click the arrow next to the **Borders,** then click **Top and Double Bottom Border**.

Now format the field titles.

10   Select cell **A3** and, on the **Home** tab, in the **Font** group, click the arrow next to **Font. Click Times New Roman**.

11   With cell **A3** still selected, on the **Home** tab, in the **Font** group, click **Bold**.

12   On the **Home** tab, in the **Clipboard** group, double-click **Format Painter**.

13   Click on each of the following cells or cell ranges to apply the same formatting:

A5 to A6
C5
A8 to A10
C9 to C10
A12 to A14
C13 to C14
A17 to A20

14   On the **Home** tab, in the **Clipboard** group, click **Format Painter** again to turn it off.

Increase the font size of two cells containing text labels.

15   Select cell **A8** and, on the **Home** tab, in the **Font** group, click the arrow next to **Font Size,** then click **14**.

16   With cell **A8** still selected, on the **Home** tab, in the **Clipboard** group, click the **Format Painter** once.

17   Click cell **A12** to apply the same formatting there.

Now change the font for the cells containing data using the format painter.

18   Select cell **B3** and then, on the **Home** tab, in the **Font** group, click the arrow next to **Font**, and click **Arial**.

19   With cell **B3** still selected, on the **Home** tab, in the **Clipboard** group, double-click **Format Painter**.

20   Click on each of the follow cells or cell ranges to apply the same formatting:

B5 to B6
D5
B9
D9
B13
D13

21   On the **Home** tab, in the **Clipboard** group, click **Format Painter** again to turn it off.

You could not use the format painter from cells containing text to cells containing dates and times—you will have to format these separately.

22   Select cell **B10** and change the **Font** to **Arial**.

23   Use the Format Painter to copy that format to cell **B14**.

24   Select cell **D10** and change the **Font** to **Arial**.

25   Use the Format Painter to copy that format to cell **D14**.

Your sheet should now look like the following:

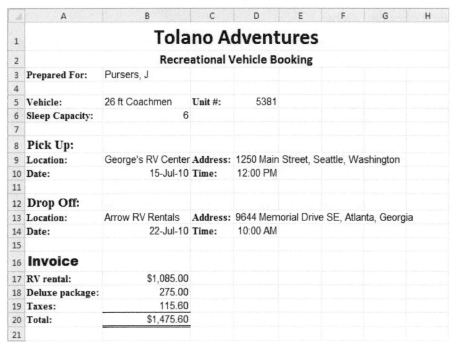

	A	B	C	D	E	F	G	H
1		**Tolano Adventures**						
2		**Recreational Vehicle Booking**						
3	**Prepared For:**	Pursers, J						
4								
5	**Vehicle:**	26 ft Coachmen	**Unit #:**	5381				
6	**Sleep Capacity:**	6						
7								
8	**Pick Up:**							
9	**Location:**	George's RV Center	**Address:**	1250 Main Street, Seattle, Washington				
10	**Date:**	15-Jul-10	**Time:**	12:00 PM				
11								
12	**Drop Off:**							
13	**Location:**	Arrow RV Rentals	**Address:**	9644 Memorial Drive SE, Atlanta, Georgia				
14	**Date:**	22-Jul-10	**Time:**	10:00 AM				
15								
16	**Invoice**							
17	**RV rental:**	$1,085.00						
18	**Deluxe package:**	275.00						
19	**Taxes:**	115.60						
20	**Total:**	$1,475.60						
21								

26   Save and close the workbook.

Clearing Cell Contents and Formatting

3.1

The Clear feature can be used to remove the contents (or certain components that you choose) from the cell. Because you have not deleted the cell, the structure of the worksheet stays intact. You can choose from different options:

All	Remove all data, cell formats and comments from the selected cell(s).
Format	Remove only the formatting from the selected cell(s). The data and comments remain. Because the cell formatting reverts to the default, Excel displays the data that way.
Contents	Remove only the data from the selected cell(s). Because the cell formatting is unchanged, any new data entered into the same cells afterward uses that formatting again.
Comments	Remove only the comments part of the selected cell(s).

A quick way to remove the contents of a cell without removing formatting is to select the cell or cells you want to clear and then use DELETE on the keyboard.

In contrast, using **Delete**, found on the **Home** tab in the **Cells** group, removes the selected cells (or the entire row or column) from the worksheet. The remaining worksheet cells then shift over to replace the deleted cells.

Learn the Skill

This exercise demonstrates the use of the Clear command on the three main types of data: numbers, dates and text. To better illustrate this feature, you will use a worksheet containing random data.

1   Open the *Clear Formats Demo* workbook and save it as `Clear Formats Demo - Student`.

	A	B	C	D
1				
2		12,345.68	June 15, 2010	Sample text
3		12,345.68	June 15, 2010	Sample text
4		12,345.68	June 15, 2010	Sample text
5		12,345.68	June 15, 2010	Sample text
6		12,345.68	June 15, 2010	Sample text

Use each of the different Clear commands to see how it affects the data.

2   Select cells **B2** to **D2** and, on the **Home** tab, in the **Editing** group, click **Clear** and click **Clear All**.

3   Select cells **B3** to **D3** and, on the **Home** tab, in the **Editing** group, click **Clear** and click **Clear Formats**.

4   Select cells **B4** to **D4** and, on the **Home** tab, in the **Editing** group, click **Clear** and click **Clear Contents**.

5   Select cells **B5** to **D5** and press (Delete).

The Clear Contents command and the (Delete) key accomplish the same result.

6   Select cells **B6** to **D6** and, on the **Home** tab, in the **Editing** group, click **Clear** and click **Clear Comments**.

	A	B	C	D
1				
2				
3		12345.6789	40344	Sample text
4				
5				
6		12,345.68	June 15, 2010	Sample text

Now re-enter different data into some of the cells.

7   Enter the following values (do not use the copy and paste functions):

Cell	Value
B2	9876.543
B4	9876.543
B5	9876.543
C2	Mar 1, 2011
C3	Mar 1, 2011
C4	Mar 1, 2011
C5	Mar 1, 2011
D2	label
D4	label
D5	label

Notice the following:

In rows **2** and **3**, the Clear command removes all cell formats to revert them to default.

In cell **C3**, the date format temporarily reverts to a numeric format until replaced with a new date value.

In row **2**, Excel deletes all of the original data, including the cell comment, whereas in row **3**, Excel retains all of the original data, even though the date value in cell **C3** initially looked odd.

In both rows **4** and **5**, Excel deletes all of the original data except for the cell comments, but Excel retains the individual cell formats.

In row **6**, Excel deletes only the cell comment.

The completed worksheet should look similar to the following example:

	A	B	C	D
1				
2		9876.543	1-Mar-11	label
3		12345.6789	1-Mar-11	Sample text
4		9,876.54	March 1, 2011	label
5		9,876.54	March 1, 2011	label
6		12,345.68	June 15, 2010	Sample text

8   Save and close the workbook.

Themes
Applying Themes

4.1

The Microsoft Office suite (Word, Excel and PowerPoint) now offers a formatting feature called themes. A document theme is a set of theme colors, theme fonts and display effects that you choose and apply to a document as a combination.

By default, Excel (as well as Word and PowerPoint) uses the Office theme for all documents, as shown in this screen example.

There are several built-in themes from which to choose. You can also search for more themes on the Microsoft web site or you can create your own themes. To display the document themes, on the **Page Layout** tab, in the **Themes** group, click **Themes.**

Themes are very useful for creating a consistent look for all of your documents, whether they are letters, spreadsheets or slide presentations. By maintaining a consistent theme for these documents, you can create an identity that external customers, suppliers and others can quickly recognize.

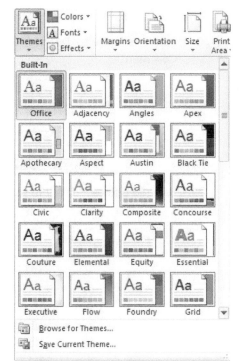

Learn the Skill

This exercise demonstrates how to apply a document theme to a worksheet.

1 Open the *Monthly Sales* workbook and save it as `Monthly Sales - Student`.

	A	B	C	D	E	F
1			Tolano Adventures			
2			Sales for July			
3						
4	Employee	Office	Units	Sales, Local Currency	Exchange Rate	Sales, US $
5	Nick Klassen	New York, USA	832	645,921	1.0000	$645,921
6	Madison Cowell	New York, USA	743	712,732	1.0000	$712,732
7	Jamie Gibson	Cape Town, South Africa	983	4,376,422	0.1339	$585,823
8	Toby Belanger	Toronto, Canada	425	582,085	0.9981	$580,952
9	Andrew McSweeney	London, England	782	562,493	1.5348	$863,292
10	Kanda Yamoto	Tokyo, Japan	884	93,742,745	0.0106	$997,329
11	Christie Akira	Tokyo, Japan	827	87,643,124	0.0106	$932,435
12	Lawrence Jang	Sydney, Australia	542	651,952	0.9203	$599,981
13	Curtis Gorski	Sydney, Australia	501	598,623	0.9203	$550,903
14	Total					$6,469,368

Notice that this worksheet is already formatted with fonts, sizes and colors.

2 On the **Page Layout** tab, in the **Themes** group, click **Themes**.

3 Point to different theme buttons and note how the Live Preview feature changes the background and border colors on this worksheet.

*Hint: The only colors changed on a worksheet are the ones selected from the **Theme Colors** section. Any colors selected from the **Standard Colors** section of the color palette remain unchanged when you select a different theme.*

4 Click the **Urban** theme.

All of the cells with background colors change to the selected theme.

Notice that not only the colors, but also the font changed as well. A Theme is actually a combination of a Color Theme with several colors and a Font Theme with two fonts.

5 Select cell **A1** and, on the **Home** tab, in the **Font** group, click the arrow for **Fill Color**.

The Theme Colors section of the color palette now shows the color scheme used by the **Urban** theme.

6 Click anywhere away from the color palette to close it.

The completed workbook should look similar to the following example:

7 Save the workbook.

Modifying Themes

Theme colors consist of four sets of text and background colors, six accent colors and two hyperlink colors.

When you modify the theme colors, the Sample pane of the **Edit Theme Colors** window shows your proposed changes. The left sample shows the Text/Background – Dark 2 selection, and the right sample shoes the Text/Background – Light 2 selection.

After you have made changes, save the theme colors with a name of your choice. You must also save the overall theme using a theme name of your choice.

Learn the Skill

This exercise demonstrates how to create a theme of your own.

1   Make sure the *Monthly Sales - Student* workbook is active on the screen.

2   On the **Page Layout** tab, in the **Themes** group, click **Colors** and then click **Create New Theme Colors** at the bottom of the list.

3   Click the arrow for **Accent 1**.

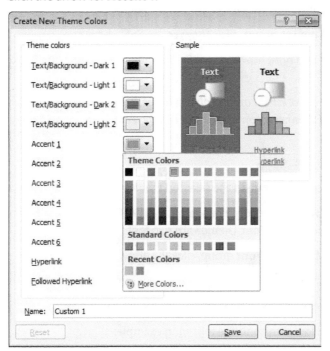

4   Click **More Colors** at the bottom of the color palette window.

5   In the Colors dialog box, click the **Standard** tab and select a bright green color of your choosing.

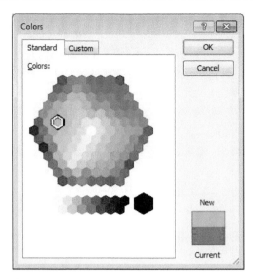

If the **Standard** tab does not contain the specific color shade that you want, you can select it from the **Custom** tab.

6   Click **OK**.

In the **Sample** section of the Create New Theme Colors dialog box, the left-most bar in the left and right sample bar charts are now displayed using the green color you selected.

7   In the **Name** box, replace the default name with: My colors.

8   Click **Save**.

The colors used on your worksheet now reflect your new selection.

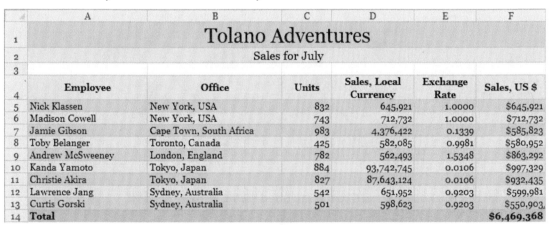

	A	B	C	D	E	F
1			Tolano Adventures			
2			Sales for July			
3						
4	Employee	Office	Units	Sales, Local Currency	Exchange Rate	Sales, US $
5	Nick Klassen	New York, USA	832	645,921	1.0000	$645,921
6	Madison Cowell	New York, USA	743	712,732	1.0000	$712,732
7	Jamie Gibson	Cape Town, South Africa	983	4,376,422	0.1339	$585,823
8	Toby Belanger	Toronto, Canada	425	582,085	0.9981	$580,952
9	Andrew McSweeney	London, England	782	562,493	1.5348	$863,292
10	Kanda Yamoto	Tokyo, Japan	884	93,742,745	0.0106	$997,329
11	Christie Akira	Tokyo, Japan	827	87,643,124	0.0106	$932,435
12	Lawrence Jang	Sydney, Australia	542	651,952	0.9203	$599,981
13	Curtis Gorski	Sydney, Australia	501	598,623	0.9203	$550,903
14	**Total**					**$6,469,368**

9   On the **Page Layout** tab, in the **Themes** group, click **Themes** and then click **Save Current Theme**.

10   In the Save Current Theme dialog box, replace the **File name** with: My Theme.

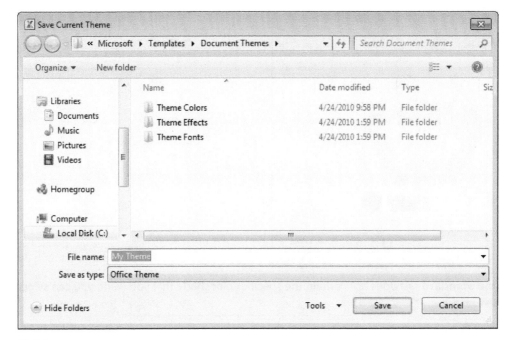

11   Click **Save**.

You have now saved the new theme to this workbook. The new theme and set of theme colors are now available to all workbooks used on this computer. You can also copy them and make them available to other users.

12   On the **Page Layout** tab, in the **Themes** group, click **Themes** to display the drop down list of all available themes.

When you no longer need your customized theme, you can delete it.

13   Right-click on **My Theme** and click **Delete**.

A message box appears with the question: "Delete this theme?"

14   Click **Yes**.

15   On the **Page Layout** tab, in the **Themes** group, click **Colors** to display the list of available colors.

16   Right-click on **My Color** and click **Delete**.

A message box appears with the question: "Delete these theme colors?"

17   Click **Yes**.

Notice that the workbook still uses the new customized color theme—until another theme is selected in the future—even though the theme has been deleted.

18   Save and close the workbook.

Using Cell Styles

3.6

You can use styles in Excel workbooks as a powerful formatting feature. Like Microsoft Word, a style is simply a grouping of specific format settings for a cell, such as font, size and color. Every time you apply this style to a cell, Excel formats it the same way. If the style is changed, Excel applies the changes to all cells with that style, maintaining a consistent look throughout the worksheet with minimal effort.

Excel provides you with a set of prebuilt styles known as **Quick Styles** because you can access them easily from the Ribbon.

Note the following restrictions:

- You define styles for a workbook. You cannot store them in a template file.

- If you change a style, Excel applies the changes to all cells using that style in every worksheet in that workbook.

- Unlike in Word, you cannot determine what style a cell is using because you cannot see the style name displayed on the Ribbon.

- You base styles on the currently selected theme. If you change the theme or the formatting of the theme, the style also changes.

You can create new styles using one of the following three methods:

- Use the formatting in a cell or cell range as an example; or

- display the Format Cells dialog box to specify the formatting; or

- merge the styles from another workbook into the current workbook.

Learn the Skill

This exercise demonstrates the format styles feature.

1   Open the *Balance Sheet* workbook and save it as Balance Sheet - Student.

	A	B	C	D
1	Tolano Adventures			
2	Consolidated Balance Sheet			
3	As at June 30			
4				
5		Current Year		Previous Year
6	Assets			
7	Cash	45430		44536
8	Customer Deposits	85930		75930
9	Equipment, Net	234824		235924
10	Buildings, Net	1927245		1927350
11	Total Assets	2293429		2283740
12				
13	Liabilities			
14	Accounts Payable	42569		36096
15	Mortgage Payable	1592742		1592850
16	Total Liabilities	1635311		1628946
17				
18	Shareholders' Equity			
19	Share Capital	100000		100000
20	Retained Earnings	558118		554794
21	Total Shareholders' Equity	658118		654794
22				
23	Total Liabilities and Equity	2293429		2283740

First, apply one of the built-in cell styles to a cell in the worksheet.

2   Select cell **B5**, then on the **Home** tab, in the **Styles** group, click **Cell Styles**.

Good, Bad and Neutral			
Normal	Bad	Good	Neutral

Data and Model					
Calculation	Check Cell	Explanatory...	Input	Linked Cell	Note
Output	Warning Text				

Titles and Headings

Heading 1	Heading 2	Heading 3	Heading 4	Title	Total

Themed Cell Styles

20% - Accent1	20% - Accent2	20% - Accent3	20% - Accent4	20% - Accent5	20% - Accent6
40% - Accent1	40% - Accent2	40% - Accent3	40% - Accent4	40% - Accent5	40% - Accent6
60% - Accent1	60% - Accent2	60% - Accent3	60% - Accent4	60% - Accent5	60% - Accent6
Accent1	Accent2	Accent3	Accent4	Accent5	Accent6

Number Format

Comma	Comma [0]	Currency	Currency [0]	Percent

New Cell Style...
Merge Styles...

3   Click **Heading 3** in the Titles and Headings section.

Apply this same style to another cell.

4   Select cell **D5** and, on the **Home** tab, in the **Styles** group, click **Cell Styles** and click **Heading 3**.

> Alternatively, you can use the Format Painter to copy a format from one cell to another.

5   Click cell **D5** and, on the **Home** tab, in the **Clipboard** group, double-click **Format Painter.**

6   Click on each of the following cells to copy the formatting to them: **A6**, **A13** and **A18**.

7   On the **Home** tab, in the **Clipboard** group, click **Format Painter** to turn it off.

Set the first and last number in each cell range to the currency format with no decimal digits.

8   Select cell **B7** and, on the **Home** tab, in the **Styles** group, click **Cell Styles**. Click **Currency [0]** in the **Number Format** section.

9   Use the **Format Painter** to copy the style in cell **B7** to each of the following cells:

B11, B14, B16, B19, B21, B23

D7, D11, D14, D16, D19, D21, D23

10   Turn off the **Format Painter**.

Set the remaining numbers in the worksheet to numeric format with commas and no decimal digits.

11   Select cell **B8** and, on the **Home** tab, in the **Styles** group, click **Cell Styles**. Click **Comma [0]** in the **Number Format** section.

12   Use the **Format Painter** to copy the style in cell **B8** to each of the following cells or cell ranges:

B9:B10, B15, B20

D8:D10, D15, D20

13   Turn off the **Format Painter**.

Use the Total style for the totals in each major account group.

14   Select cell **B11** and, on the **Home** tab, in the **Styles** group, click **Cell Styles.** Click **Total** in the **Titles and Headings** section.

15   Use the **Format Painter** to copy the style in cell **B11** to each of the following cells or cell ranges: D11, B23 and D23.

16   Turn off the **Format Painter**.

Use the Heading 4 style for the row titles in each major account group.

17   Select cell **A11** and, on the **Home** tab, in the **Styles** group, click **Cell Styles.** Click **Heading 4** in the **Titles and Headings** section.

18   Use the **Format Painter** to copy the style in cell **A11** to each of the following cells or cell ranges: A16, A21 and A23.

19   Turn off the **Format Painter**.

The subtotal numbers need a new style with a single border at the top and bottom of the cell.

20   Select cell **B16**.

21   On the **Home** tab, in the **Styles** group, click **Cell Styles** and then click **New Cell Style**.

Excel displays the Style dialog box to allow you to create this new style. Because you had selected a cell with another style applied to it, this new style inherits the same settings. Any changes to the parent style automatically flow through to this style as well.

22   In the **Style Name** list box, overtype the contents with: Subtotal.

23   Click **Format** in the Style dialog box.

Excel displays the Format Cells dialog box so that you can specify your formatting options.

24   Click the **Border** tab.

25   Click the arrow for the **Line Color**, select **Blue, Accent 1** (top row in the **Theme Colors** section, fifth from the left).

26   Click **Top Border** and **Bottom Border** to place the border at the top and bottom edges of the cell and click **OK**.

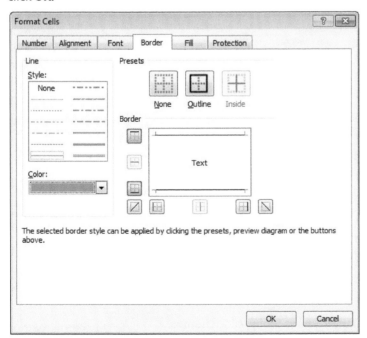

Alternatively, you can click on the top and bottom edges in the preview box.

You have now completed your formatting changes. The next step is to save the new style.

27 Click **OK** to save and close the Style dialog box.

Apply this new style to the subtotal numbers.

28 Select cell **B16**, then on the **Home** tab, in the **Styles** group, click **Cell Styles** and click **Subtotal** in the **Custom** section.

29 Use the **Format Painter** to copy the style in cell **B16** to each of the following cells: D16, B21 and D21.

30 Turn off the **Format Painter**.

Your worksheet should now look similar to the following:

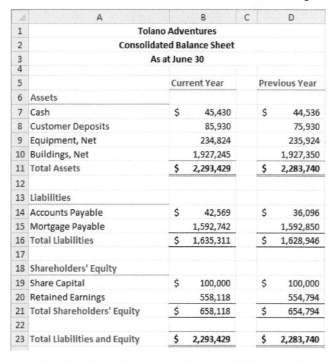

Now see what the effect of changing themes will do to the formatting.

31 On the **Page Layout** tab, in the **Themes** group, click **Themes**.

32 Point the mouse cursor over some of the themes listed and note how the cell style changes again.

33 Click on an empty part of the worksheet to close the Themes list.

You do not have to select any cell to modify the formatting in a style—Excel does not automatically apply the style to the current cell.

Excel indents all the numbers a little to the left. You can change this by modifying the style.

34 On the **Home** tab, in the **Styles** group, click **Cell Styles**, right-click **Comma [0]** and select **Modify**.

35 Click **Format** in the Style dialog box.

Excel now displays the Format Cells dialog box to allow you to specify your formatting options.

36 In the Format Cells dialog box, click the **Number** tab.

37 Click **Number** in the **Category** list and click **-1,234** in the **Negative Numbers** list.

38 Click **OK** to close the Format Cells dialog box, and click **OK** to close the Style dialog box.

> Notice that the change to the style affects __all__ the cells in the worksheet with that selected cell style.

Excel indents all the numbers a little to the left. You can change this by modifying the style.

39 On the **Home** tab, in the **Styles** group, click **Cell Styles**, right-click **Currency [0]** and select **Modify**.

40 Click **Format** in the Style dialog box.

Excel now displays the Format Cells dialog box to allow you to specify your formatting options.

41 In the Format Cells dialog box, click the **Number** tab.

42 Click **Currency** in the **Category** list, and click **-1,234** in the **Negative Numbers** list.

43 Click **OK** to close the Format Cells dialog box and click **OK** to close the Style dialog box.

This change does not affect the cells using the Currency [0] style along with another style. You will have to apply that change manually.

44 Select cell **B11** and then, on **Home** tab, in the **Styles** group, click **Cell Styles** and click **Currency [0]**.

45 Use the Format Painter to copy this format to cells: B23, D11 and D23.

46 Select cell **B16** and then, on **Home** tab, in the **Styles** group, click **Cell Styles** and click **Currency [0]**.

47 Use the Format Painter to copy this format to cells: B21, D16 and D21.

	A	B	C	D
1	Tolano Adventures			
2	Consolidated Balance Sheet			
3	As at June 30			
4				
5		Current Year		Previous Year
6	Assets			
7	Cash	$45,430		$44,536
8	Customer Deposits	85,930		75,930
9	Equipment, Net	234,824		235,924
10	Buildings, Net	1,927,245		1,927,350
11	Total Assets	$2,293,429		$2,283,740
12				
13	Liabilities			
14	Accounts Payable	$42,569		$36,096
15	Mortgage Payable	1,592,742		1,592,850
16	Total Liabilities	$1,635,311		$1,628,946
17				
18	Shareholders' Equity			
19	Share Capital	$100,000		$100,000
20	Retained Earnings	558,118		554,794
21	Total Shareholders' Equity	$658,118		$654,794
22				
23	Total Liabilities and Equity	$2,293,429		$2,283,740

48 Save and close the workbook.

Conditional Formatting

Using the Ribbon

8.3

You use cell formatting to enhance the visual appeal of a worksheet. However, highlighting certain cells to differentiate them from the rest of the worksheet also draws attention to them or conveys the data they contain in a visual manner.

Conditional formatting is a powerful tool you can use to display the data in cells one way for some values, but another way for others, without the additional effort of manually changing the formatting each time you modify data or add new data to a worksheet.

The Ribbon offers several choices for setting up conditional formats.

Highlight Cell Rules

Use this option to highlight cell values based on their relation to specific values you enter. In this example, you specified that Excel should highlight cell values of greater than 12000 with a green background, while cells with less than 9000 would be highlighted with a pink background, and cells with in-between values would be in dark yellow text with a light yellow background.

	A	B
1	Sales By Customer, Year To Date	
2		
3	Air Wing Fuels Inc.	5,025.74
4	Awesome Bikes Ltd.	6,100.02
5	Boat Brokerage Sales Corp.	14,559.50
6	Consolidated Amalgamated Corp.	11,290.13
7	Daring Swimsuits Unlimited	11,341.36
8	Ecological Bicycles Ltd.	6,346.47
9	Exotic Lingerie Inc.	5,053.12
10	Farley's Farm Supplies Inc.	13,259.16
11	Flaming Hot Skis Ltd.	9,890.61
12	Fraser Glen College	10,296.38
13	Gas Tank Wholesalers Inc.	6,806.98
14	Hole In The Wall Computers Inc.	9,041.47
15	Humongous Holdings Ltd.	12,369.33
16	Les's Tailors Ltd	13,062.72
17	Megatron Entertainment Corp.	13,127.39
18	Millennium Holdings Ltd.	10,287.27
19	Office Supplies Unlimited	8,118.71
20	Paint The World Ltd.	8,628.84
21	Pullemout Dental Suppliers Inc.	10,020.39
22	Sweet Stuff Manufacturing Corp.	11,535.14
23	The Potato Chipper Ltd.	14,273.87

Top/Bottom Rules

Use this option to activate the conditional formatting on the top or bottom ranking cells in a range. In this example, the conditional formatting is set so that Excel highlights the top 10% of cells in red with a pink background, and the bottom 10% in dark green with a light green background. There are 20 cells selected in the range, so 10% is 2 cells each. If the range comprises 50 cells, the top and bottom 10% would be 5 cells each.

You can choose to highlight any percentage of cells for conditional formatting.

	A	B
1	Sales By Customer, Year To Date	
2		
3	Air Wing Fuels Inc.	5,025.74
4	Awesome Bikes Ltd.	6,100.02
5	Boat Brokerage Sales Corp.	14,559.50
6	Consolidated Amalgamated Corp.	11,290.13
7	Daring Swimsuits Unlimited	11,341.36
8	Ecological Bicycles Ltd.	6,346.47
9	Exotic Lingerie Inc.	5,053.12
10	Farley's Farm Supplies Inc.	13,259.16
11	Flaming Hot Skis Ltd.	9,890.61
12	Fraser Glen College	10,296.38
13	Gas Tank Wholesalers Inc.	6,806.98
14	Hole In The Wall Computers Inc.	9,041.47
15	Humongous Holdings Ltd.	12,369.33
16	Les's Tailors Ltd	13,062.72
17	Megatron Entertainment Corp.	13,127.39
18	Millennium Holdings Ltd.	10,287.27
19	Office Supplies Unlimited	8,118.71
20	Paint The World Ltd.	8,628.84
21	Pullemout Dental Suppliers Inc.	10,020.39
22	Sweet Stuff Manufacturing Corp.	11,535.14
23	The Potato Chipper Ltd.	14,273.87

Data Bars

You can use conditional formatting to embed a bar chart into a selected range of cells, based on the value in each cell.

This type of formatting offers a quick visual representation of each cell value in relation to the others.

	A	B
1	Sales By Customer, Year To Date	
2		
3	Air Wing Fuels Inc.	5,025.74
4	Awesome Bikes Ltd.	6,100.02
5	Boat Brokerage Sales Corp.	14,559.50
6	Consolidated Amalgamated Corp.	11,290.13
7	Daring Swimsuits Unlimited	11,341.36
8	Ecological Bicycles Ltd.	6,346.47
9	Exotic Lingerie Inc.	5,053.12
10	Farley's Farm Supplies Inc.	13,259.16
11	Flaming Hot Skis Ltd.	9,890.61
12	Fraser Glen College	10,296.38
13	Gas Tank Wholesalers Inc.	6,806.98
14	Hole In The Wall Computers Inc.	9,041.47
15	Humongous Holdings Ltd.	12,369.33
16	Les's Tailors Ltd	13,062.72
17	Megatron Entertainment Corp.	13,127.39
18	Millennium Holdings Ltd.	10,287.27
19	Office Supplies Unlimited	8,118.71
20	Paint The World Ltd.	8,628.84
21	Pullemout Dental Suppliers Inc.	10,020.39
22	Sweet Stuff Manufacturing Corp.	11,535.14
23	The Potato Chipper Ltd.	14,273.87

Color Scales

Use this type of conditional formatting to show the relative value of each cell to each other cell using color gradients. This example shows the red-yellow-green option, with the lowest value highlighted with dark red, dark green for the highest value and yellow for the middle values.

	A	B
1	Sales By Customer, Year To Date	
2		
3	Air Wing Fuels Inc.	5,025.74
4	Awesome Bikes Ltd.	6,100.02
5	Boat Brokerage Sales Corp.	14,559.50
6	Consolidated Amalgamated Corp.	11,290.13
7	Daring Swimsuits Unlimited	11,341.36
8	Ecological Bicycles Ltd.	6,346.47
9	Exotic Lingerie Inc.	5,053.12
10	Farley's Farm Supplies Inc.	13,259.16
11	Flaming Hot Skis Ltd.	9,890.61
12	Fraser Glen College	10,296.38
13	Gas Tank Wholesalers Inc.	6,806.98
14	Hole In The Wall Computers Inc.	9,041.47
15	Humongous Holdings Ltd.	12,369.33
16	Les's Tailors Ltd	13,062.72
17	Megatron Entertainment Corp.	13,127.39
18	Millennium Holdings Ltd.	10,287.27
19	Office Supplies Unlimited	8,118.71
20	Paint The World Ltd.	8,628.84
21	Pullemout Dental Suppliers Inc.	10,020.39
22	Sweet Stuff Manufacturing Corp.	11,535.14
23	The Potato Chipper Ltd.	14,273.87

Icon Sets

You can use this type of conditional formatting to highlight values using icons. In this example, a 5-bar strength meter (similar to the wireless network strength indicator on laptop computers) indicates the relative value of each cell to each other cell. The cells with the lowest values have no bars filled, while the highest values have all bars filled.

	A	B
1	Sales By Customer, Year To Date	
2		
3	Air Wing Fuels Inc.	5,025.74
4	Awesome Bikes Ltd.	6,100.02
5	Boat Brokerage Sales Corp.	14,559.50
6	Consolidated Amalgamated Corp.	11,290.13
7	Daring Swimsuits Unlimited	11,341.36
8	Ecological Bicycles Ltd.	6,346.47
9	Exotic Lingerie Inc.	5,053.12
10	Farley's Farm Supplies Inc.	13,259.16
11	Flaming Hot Skis Ltd.	9,890.61
12	Fraser Glen College	10,296.38
13	Gas Tank Wholesalers Inc.	6,806.98
14	Hole In The Wall Computers Inc.	9,041.47
15	Humongous Holdings Ltd.	12,369.33
16	Les's Tailors Ltd	13,062.72
17	Megatron Entertainment Corp.	13,127.39
18	Millennium Holdings Ltd.	10,287.27
19	Office Supplies Unlimited	8,118.71
20	Paint The World Ltd.	8,628.84
21	Pullemout Dental Suppliers Inc.	10,020.39
22	Sweet Stuff Manufacturing Corp.	11,535.14
23	The Potato Chipper Ltd.	14,273.87

In all of these examples, you see the same conditional format applied to the entire cell range. If you change a value in any of these cells, the conditional format is automatically re-evaluated and the highlighting may change.

A cell may have both a manual format and a conditional format. If the cell contains a value that does not meet any of the specified conditions, the cell uses the manual format.

Formatting options include only the font styles (regular, bold, italics or bold and italics), font colors, borders and background fill patterns. You may not choose different font names or font sizes in a conditional format.

Learn the Skill

This exercise demonstrates how to apply conditional formats to a range of cells.

You have been asked to prepare a report for your manager, identifying your best corporate customers based on the amount of sales this year. In addition, you need to identify mid-level corporate customers because the Marketing department may want to work closely with them during the latter half of the year.

You will identify the best customers as having generated more than $12,000 of sales this year, and the mid-level customers as having generated more than $9,000 but less than $12,000.

1   Open the *Sales By Customer* workbook, and save it as Sales By Customer - Student.

Add a conditional format to identify the mid-level customers.

2   Select cells **B3:B23**. On the **Home** tab, in the **Styles** group, click **Conditional Formatting**.

3   Click **Highlight Cells Rules** and then click **Between**.

4   In the Between dialog box, replace the value in the left-most text box with: 9000.

5   Press (Tab) and replace the value in that text box with: 12000.

6   Click the arrow for the right-most list box and click **Yellow Fill with Dark Yellow Text**.

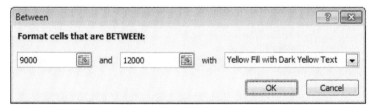

7   Click **OK**.

Now add another conditional format to identify the best customers.

8   With cells **B3:B23** still highlighted, on the **Home** tab, in the **Styles** group, click **Conditional Formatting**, click **Highlight Cell Rules** and click **Greater Than**.

9   In the Greater Than dialog box, replace the value on the left with: 12000.

10   Click the arrow for the right-most list box and click **Custom Format**.

Excel displays the Format Cells dialog box to allow you to select from a wide variety of formatting options.

11   Click the **Fill** tab.

12   Click the light green color (fifth from the left, bottom row) in the **Background Color** section and click **OK**.

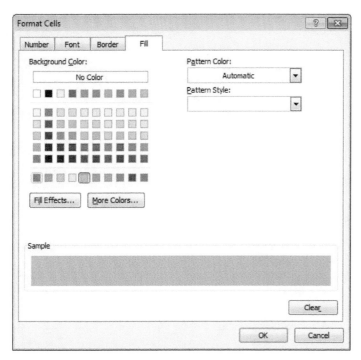

13   Click **OK** in the Greater Than dialog box.

14   Click in an empty cell outside of the cell range to view the data.

The completed worksheet should now appear similar to the following:

	A	B
1	Sales By Customer, Year To Date	
2		
3	Air Wing Fuels Inc.	5,025.74
4	Awesome Bikes Ltd.	6,100.02
5	Boat Brokerage Sales Corp.	14,559.50
6	Consolidated Amalgamated Corp.	11,290.13
7	Daring Swimsuits Unlimited	11,341.36
8	Ecological Bicycles Ltd.	6,346.47
9	Exotic Lingerie Inc.	5,053.12
10	Farley's Farm Supplies Inc.	13,259.16
11	Flaming Hot Skis Ltd.	9,890.61
12	Fraser Glen College	10,296.38
13	Gas Tank Wholesalers Inc.	6,806.98
14	Hole In The Wall Computers Inc.	9,041.47
15	Humongous Holdings Ltd.	12,369.33
16	Les's Tailors Ltd	13,062.72
17	Megatron Entertainment Corp.	13,127.39
18	Millennium Holdings Ltd.	10,287.27
19	Office Supplies Unlimited	8,118.71
20	Paint The World Ltd.	8,628.84
21	Pullemout Dental Suppliers Inc.	10,020.39
22	Sweet Stuff Manufacturing Corp.	11,535.14
23	The Potato Chipper Ltd.	14,273.87

Now observe what happens when you change data values. Assume that two of the cell values are correct.

15   Select cell **B3** and enter: 13,000.

16   Select cell **B10** and enter: 2,000.

Even though the formatting has not changed for any of these cells, the highlighting has changed based on the new cell values.

17   Save and close the workbook.

Using the Rules Manager

8.3

When you use the Ribbon to set up conditional formatting in your worksheet, Excel creates the conditional formatting rules in the background.

You can use the Rules Manager directly to create new rules that are more customized to your needs, The Rules Manager can also be used to modify existing rules or delete rules no longer needed.

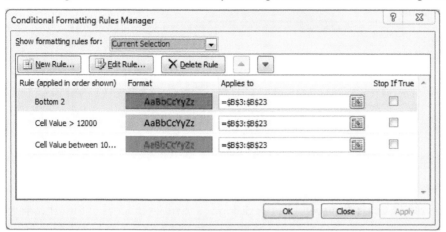

Learn the Skill

This exercise demonstrates how to add, modify and delete conditional formats for a range of cells using the Rules Manager.

1   Select the *Sales By Customer - Student* workbook.

Use the Rules Manager to display the existing conditional formatting rules.

2   Select cells **B3:B23**.

3   On the **Home** tab, in the **Styles** group, click **Conditional Formatting**, and click **Manage Rules**.

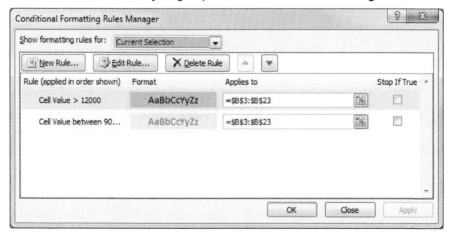

Change one of the existing conditional formatting rules.

4   Click on the bottom rule (**Cell Value between 9000 and 12000**) to select it, then click **Edit Rule**.

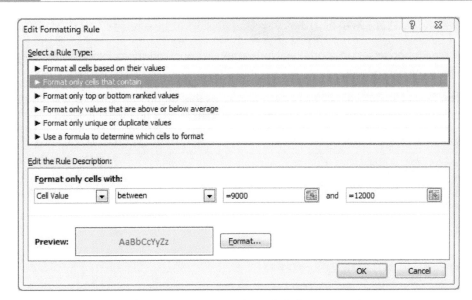

5   Change the left value from 9000 to 10000, then click the **Format** button.

     The Format Cells dialog box is displayed. Use this dialog box to make changes to the cell formatting.

6   Click the **Fill** tab, then select blue (third from the right in the Standard Colors section) as the fill color, and click **OK**.

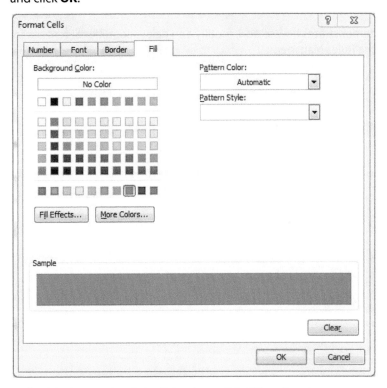

7   In the Edit Formatting Rule dialog box, click **OK** to close it.

8   In the Conditional Formatting Rules Manager dialog box, click **Apply** to see the changes take effect on the worksheet.

Add a new conditional formatting rule using the Rules Manager.

9   In the Conditional Formatting Rules Manager dialog box, click **New Rule**.

10   In the New Formatting Rule dialog box, click on each of the options in the **Select a Rule Type** section and observe the options available in the lower half of the dialog box.

11 Select the **Format only top or bottom ranked values** option, then select **Bottom 2** (do not choose **% of the selected range**) in the **Edit the Rule Description** section.

12 Click **Format**, click the **Fill** tab and select dark red in the Standard Colors section. Click **OK**.

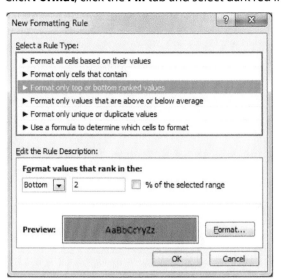

13 Click **OK** to close the New Formatting Rule dialog box, and click **OK** to close the Conditional Formatting Rules Manager dialog box.

14 Click on an empty cell to view the worksheet data.

The completed worksheet should now appear similar to the following:

Delete one of the formatting rules using the Rules Manager dialog box.

15 Select cells **B3:B23**, then on the **Home** tab, in the **Styles** group, click **Conditional Formatting**, and click **Manage Rules**.

16 Select the bottom rule (Cell Value between 10000 and 12000), and click **Delete Rule**.

17 Click **OK** in the Conditional Formatting Rules Manager dialog box.

18 Save and close the workbook.

Using Conditional Formatting with IF Function

8.3

In most situations, you will set up a conditional format using the value in the same cell. Occasionally you may need to create the conditional format using the value from a different cell in the worksheet. This capability can be combined with the IF function to create indicators on your worksheet that draw readers attention.

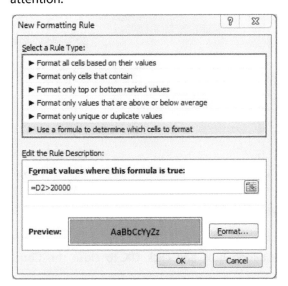

Because of the complexity of this type of conditional format, Excel requires the conditional format rule to be calculated as a logical (i.e. True or False) value. This is a very flexible arrangement that allows you to use any type of formula that uses functions, comparison operators, and others, as long as they resolve down to a simple True or False result. This coincides with the capabilities of the IF function which also delivers a result based on a True or False calculation.

Learn the Skill

This exercise demonstrates how to create a conditional format with an IF function.

1 Open the *Customer Feedback* workbook and save it as Customer Feedback - Student.

▲	A	B	C	D	E
1		Yes	No	Difference	Flag
2	January	30,713	3,449	27,264	
3	February	19,599	3,830	15,769	
4	March	17,303	9,450	7,853	
5	April	28,004	15,225	12,779	
6	May	29,299	6,151	23,148	
7	June	21,689	18,677	3,012	

This spreadsheet is used by Tolano Adventures to track the number of satisfied customers each month for one of their challenging "bootcamp" vacations. Due to the nature of that vacation, there will always be some customers who are not fully satisfied with every aspect. However, if the number of No responses is too high, then management wants to be alerted so that changes can be made quickly.

Enter an IF formula that will display a specific color (as a word) when a value in column D falls within a certain range:

Column D Value	Column E Displays
Difference > 20,000	Green
Difference between 10,000 and 20,000	Yellow
Difference < 10,000	Red

Notice that column E could display one of three possible colors. However, a single IF formula can only display one of two possible values; therefore, one IF formula will be "nested" inside another one. Note that the "between" logic is met by the fact that Excel reads formulas from left to right; that is, Excel has already determined that the value in D2 is less than or equal to 20,000 when the D2 > 10,000 comparison is being calculated.

2   Select cell **E2** and enter: =IF(D2>20000,"Green",IF(D2>10000,"Yellow","Red")).

3   Copy this formula in cell **E2** down to the cell range **E3:E7**.

Create three new conditional formatting rules so that the cells displaying the word "green" will have a fill color of green, yellow will appear as yellow, and red will appear as red.

4   Select the cell range **E2:E7**.

5   On the **Home** tab, in the **Styles** group, click **Conditional Formatting**, and click **Manage Rules**.

6   In the Conditional Formatting Rules Manager dialog box, click **New Rule**.

7   Select the **Use a formula to determine which cells to format** option.

This first rule will be true if the value in column D is greater than 20,000.

8   Click in the text box below **Format values where this formula is true** and enter: =D2>20000.

9   Click **Format**. Click the **Fill** tab, then select green in the Standard Colors section and click **OK**.

10   Click **OK** to close the New Formatting Rule dialog box.

Enter the second conditional format that will display the yellow fill color if the value in column D is between 10,000 and 20,000.

11   Click **New Rule** and select the **Use a formula to determine which cells to format** option.

12   Enter the formula: =AND(D2>10000,D2<20000) and select yellow as the fill color. Click **OK** to save this new rule.

Enter the third conditional format that will display the red fill color if the value in column D is less than 10,000.

13   Click **New Rule** and select the **Use a formula to determine which cells to format** option.

14   Enter the formula: =D2<10000 and select red as the fill color. Click **OK** to save this new rule.

15   Click **OK** to close the Conditional Formatting Rules Manager dialog box.

The completed worksheet should now appear similar to the following:

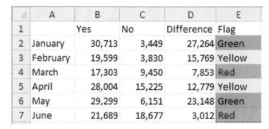

	A	B	C	D	E
1		Yes	No	Difference	Flag
2	January	30,713	3,449	27,264	Green
3	February	19,599	3,830	15,769	Yellow
4	March	17,303	9,450	7,853	Red
5	April	28,004	15,225	12,779	Yellow
6	May	29,299	6,151	23,148	Green
7	June	21,689	18,677	3,012	Red

16   Save and close the workbook.

Lesson Summary

In this lesson, you looked at how to use a variety of methods to format cells in a worksheet to emphasize different worksheet areas. You should now be able to:

☑ format numbers and decimal places

☑ change the alignment of cell contents

☑ change fonts and font size

☑ apply borders around cell(s)

☑ apply background colors and patterns to cell(s)

☑ use the Format Painter

☑ clear cell contents and formatting

☑ apply and modify themes

☑ apply and modify cell styles

☑ apply conditional formatting

Review Questions

MMM
Go online for
Additional
Review and
Activities

1. What is Live Preview?

2. How do data appear in a cell if the alignment is set to General?

3. How can applying colors or patterns be useful in a worksheet?

4. How does applying themes differ from applying different formatting features individually?

5. Give an example of when you might want to use a theme in a worksheet.

6. What is the difference between clicking the Format Painter once and clicking it twice?

7. Give some examples of why you might want to use styles on cells in the worksheet.

8. Explain what conditional formatting is and provide examples of how you can use it to find or enhance data.

Microsoft®
Excel® 2010
Core Certification

Lesson 5: Viewing and Printing Workbooks

Lesson Objectives

This lesson introduces how to change the views in preparation for printing worksheets, print and preview worksheets, customize the page setup for printing worksheets, and change the Excel Backstage options. Upon successful completion of this lesson, you should be able to:

☐ create worksheet windows

☐ arrange worksheet windows

☐ split panes

☐ freeze panes

☐ zoom in and out of worksheets

☐ print and preview worksheets

☐ use different workbook views

☐ add and preview page breaks

☐ change printing margins, orientation, paper size and scale

☐ print column and row titles or selected range of cells

☐ add and modify headers and footers

☐ printing selected worksheets

☐ change Excel default settings

Changing Worksheet Views

4.2
4.3

In previous years, computer monitors were relatively small; they have grown slowly from 14 inches to more than 20 inches. The screen resolution (and therefore the ability to display many rows and columns of a spreadsheet clearly) has also increased from a paltry 640 by 480 pixels to 1024 by 768 pixels and more. LCD monitors now have even larger screens with the ability to display large portions of a spreadsheet at the same time.

To overcome the limited size of smaller monitors (such as those used with netbook computers), Excel provides you with the ability to change how Excel displays the worksheet. If you are doing some "What-if" evaluations, for example, you may want to see distant parts of one large worksheet or workbook on the screen at the same time. On the other hand, you may wish to have more than one workbook on the screen to cut and paste from one worksheet to another. Alternatively, you may experience difficulty working on your large worksheet because you cannot see the row and column headings when making entries.

The **View** tab offers a number of tools to facilitate different views:

Zoom	Change the magnification percentage to zoom closer or further away from the worksheet.
100%	Force the zoom back to 100% immediately.
Zoom to Selection	Zoom into the selected block of cells on the worksheet.
New Window	Create a new window containing a copy of the worksheet.
Arrange All	Arrange all of the windows on the screen in one of several layouts: tiled, horizontal, vertical or cascade.
Freeze Panes	Lock in place the rows above and the columns to the left of a selected cell, while you scroll in the worksheet. This option is useful to keep the headings on the screen when you are working in cells remote from those headings.
Split	Split the worksheet into two or four panes.
Hide	Hide the active window from the screen; this is useful when you are working with multiple windows and you want Excel to display only specific windows.
Unhide	Display a dialog box listing the windows you have hidden so that you can select individual windows and redisplay them.
View Side by Side	Place two open workbooks side by side in the Excel document window. You can place the two side by side in a vertical or horizontal position.
Synchronous Scrolling	Scroll through the worksheets in each pane simultaneously.
Reset Window Position	Reset the displayed worksheets to equal sizes.
Save Workspace	Save the current layout of windows or the workspace so that you can use it later.
Switch Windows	Present a list of the documents currently open in Excel. Excel numbers the documents, which you can access by clicking the document you want to view.

Even though you may have multiple workbooks open at the same time, only one can be active at a time. That is, you can only work on one workbook at a time; if you need to update two of them at essentially the same time, you must switch back and forth between workbooks to do the entries.

To increase the amount of display area available to view all of your document windows, you can also minimize the Ribbon temporarily.

Creating and Arranging Worksheet Windows

The **New Window** button enables you to open another view of the active workbook. You can then arrange the workbook windows to view different parts of the workbook (either the same worksheet, or different worksheets of the same workbook) at the same time without having to scroll around the worksheet continuously to view cells that are far from each other.

For example, you may want to do some "What-if" evaluations on a workbook. These evaluations may require that you make changes at the top of your worksheet while you view the effects on the totals at the bottom of the worksheet. Using at least two windows on the same workbook facilitates this process.

Every open workbook will have its own window in the Excel screen. If you use the New Window feature to create a second (or more) view of any of the workbooks, you will quickly run out of available space on the screen to display all of these windows.

The **Arrange All** button in the Ribbon enables you to quickly reposition all open workbook views on the screen at the same time. When arranging the windows on the screen, you can choose from several options:

Tiled	Re-arrange worksheet windows on the screen so that all windows are as square as possible and positioned next to each other.

Horizontal   Re-arrange worksheet windows on the screen so that each window stretches across the entire width of the Excel screen. Excel lays them horizontally so that you can see as many columns as possible in each worksheet.

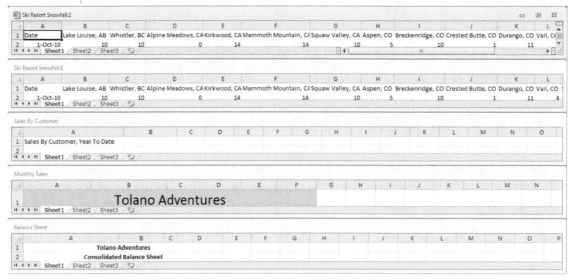

Vertical   Re-arrange worksheet windows on the screen so that each window stretches from the top to the bottom of the Excel screen. Excel lines up these windows vertically so that you can see as many rows as possible in each worksheet.

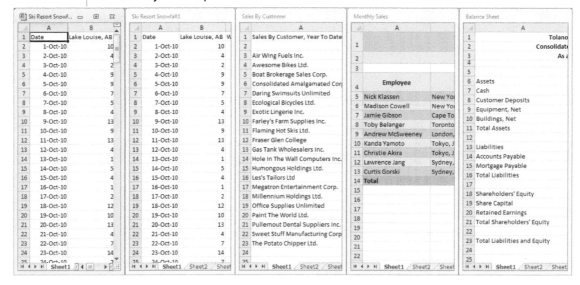

Cascade   Re-arrange worksheets so that each one is on top of the next and slightly offset to give you a three-dimensional view of all open workbooks. This kind of arrangement is best when you do not want to reduce the size of each worksheet window, and you can flip between the open windows as needed.

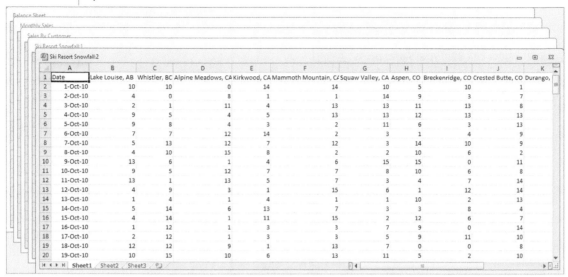

In all of these view options, the active workbook is the one with the darker colored title bar and the scroll bars. The other open workbooks have a title bar with a lighter shade, and no scroll bars.

Learn the Skill

In this exercise, you will practice creating another window for a workbook, moving between workbooks and arranging workbooks.

1   Open the *Ski Resort Snowfall* workbook and save as it `Ski Resort Snowfall - Student`.

2   On the **View** tab, in the **Window** group, click **New Window**.

Note that if you have maximized the document window, nothing seems to happen when you select this option.

This new window is identified in the title bar as *Ski Resort Snowfall - Student.xlsx:2*, while the original window is identified as *Ski Resort Snowfall - Student.xlsx:1*. You can change the arrangement of these windows to view both at the same time.

3   On the **View** tab, in the **Window** group, click **Arrange All**.

Excel displays the Arrange Windows dialog box.

4   Click **Tiled** and click **OK**.

Excel arranges the two workbook windows on your screen side by side. If you had more than two windows or had other files open, Excel would tile them in several same-sized rectangles. You can identify the active window by the scroll bars in that window. The inactive windows do not have any scroll bars.

Both of these windows are views of the same workbook. If you change a cell value in one window, the view in the other window is updated at the same time.

5   Select cell **B3**. Type: 5 and press (Enter).

You can move around the worksheet in each of these windows independently of each other, allowing you to view different parts of the same worksheet (or even different worksheets) at the same time.

6   Drag the horizontal scroll bar of the active window (the one on the left) to move to the right of the worksheet.

7   Click anywhere in the other window to make it the active worksheet.

8   Drag the vertical scroll bar to move down the worksheet.

This demonstrates that you can scroll through the two windows independently of each other, even though they are both showing the same worksheet. The screen should now appear similar to the one shown in this example:

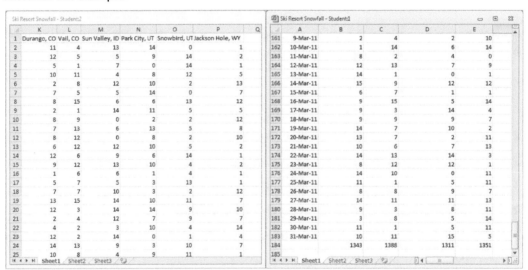

9   Close all of the workbook windows and discard all changes made to the workbook.

Splitting Panes

The split feature enables you to slice a worksheet into two or four smaller window views of that worksheet. In each of the split window views, you can move around to see different (or even the same) parts of the worksheet without having to continuously shift from one of the worksheets to the other, or move rows and columns around to see the related data closer together. The operation is like using four different cameras simultaneously, with the ability to manipulate each one independently of one another—you can point them to any part of the worksheet whether they are close or far away from each other.

You can split a worksheet into two panes, either horizontally or vertically, or into four panes with one horizontal and one vertical component.

The following illustrates the position of the horizontal and vertical split bars:

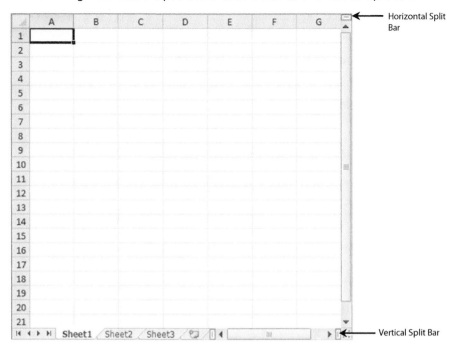

Horizontal Split Bar

Vertical Split Bar

You can only alter the position of the split bar using the mouse. To move a split bar, position your mouse pointer over the bar. When the double-headed arrow appears, press and hold the mouse button and move the bar to the desired location.

Learn the Skill

In this exercise, you will use the split bars to view separate parts of a worksheet.

1   Open the *Ski Resort Snowfall - Student* workbook.

2   Select cell **D7**.

3   On the **View** tab, in the **Window** group, click **Split**.

	A	B	C	D	E	F	G	H
1	Date	Lake Louise, AB	Whistler, BC	Alpine Meadows, CA	Kirkwood, CA	Mammoth Mountain, CA	Squaw Valley, CA	Aspen, CO
2	1-Oct-10	10	10	0	14	14	10	5
3	2-Oct-10	4	0	8	1	1	14	9
4	3-Oct-10	2	1	11	4	13	13	11
5	4-Oct-10	9	5	4	5	13	13	12
6	5-Oct-10	9	8	4	3	2	11	6
7	6-Oct-10	7	7	12	14	2	3	1
8	7-Oct-10	5	13	12	7	12	3	14
9	8-Oct-10	4	10	15	8	2		
10	9-Oct-10	13	6	1	4	6		
11	10-Oct-10	9	5	12	7	7		
12	11-Oct-10	13	1	13	5	7		
13	12-Oct-10	4	9	3	1	15		
14	13-Oct-10	1	4	1	4	1		
15	14-Oct-10	5	14	6	13	7		

4   Drag the horizontal split line down so that it is in the middle of the screen.

5   Use the vertical scroll bar in the upper right pane to scroll down the worksheet.

Notice how the upper two panes in the window scroll down together.

You can also activate the split mode by dragging the horizontal split bar from above the vertical scroll bar or by dragging the vertical split bar on the far right of the horizontal scroll bar.

6 Click the horizontal scroll bar in the bottom left and bottom right panes to observe how the windows change.

Notice how the two panes in the window scroll left or right together.

7 Click the scroll bars so that cell **H10** is visible in the middle of each of the four panes.

8 Select cell **H10** in any one of the panes.

9 Type: 9 and press ⬚Enter⬚.

> *You can also turn off the split mode by dragging the horizontal split bar to the top or bottom, and the vertical split bar to the extreme left or right of the worksheet, or by double-clicking on a split bar.*

The worksheet should now appear as shown in the following example:

	G	H	I		F	G	H	I	J	
5	13	12			13	13	12	13	13	
6	11	6			2	11	6	3	13	
7	3	1			2	3	1	4	9	
8	3	14			12	3	14	10	9	
9	2	10			2	2	10	6	7	
10	15	9			6	15	9	0	11	
11	8	10			7	8	10	6	8	
12	3	4			7	3	4	7	14	
13	6	1			15	6	1	12	14	
14	1	10			1	1	10	2	13	
7	3	1			2	3	1	4	9	
8	3	14			12	3	14	10	9	
9	2	10			2	2	10	6	7	
10	15	9			6	15	9	0	11	
11	8	10			7	8	10	6	8	
12	3	4			7	3	4	7	14	
13	6	1			15	6	1	12	14	
14	1	10			1	1	10	2	13	
15	3	3			7	3	3	8	4	
16	2	12			15	2	12	6	7	
17	7	9			3	7	9	0	14	

Sheet1 / Sheet2

10 On the **View** tab, in the **Window** group, click **Split** to remove the split bars.

11 Save the workbook.

Freezing Panes

As your worksheet grows in size, it will become increasingly difficult to view all of the entries. More importantly, you will reach a point when you can no longer keep the row and column headings on the screen as you scroll down or across your large worksheet. It can become difficult to determine, for example, whether you are entering data in the February or March column, or in the Taxes or Travel row. To help you overcome this, Excel enables you to lock the titles on the screen, while you scroll to a remote part of the worksheet.

Freezing panes refers to the feature that enables you to lock the top row(s) or left-most column(s). This feature provides you with three options from which to choose:

> *Excel does not enable frozen and split panes at the same time.*

Freeze Panes	In this option, the active cell serves as an anchor—when the feature is activated, all rows above and all columns to the left of the active cell remain in view until the feature is turned off. You may freeze more than one row or column in place. You can also freeze just the top row(s) or just the leftmost column(s).
Freeze Top Row	When you select this option, the selection of the active cell is not important. Excel will always freeze only the one row currently displayed at the top of the worksheet window. Note that if the top row currently displayed on the screen is not row 1 (e.g. row 20), Excel will freeze that row, even though your column titles may be in row 1
Freeze First Column	When you select this option, the selection of the active cell is not important. Excel will always freeze only the one column currently displayed at the far left of the worksheet window. Like the Freeze Top Row option, be sure to verify that the left column currently displayed is the correct one to freeze

When freezing panes using the current cell, Excel locks *all* rows above and *all* columns to the left so that they will not move. Therefore, you should not freeze a block of rows and columns in the middle of the worksheet, as you will not have much space in which to move the rest of your worksheet.

Learn the Skill

In this exercise, you will practice freezing panes.

1   Make sure the *Ski Resort Snowfall - Student* workbook is active.

2   Select cell **B2**.

3   On the **View** tab, in the **Window** group, click **Freeze Panes**, and then click **Freeze Panes**.

4   Scroll to the right of the worksheet so that columns **M** and **N** are displayed.

Note that the dates in column **A** remain in view.

5   Scroll down the worksheet.

Note that row **1** remains in place.

The worksheet should now appear as shown in the following example:

	A	J	K	L	M	N	O
1	Date	Crested Butte, CO	Durango, CO	Vail, CO	Sun Valley, ID	Park City, UT	Snowbird, UT
29	28-Oct-10	1	0	5	1	14	3
30	29-Oct-10	10	13	7	7	3	14
31	30-Oct-10	13	12	5	5	7	13
32	31-Oct-10	10	13	4	11	14	14
33	1-Nov-10	9	5	3	1	2	10
34	2-Nov-10	11	2	7	9	6	2
35	3-Nov-10	6	6	13	6	8	4
36	4-Nov-10	11	3	5	6	11	13
37	5-Nov-10	14	3	11	11	13	8
38	6-Nov-10	4	1	8	9	1	13
39	7-Nov-10	2	10	12	10	13	2
40	8-Nov-10	10	12	11	5	1	2
41	9-Nov-10	13	5	7	14	14	9
42	10-Nov-10	9	11	8	13	8	2

If you need to change the location of the titles, unfreeze the panes, relocate the cell marker and then freeze the panes again.

6   On the **View** tab, in the **Window** group, click **Freeze Panes** and then click **Unfreeze Panes**.

7   Save the workbook.

Changing the Zoom

The Zoom feature changes the display magnification of the worksheet on the screen. A higher magnification level is useful for looking at small objects close up or to highlight an area. A lower magnification level helps you to see the format and structure of the overall worksheet.

Several preset magnification levels are available using one of the following methods:

- On the **View** tab, in the **Zoom** group, click the appropriate zoom option; or
- on the Status bar, click **Zoom Out** or **Zoom In** or drag the Zoom marker on the slider to the required zoom percentage.

Alternatively, you can select different magnification levels using one of the following methods:

- On the **View** tab, in the **Zoom** group, click **Zoom;** or
- on the Status bar, click **Zoom Level**.

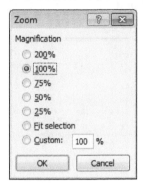

Alternatively, you can have Excel calculate the right level for the cell range selected using the **Fit selection** option. You can also type a value in the **Custom** box if you want a different percentage than is available here.

Learn the Skill

In this exercise, you will practice changing the zoom setting for the worksheet.

1   Make sure the *Ski Resort Snowfall - Student* workbook is active.

Select a magnification level to see more of the worksheet.

2   On the **View** tab, in the **Zoom** group, click **Zoom**.

3   In the Zoom dialog box, click **50%** and then click **OK**.

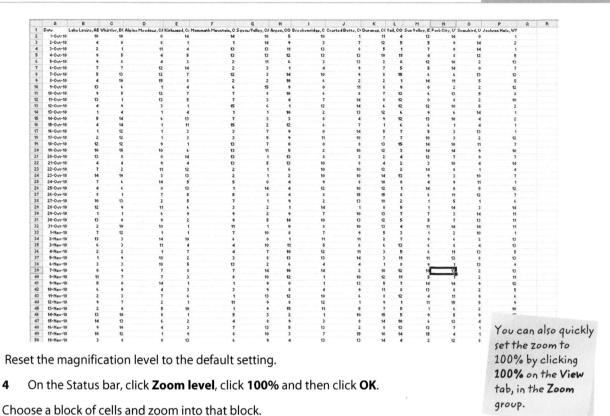

Reset the magnification level to the default setting.

4   On the Status bar, click **Zoom level**, click **100%** and then click **OK**.

Choose a block of cells and zoom into that block.

5   Select cells **E12** to **G19**. On the **View** tab, in the **Zoom** group, click **Zoom to Selection**.

	E	F	G
12	5	7	3
13	1	15	6
14	4	1	1
15	13	7	3
16	11	15	2
17	3	3	7
18	3	3	5
19	1	13	7

6   On the **View** tab, in the **Zoom** group, click **100%**.

7   Save the workbook.

Printing and Previewing the Workbook

1.2

To print your workbook, use one of the following methods:

- Click **File** and then click **Print;** or
- press Ctrl + P .

Excel will display this screen:

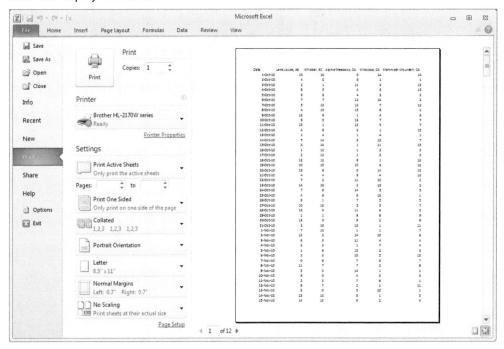

By default, Excel will only print the current active worksheet(s) of the workbook. You can also choose to print all worksheets in the workbook, a selected group of pages or only a selected range of cells.

*You can customize the Quick Access Toolbar to display the **Quick Print** button. Clicking this button will print the worksheet immediately using the current page layout settings.*

Excel takes advantage of a printer's ability to produce presentation quality work. Whether you are printing on an inkjet or laser printer, Excel uses the special fonts, borders and shading to their maximum potential. Excel takes the WYSIWYG (What You See Is What You Get) screen display and delivers it to the printer for a very professional presentation.

Prior to sending your worksheet to the printer, you should look at the preview area of the screen because the printer output will look almost exactly as it appears. Previewing a worksheet before printing is cost-effective and environmentally sound because it can reduce the paper waste that often results from page layout mistakes.

Changing the Workbook Views

Excel allows you to select different ways of viewing your workbook on the screen:

Normal   You will see this view by default. In this view, only the worksheet rows, columns and headers appear. The page break lines only appear if you activate a print-related feature such as inserting page breaks or seeing a print preview of the workbook.

	A	B	C	D	E	F	G	H	I
1	Date	Lake Louise, AB	Whistler, BC	Alpine Meadows, CA	Kirkwood, CA	Mammoth Mountain, CA	Squaw Valley, CA	Aspen, CO	Breckenridg
2	1-Oct-10	10	10	0	14	14	10	5	
3	2-Oct-10	4	0	8	1	1	14	9	
4	3-Oct-10	2	1	11	4	13	13	11	
5	4-Oct-10	9	5	4	5	13	13	12	
6	5-Oct-10	9	8	4	3	2	11	6	
7	6-Oct-10	7	7	12	14	2	3	1	
8	7-Oct-10	5	13	12	7	12	3	14	
9	8-Oct-10	4	10	15	8	2	2	10	
10	9-Oct-10	13	6	1	4	6	15	9	
11	10-Oct-10	9	5	12	7	7	8	10	
12	11-Oct-10	13	1	13	5	7	3	4	
13	12-Oct-10	4	9	3	1	15	6	1	
14	13-Oct-10	1	4	1	4	1	1	10	
15	14-Oct-10	5	14	6	13	7	3	3	
16	15-Oct-10	4	14	1	11	15	2	12	
17	16-Oct-10	1	12	1	3	3	7	9	
18	17-Oct-10	2	12	1	3	3	5	9	
19	18-Oct-10	12	12	9	1	13	7	0	
20	19-Oct-10	10	15	10	6	13	11	5	
21	20-Oct-10	13	8	0	14	13	1	13	
22	21-Oct-10	4	4	9	4	13	5	13	

Page Layout	Display the workbook as it will appear on the printer. For example, you can see which rows and columns will appear on which page, how wide the margins are, and the contents of the header and footer on each page. The vertical and horizontal rulers are also displayed to show the placement of all output on the page.
	Note that this view is only a mockup, without considering the capabilities of your printer. The print preview view (on the **File** tab, under the **Print** option) previews your worksheet on the screen more accurately because Excel can then identify what type of printer you are using.

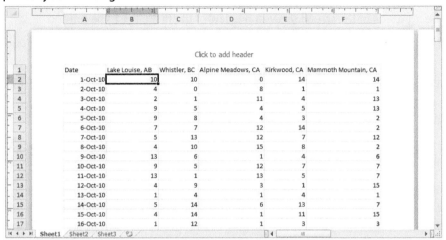

Page Break Preview	Display watermarks on your worksheet to identify which rows and columns will appear on which pages, with the page break lines to mark the boundaries.

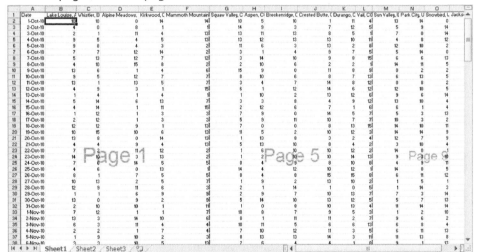

Custom Views	Save your current page layout settings with a name so that you can activate them later at any time.
Full Screen	Change the size of the Excel window or your worksheet window; this will provide you with the maximum viewing area possible. Excel turns off the Ribbon, Quick Access Toolbar and Status Bar in this mode to give you more space to view the worksheet data.

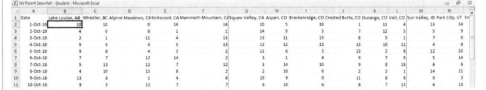

These different views are very useful to help you format your workbook prior to printing.

Learn the Skill

This exercise will demonstrate how to access each of the different workbook layouts as well as the print feature in Excel.

1   Make sure the *Ski Resort Snowfall - Student* workbook is active on the screen.

2   Click **File** and then click **Print**.

The right side of the screen shows a preview of the first page to be printed.

3   Click the **Zoom to Page** toggle switch at the bottom right corner of the print preview section to turn it off.

When turned on, this switch automatically resizes the worksheet preview so that you can see the overall worksheet.

4   Click the **Zoom to Page** toggle switch again to turn it back on.

5   Click the **Next Page** and **Previous Page** buttons at the bottom of the print preview section to scroll through the different pages of the workbook.

The workbook is not ready for printing yet; you need to make formatting changes to the page layout. On many pages, there are just rows and columns of numbers on the page and it is difficult to understand them without the row and column titles. Look at the Page Layout view to see what it looks like.

6   On the **View** tab, in the **Workbook Views** group, click **Page Layout**.

7   Use the horizontal and vertical scroll bars to scroll up and down, and to the left and right to view different parts of the worksheet.

Now look at the Page Break Preview layout.

8   On the **View** tab, in the **Workbook Views** group, click **Page Break Preview**.

9   If Excel displays the Welcome to Page Break Preview, click **OK** to close it.

Now try the Full Screen layout.

10   On the **View** tab, in the **Workbook Views** group, click **Full Screen**.

Since the last view was the Page Break Preview, this view now occupies the entire screen.

11   Scroll up and down the worksheet.

12   Click the Esc key to exit from the Full Screen layout view.

13   On the **View** tab, in the **Workbook Views** group, click **Normal**.

14   Close the workbook and discard any changes.

Customizing the Page Layout

1.2
3.5

By default, Excel creates every new workbook with the same print settings:

- The top and bottom margins are set to 0.75", and the left and right margins to 0.7".
- The orientation is portrait (vertical) rather than landscape (horizontal).
- The paper size is set to letter or A4, depending on the regional setting.
- The scaling is set to 100% (no zoom).
- There is no header or footer.
- There are no gridlines, or row and column headings.
- If the worksheet prints on more than one page, the page order sequence is set to top-down, and then left-to-right.

If you find the page order sequence confusing at first, visualize it as dividing the worksheet into vertical strips. Excel prints down each consecutive strip, starting from the left-most strip, and then starts at the top of the next strip, and the next, until the entire worksheet is printed. A nine-page worksheet therefore prints in this sequence:

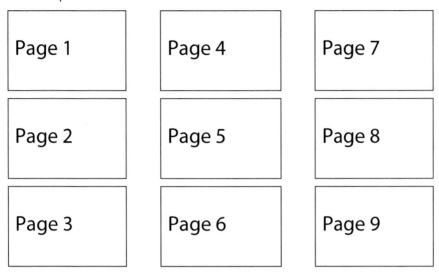

You can change most of these settings on the **Page Layout** tab in any one of the **Page Setup**, **Scale to Fit** or **Sheet Options** groups, or on the **Insert** tab in the **Text** group.

Setting Page Breaks

It is common to have worksheets that are too large to fit on a single sheet of paper. In those situations, Excel automatically inserts page breaks where one or more rows or columns do not fit within the printable area of the page. In many cases, these page breaks do not coincide with the natural grouping of the data. You can overcome this by manually inserting page breaks where you want them in the worksheet.

When you manually insert a page break, Excel positions it in the upper left corner of the active cell. This is important to understand because the page break applies to both the current row and the current column. Not only does Excel force the current row to the next page, it also forces all data in the current column and to its right to the next strip of the printed pages. When you need to remove a manually inserted page break, you must do so in the cell into which you inserted it. To find this cell, look for the place where the page break lines cross. Alternatively, you can remove all manual page breaks in the worksheet and insert new ones.

You can also try other techniques to fit more data onto a single page, such as reducing the page margins or reduce the printing scale.

▲	A	B	C	D
21	20-Oct-10	13	8	0
22	21-Oct-10	4	4	9
23	22-Oct-10	7	2	11

If you select the Fit to option, Excel ignores all manual page breaks when you print the worksheet.

The positioning of page breaks is often a trial-and-error process. The **Page Break Preview** layout is an excellent tool that greatly simplifies this task. In this mode, you can drag the page breaks to a new position. Excel makes the adjustments necessary to accommodate the information in the space you have indicated.

The default page breaks appear as dotted lines in the Print Preview mode, whereas manually inserted page breaks appear as solid lines.

Learn the Skill

In this exercise, you will practice manually inserting page breaks into a worksheet in order to group similar columns together on the same page.

1   Open the *Ski Resort Snowfall - Student* workbook.

Select a cell and insert a page break there.

2   Select cell **D23**.

3   On the **Page Layout** tab, in the **Page Setup** group, click **Breaks** and then click **Insert Page Break**.

Notice that the page break lines now appear in the worksheet to indicate where the page breaks are. However, in this view it is difficult to distinguish between a manual page break and an automatic one.

4   Click the **File**, and then click **Print**.

5   Click **Next Page** and **Previous Page** to view the different pages of the worksheet.

Notice that the first page has only three short columns of data with a lot of empty space on the page below and to the right. This is the result of inserting a page break too high and too far to the left by selecting cell **D23**. It is in the wrong location, so remove this manual page break.

Date	Lake Louise, AB	Whistler, BC
1-Oct-10	10	10
2-Oct-10	4	0
3-Oct-10	2	1
4-Oct-10	9	5
5-Oct-10	9	8
6-Oct-10	7	7
7-Oct-10	5	13
8-Oct-10	4	10
9-Oct-10	13	6
10-Oct-10	9	5
11-Oct-10	13	1
12-Oct-10	4	9
13-Oct-10	1	4
14-Oct-10	5	14
15-Oct-10	4	14
16-Oct-10	1	12
17-Oct-10	2	12
18-Oct-10	12	12
19-Oct-10	10	13
20-Oct-10	13	8
21-Oct-10	4	4

6   Click the **Page Layout** tab to exit the Print facility.

7   With cell **D23** selected, on the **Page Layout** tab, in the **Page Setup** group, click **Breaks** and then click **Remove Page Break**.

Go to the Page Break Preview to see what it looks like.

8   On the **View** tab, in the **Worksheet Views** group, click **Page Break Preview**.

The Welcome to Page Break Preview message box may appear over the preview screen.

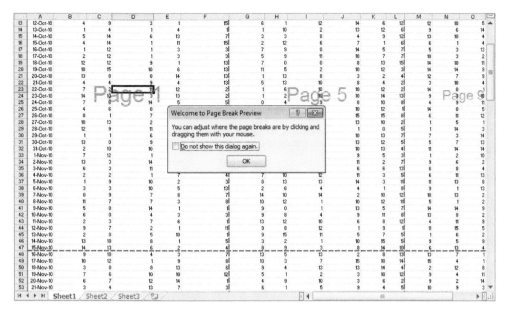

9   Click **OK** to close the Welcome to Page Break Preview message box.

In this view, Excel displays the page numbers as a watermark on each section of data to identify which rows and columns it will print on each page. All of the page break lines are dotted, which indicates that none of them are set manually.

10   Position the mouse pointer over the page break line between pages 1 and 5 until a ←→ arrow appears. Click the mouse button and drag the page break to the left by one column.

You have now set a manual page break to the left side of column F. Notice that the automatic page break between pages 5 and 9 (and the pages below them) has moved from column M to column K because of your manual page break.

11   Drag the page break line at the left side of column **K** to the left by two columns.

You can also set a manual page break between rows.

12   Drag the horizontal page break line at the top of row 48 up to row 33.

If you want to remove a manual page break, you can do so in this view.

13   Select any cell on the right side of the page break on page 11 (column I).

14   On the **Page Layout** tab, in the **Page Setup** group, click **Breaks** and then click **Remove Page Break**.

The worksheet now looks similar to the following example:

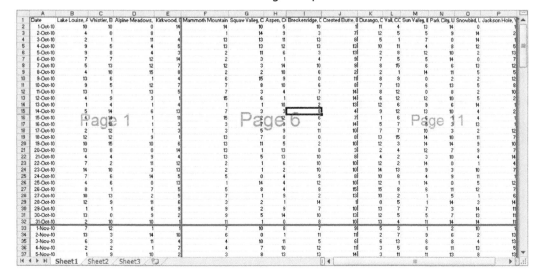

The data appears evenly divided between three pages across, and the data for all of October is on each of these pages.

You can also remove all manual page breaks.

15   On the **Page Layout** tab, in the **Page Setup** group, click **Breaks** and then click **Reset All Page Breaks**.

Excel allows you to add more columns to print on a page. It accomplishes this by changing the scaling.

16   Drag the vertical page break line at the left side of column G to column H.

17   Drag the vertical page break line at the left side of column P to the right by one column (the end of the data).

18   Drag the horizontal page break line at the top of row 61 down to the top of row **63**.

The worksheet should look similar to the following example:

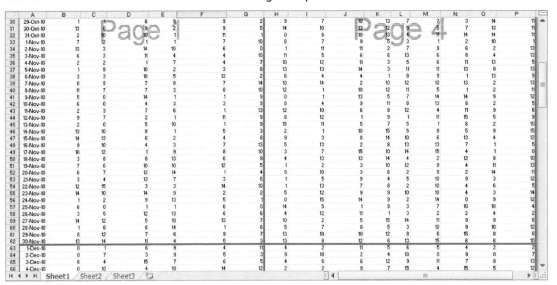

Scroll down the worksheet and verify that the next horizontal page break is set at a natural break between months.

19   Scroll down the worksheet and look at the horizontal page break set at row 125.

20   On the **Page Layout** tab, look at the **Scale** setting in the **Scale to Fit** group.

Excel has automatically adjusted it down from 100% to about 75% to fit all of the data on each page.

21   Click the **File** tab and click **Print**.

22   Click the **Next Page** and **Previous Page** buttons to view each of the pages.

Now go back to the normal page view and remove all page breaks.

23   On the **View** tab, in the **Worksheet Views** group, click **Normal View**.

24   On the **Page Layout** tab, in the **Page Setup** group, click **Breaks** and then click **Reset All Page Breaks**.

25   Save the workbook.

Page Formatting

The Page Layout tab has several page formatting settings that you can modify.

| **Margins** | The Top, Bottom, Left and Right settings are the amount of white space (measured in inches) from the edge of the page. Many printers—especially laser printers—require a minimum page margin because they are not able to print to the edges of the page. Reports are not visually appealing when data appears up to the edges of the page; you also need to allow space for holes if you are going to insert the pages are into a notebook or ring binder. The Header sets the distance between the Header and the top edge of the page, and between the Footer and the bottom edge of the page, to allow space for the page header and footer to appear. |

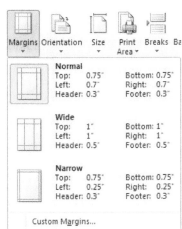

If **Custom Margins** is selected at the bottom of this menu, a Page Setup dialog box is displayed to show all Margin options available:

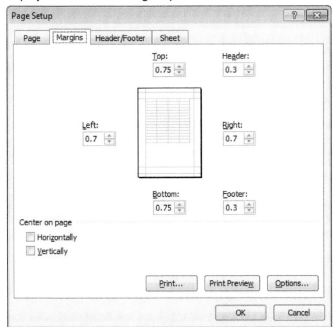

| **Orientation** | The page orientation options are **Portrait** (vertical) or **Landscape** (horizontal). |

Size	This option lets you specify what size of paper to use for printing. You must choose options that are within the print capabilities of your printer, and you must remember to load the appropriate paper or select the correct tray from which to print. If you select **More Paper Sizes**, Excel displays the Page Setup dialog box: 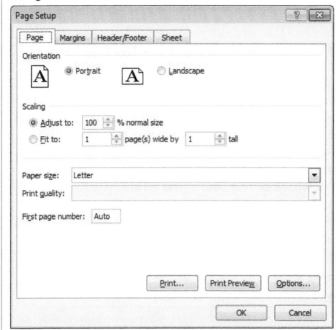	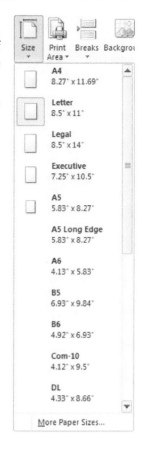
Scale, Width, Height	The **Scale** option enables you to magnify or shrink the size of the worksheet proportionally on the page. The Zoom feature only affects the display of the workbook on the screen. Scale is the equivalent for printing. You can use the **Width** and **Height** options to calculate the correct scale value to fit the worksheet into the specified number of pages automatically. For example, you can scale down a worksheet that requires nine pages to fit into a width of two pages and a height of three pages, so that it will print on six pages.	
Gridlines, Headings	The **Gridlines** option causes lines to display around each cell. By default, they are turned on for the screen (View) and turned off when printing. Similarly, the **Headings** option is turned on by default on the screen and turned off for printing. This option identifies columns to be labeled as A, B, C and so on, and rows are labeled as 1, 2, 3 and so on.	

All of these page-formatting options are also available from the **Print** option on the **File** tab.

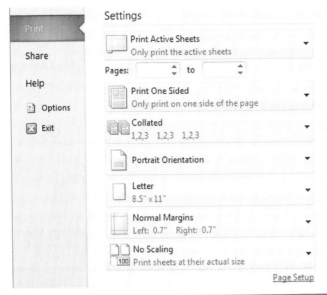

Settings

Print Active Sheets
Only print the active sheets

Pages: [ ] to [ ]

Print One Sided
Only print on one side of the page

Collated
1,2,3 1,2,3 1,2,3

Portrait Orientation

Letter
8.5" x 11"

Normal Margins
Left: 0.7"   Right: 0.7"

No Scaling
100 Print sheets at their actual size

Page Setup

```
MMM
Setting Page
Breaks Online
Exercise
```

Learn the Skill

In this exercise, you will examine the effects of changing some of the page print settings.

1   Make sure the *Ski Resort Snowfall - Student* workbook is active on the screen.

2   On the **Page Layout** tab, in the **Page Setup** group, click **Orientation** and click **Landscape**.

3   On the **Page Layout** tab, in the **Page Setup** group, click **Size** and click **Legal** (or **A4 Long**, if this is the page size for your region).

4   Click the **File** tab and click **Print**.

5   Click the **Next Page** and **Previous Page** buttons to view each of the pages.

   Note that the worksheet now appears sideways and the page is wider at 14 inches (legal size paper). More columns now fit onto each page, but some columns still need to overflow to a second set of pages.

Your printer may show paper sizes (8.5 x 11), or only show the paper size name (Letter or Legal).

6   On the **Page Layout** tab, in the **Scale to Fit** group, click the arrow next to **Width** and click **1 page**.

7   Click the **File** tab and click **Print**.

8   Click the **Next Page** and **Previous Page** buttons to view each of the pages.

   Excel has automatically scaled the data down to fit all columns onto one page.

9   Click **Fit All Columns on One Page** to view the options displayed.

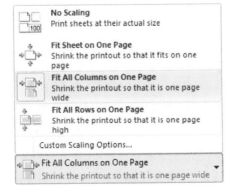

10 Click in a blank area of the Excel window to close this pop-up list.

11 Click **Landscape Orientation and** then click **Portrait Orientation**.

The entire worksheet now fits onto two pages, but the size of the text is very small. You can enter your own scale value.

12 Click **Fit All Columns on One Page and** then click **Custom Scaling Options**.

13 On the **Page** tab, click **Adjust to** and replace the number in the text box with: 65. Click **OK**.

14 Click the **Zoom to Page** button in the lower right corner of the window to zoom in closer.

15 Click **Zoom to Page** to zoom out again.

16 Click the **Show Margins** button in the lower right corner of the window to display the margin markers in the preview.

> *You can also set the **Adjust to** value by entering it into the **Scale** field, on the **Page Layout** tab, in the **Scale to Fit** group.*

The margin markers are useful when you set custom margins, and when you accidentally set one or more margins incorrectly.

17 Click **Normal Margins** and then click **Narrow**.

The worksheet will look similar to the following example:

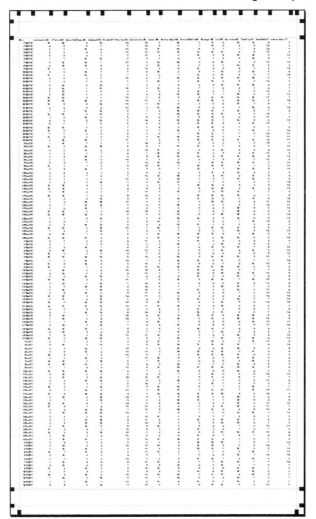

If you print this worksheet, the first page will appear cramped because of the narrow margins and the amount of data. Now revert to the default page settings.

18   Click **Show Margins** again to remove the margin markers in the preview.

19   On the **Page Layout** tab, in the **Scale to Fit** group, click the arrow next to **Width** and click **Automatic**.

20   On the **Page Layout** tab, in the **Scale to Fit** group, click in the **Scale** text box and type: 100. Press
      Enter.

21   On the **Page Layout** tab, in the **Page Setup** group, click **Size** and click **Letter** (or **A4** if that is your
      standard paper size).

22   On the **Page Layout** tab, in the **Page Setup** group, click **Margins** and click **Normal**.

Now print the worksheet with the row and column headings.

23   On the **Page Layout** tab, in the **Sheet Options** group, click the **Print** check box under **Headings** to
      turn it on.

24   Click the **File** tab and click **Print**.

25   Enter: 1 in both text boxes for **Pages** so that only page 1 of the worksheet is
      printed.

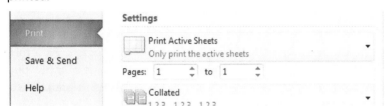

Remember to remove or change the first and last page numbers after you have finished printing. They will remain there until the workbook is closed.

26   Click **Print** to print this page.

27   On the **Page Layout** tab, in the **Sheet Options** group, click the **Print** check box under **Headings** to
      turn it off.

28   Save the workbook.

Adding a Header or Footer

A header is the text you insert to be printed at the top of every page; a footer is the text you insert to be printed at the bottom of every page of a worksheet. If you do not insert text into the header and footer, they remain blank.

Any header or footer that you set up will only apply to the active worksheet. Therefore, if two or more worksheets in a workbook have data that you need to print, you must set up the header and footer for each of the worksheets, even if they all contain the same information.

To add or modify a worksheet header or footer, use one of the following methods:

• On the **Insert** tab, in the **Text** group, click **Header & Footer;** or

• on the **View** tab, in the **Worksheet Views** group, click **Page Layout** and then click in the header or
  footer section of the worksheet; or

• on the **Page Layout** tab, in the **Page Setup** group, click the **Dialog box launcher** and click
  Header/Footer.

The header or footer consists of three sections: **Left**, **Center** and **Right**.

Header

Footer

You can add or modify headers and footers directly using the Page Layout view. In this view, when you click in the Header or Footer section, the Ribbon displays the **Design** tab under **Header & Footer Tools**.

In this tab, you can select from one of several standard header or footer options.

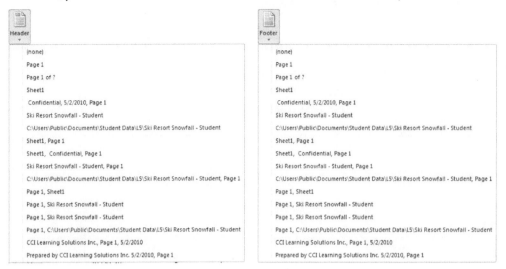

Alternatively, you can create custom configurations for your headers and footers. As a minimum, you should add a header and footer to your worksheet displaying the current page number, print date and workbook name, whether or not the worksheet requires one or more pages to print. This information makes the page appear more professional.

In the **Header & Footer Elements** group of the **Header & Footer Tools Design** tab, there are nine buttons. You can use these buttons to insert commonly used variables into the header or footer.

Page Number	Click this button to display the code (**&[Page]**) in the selected section of the header or footer. The page number will start at 1 by default; you can change this in the Page Setup dialog box.
Number of Pages	Click this button to display the code **&[Pages]**. This calculates the total number of pages in the selected worksheet(s) to be printed. This is often used with the Page number code to show each page number as one among the total of all the pages (i.e., Page 1 of 4).
Current Date	Insert the current date (from the computer) into the report, displayed as the code **&[Date]**.
Current Time	Insert the current time (from the computer) into the report, displayed as the code **&[Time]**.
File Path	Insert the current path (drive and folder location) and file name into the header or footer, displayed as the code **&[Path]&[File]**.
File Name	Insert the name of the file into the header or footer, displayed as the code **&[File]**.
Sheet Name	Insert the name of the tab for the current worksheet, displayed as the code **&[Tab]**.
Picture	Insert a picture into the header or footer, displayed as the code **&[Picture]**.
Format Picture	Provide options to change the properties for the picture.

The Options group in the Ribbon gives you more flexibility with the headers and footers, such as creating a different header and footer for the first page, and different headers and footers for odd and even pages.

Learn the Skill

In this exercise, you will create headers and footers on your printed output.

1   Make sure the *Ski Resort Snowfall - Student* workbook is active on the screen.

2   Click the **File** tab and click **Print**.

3   Click the **Next Page** and **Previous Page** buttons to view each of the pages.

You may find that, without any page number references, if you inadvertently mix up pages, you will have a hard time reassembling them in the correct sequence.

4   On the **Insert** tab, in the **Text** group, click **Header & Footer**.

Excel automatically displays the Page Layout view with the cursor in the middle section of the header.

5   On the **Header & Footer Tools Design** tab, in the **Header & Footer** group, click **Header** and then click the preformatted header that appears as *Ski Resort Snowfall - Student*.

Excel will return the cursor to the active cell of the worksheet.

6   Click on the header.

The header shows a code: &[File] instead of the file name. This ensures that, if the file name changes, the header will change automatically to show the new name.

7   On the **Header & Footer Tools Design** tab, in the **Navigation** group, click **Go to Footer**.

The cursor is now in the center section of the footer.

Alternatively, you can manually scroll down the worksheet and click in the footer area.

8   On the **Header & Footer Tools Design** tab, in the **Header & Footer** group, click **Footer** and then click the preformatted footer near the bottom of the list (*student name, Page 1, <today's date>*).

Now add the company logo to the header.

9   Scroll up the worksheet and click in the left section of the header area of the page.

10   Click on the **Header & Footer Tools Design** tab.

11   On the **Header & Footer Tools Design** tab, in the **Header & Footer Elements** group, click **Picture**.

12   In the Insert Picture dialog box, navigate to the folder where the *tolano logo.jpg* file is located.

13   Select the *tolano logo file* and click **Insert**.

14   Click in the worksheet area.

Note that the logo is too tall and is covering some of the data.

15   Click in the left section of the header again. Then, on the **Header & Footer Tools Design** tab, in the **Header & Footer Elements** group, click **Format Picture**.

16   Ensure that the **Lock aspect ratio** box is checked and then reduce the **Scale Height** or **Scale Width** to 33%.

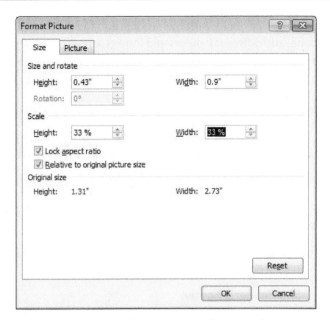

17 Click **OK** and then click anywhere in the worksheet.

Now view the results of adding the header and footer to this worksheet.

18 Click the **File** tab and click **Print**.

19 Click the **Next Page** and **Previous Page** buttons to view each of the pages.

Note the preformatted header and footer entries on each page. The screen should look similar to the following example:

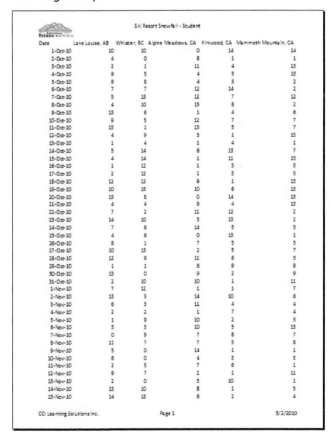

20 Click the **Home** tab to return to your worksheet.

21 Save the workbook.

Printing Titles or Range of Cells

With large worksheets you have the ability to freeze row and column titles so that you can always relate any cell to their descriptions. However, the Freeze Panes feature only applies to the screen. The equivalent feature when printing is to set Print Titles.

When working with large worksheets, at times you may want to only print a section. Excel provides an option to select a range of cells as the print range.

You can also set the print area for specific areas of a large worksheet. Be sure to turn it off afterwards because the setting stays until it is cleared or changed. In most cases you should expect to print the entire contents of a worksheet – Excel will automatically select only the range of cells containing data in a worksheet for printing. If you are setting the print area because you have more than one group of data (each group is really their own standalone spreadsheet) on the same worksheet, you should consider putting them on different worksheets.

Learn the Skill

In this exercise, you will display the column and row titles on every page and select a range of cells for printing.

1   Make sure the *Ski Resort Snowfall - Student* workbook is active on the screen.

2   Click the **File** tab and click **Print**.

3   Click the **Next Page** and **Previous Page** buttons to view each of the pages.

While looking at each of the pages, you will notice that some of the pages are just rows and columns of numbers. As a result, you are unable to relate these numbers to dates and locations. This can be resolved by displaying row and column titles.

4   On the **Page Layout** tab, in the **Page Setup** group, click **Print Titles**.

Excel displays the Page Setup dialog box.

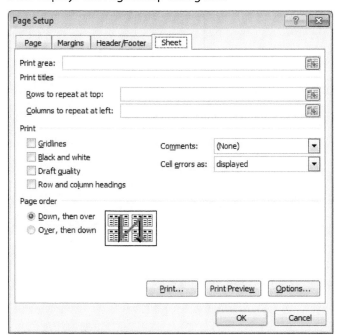

You can also display the **Dialog box launcher** in the **Page Setup** group and then click the **Sheet** tab.

You can now select column or row headers or the range of cells you want to print by selecting these cells directly from the worksheet.

5　Click the **Collapse** button for the **Rows to repeat at top** field.

6　Click the row **1** header on the worksheet behind the Page Setup - Rows to repeat at top dialog box.

Excel enables you to select any number of rows to display at the top of every page provided they are contiguous (all rows are together).

You can also press ENTER to expand this dialog box.

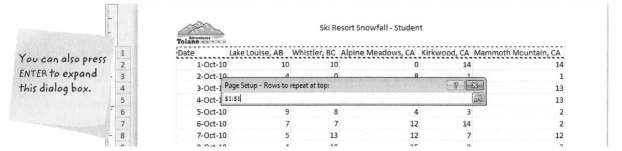

7　Click the **Expand** button in the **Page Setup - Rows to repeat at top** window.

8　In the Page Setup dialog box, click the **Collapse** button for the **Columns to repeat at left** field.

9　Click the column **A** header on the worksheet behind the Page Setup - Columns to repeat at left dialog box, then press Enter.

10　Click **Print Preview**. Click the **Next Page** and **Previous Page** buttons to view each of the pages.

The print preview screen for the last page should appear similar to the following example:

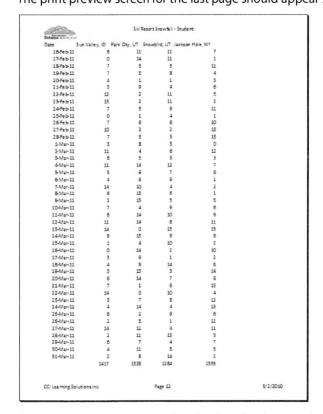

Suppose you only want to print the data for the month of November for a small group of ski resorts. You can do this by designating a range of cells as a print area.

11　Click the **Page Layout** tab.

12　Select the cell range G33 to L62.

13　On the **Page Layout** tab, in the **Page Setup** group, click **Print Area** and click **Set Print Area**.

14   Click the **File** tab and click **Print**.

There will only be one page to print in this case. The screen should look similar to the following example:

Ski Resort Snowfall - Student						
Date	Squaw Valley, CA	Aspen, CO	Breckenridge, CO	Crested Butte, CO	Durango, CO	Vail, CO
1-Nov-10	10	8	7	9	5	3
2-Nov-10	0	1	11	11	2	7
3-Nov-10	10	11	5	6	6	13
4-Nov-10	7	10	12	11	3	5
5-Nov-10	8	13	13	14	3	11
6-Nov-10	2	6	4	4	1	8
7-Nov-10	14	10	14	2	10	12
8-Nov-10	10	12	1	10	12	11
9-Nov-10	9	0	1	13	5	7
10-Nov-10	9	8	4	9	11	8
11-Nov-10	13	12	10	6	8	12
12-Nov-10	9	8	12	1	9	1
13-Nov-10	9	15	11	5	7	5
14-Nov-10	3	2	1	10	15	5
15-Nov-10	8	9	3	8	14	10
16-Nov-10	13	5	13	2	8	13
17-Nov-10	10	3	7	15	10	14
18-Nov-10	9	4	13	13	14	4
19-Nov-10	5	1	2	3	10	12
20-Nov-10	4	9	10	3	6	2
21-Nov-10	6	1	5	9	4	5
22-Nov-10	10	1	13	7	8	2
23-Nov-10	2	5	12	9	9	10
24-Nov-10	1	0	15	14	9	2
25-Nov-10	0	14	5	1	9	3
26-Nov-10	6	4	12	11	1	3
27-Nov-10	7	10	2	5	15	14
28-Nov-10	6	5	7	0	5	3
29-Nov-10	7	13	10	10	12	8
30-Nov-10	3	13	8	12	6	13

Now print this page.

15   On the **File** tab, in the **Print** group, click **Print**.

When you have printed the range that you selected, you must go back and clear the selected area. Otherwise, Excel will keep the worksheet locked so that it will print only this range of cells until it is changed.

16   On the **Page Layout** tab, in the **Page Setup** group, click **Print Area** and click **Clear Print Area**.

17   Save and close the workbook.

Printing Selected Worksheets

The File Print settings allow you to select one of three options for printing:

- print the current active worksheet(s),
- print the entire workbook, or
- print the currently selected range of cells in the current active worksheet.

You will usually have only one worksheet (e.g. Sheet1) as your active worksheet. Therefore when you print the active sheet, Excel will only print the contents of that worksheet.

If you want to print more than one worksheet (but not the entire workbook) at the same time, then you must select all of these worksheets as a group first, and then print them. Use the $\boxed{\text{Ctrl}}$ key to add the worksheets to the group of active worksheets. You can also use the $\boxed{\text{Shift}}$ key to select a range of worksheets as the active group.

Learn the Skill

In this exercise, you will print a selected group of worksheets in a workbook.

1   Open the *Quarterly Income Statement* workbook.

2   Click the *Quarter 1* worksheet tab.

3   Hold down the Ctrl key and click the *Quarter 3* and *Quarter 4* worksheet tabs to select them as part of the group.

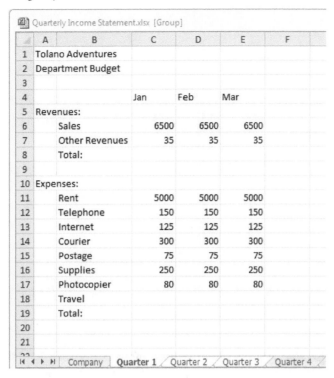

Notice the word [Group] appearing in the title bar of the worksheet.

4   Click the **File** tab and click **Print**.

5   Verify that **Print Active Sheets** is currently selected.

6   Click **Print** to print these worksheets.

7   Close the workbook and discard any changes.

Changing Excel Default Settings

1.3

You can personalize Excel to your needs by using the Backstage to display the Excel Options. The Excel Options dialog box has eight categories with a variety of options to make changes that affect how spreadsheets look or how Excel will behave.

3243-1 v1.00 © CCI Learning Solutions Inc.

To access the Excel Options, click the **File** tab, then click **Options**.

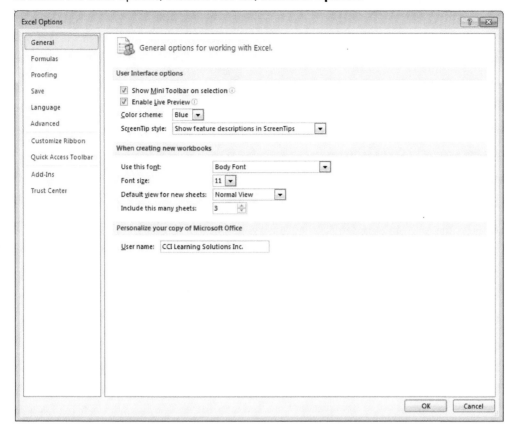

The eight categories of options are:

General	Options that affect how Excel and workbooks are set up or appear on the screen.
Formulas	Options relating to how formulas are calculated and how to handle formula errors.
Proofing	Options that affect how Excel formats and makes corrections to text data.
Save	Options that control how workbooks are saved and recovered in case of a system error.
Language	Sets the language options used.
Advanced	A collection of advanced settings that control how Excel operates.
Customize Ribbon	Controls what commands are displayed in the Ribbon. Additional commands can be added or removed. Note that certain core commands cannot be removed.
Quick Access Toolbar	Controls what commands are displayed in the Quick Access Toolbar. Additional commands can be added or removed. Note that certain core commands cannot be removed.
Add-Ins	Enables you to install additional Microsoft Office Add-in modules.
Trust Center	Options that control security and privacy settings in Excel.

Learn the Skill

This exercise demonstrates how to make changes to Excel Options and view the effects.

1   Click the **File** tab and then click **Options**.

2   If necessary, click **General**.

3   Click the arrow next to **Color scheme** and change it to **Blue**.

4   Change the **Font size** to: 20.

5   Increase the **Include this many sheets** to: 5 and click **OK**.

Excel displays the following message box because you have increased the font size to 20.

6   Click **OK** and exit from Excel. Start up Excel again.

Excel creates a new workbook with five worksheets and the font size is set to 20 by default. The Excel window now displays in a blue color.

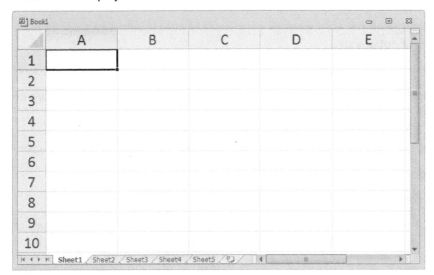

7   Click the **File** tab and then click **Options**.

8   Change the following options back to their defaults:

Color scheme   Silver

Font size   11

Include this many sheets   3

9   Click the **Proofing** category.

The default options in this dialog box are usually appropriate for most users. Excel uses these options to flag and correct words that it believes are incorrect, such as spelling errors. An interesting area is the **AutoCorrect Options**.

10 Click **AutoCorrect Options** and view the settings available in this dialog box.

11   Click the **Cancel** button to close the AutoCorrect dialog box.

12   Click the **Save** category.

As with the Proofing category, you can leave most of the default options unchanged. The one that you will most likely change after installing Excel on a computer for the first time is Default file location. Changing this will save time in selecting the location of your data folders whenever you start Excel.

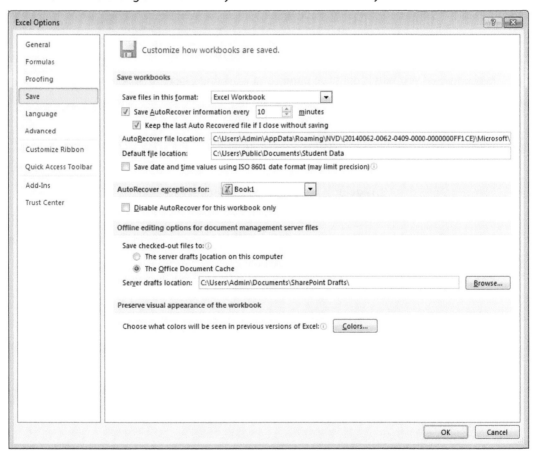

Excel displays the message box again to warn you that you changed the font size.

13   Click the **OK** button to close the Excel Options dialog box.

14   Click the **OK** button.

15   Exit out of Excel.

Lesson Summary

This lesson introduced how to change the views in preparation for printing worksheets, print and preview worksheets, customize the page setup for printing worksheets and change the Excel Backstage options. You should now be able to:

☑ create worksheet windows

☑ arrange worksheet windows

☑ split panes

☑ freeze panes

☑ zoom in and out of worksheets

☑ print and preview worksheets

☑ use different workbook views

☑ add and preview page breaks

☑ change printing margins, orientation, paper size and scale

☑ print column and row titles or selected range of cells

☑ add and modify headers and footers

☑ printing selected worksheets

☑ change Excel default settings

Review Questions

MMM
Go online for
Additional
Review and
Activities

1. Give examples of when it can be helpful to use the different types of worksheet window arrangement, e.g. tiled, horizontal, vertical or cascade.

2. Explain when you would split the panes of a worksheet instead of setting up a tiled arrangement of two or four windows.

3. Give examples of when you might freeze the panes.

4. Explain why you should preview a worksheet prior to printing.

5. Explain how the different worksheet views can help you with previewing or printing worksheets.

6. Give examples of when adding a header or footer can be helpful in the worksheet.

7. What is the difference between using the Scale and the Width and Height settings in the Ribbon?

8. Explain what are the similarities and differences between printing a header and printing titles for a worksheet.

9. Explain why you may want to access the Excel Options in the Backstage.

Microsoft
Excel® 2010
Core Certification

Lesson 6: Working with Charts

Lesson Objectives

This lesson introduces you to working with charts. You will look at how to create a chart, how to change the type, layout and design of a chart, and how to manipulate a chart. Upon successful completion of this lesson, you will be able to:

☐ create charts

☐ change the chart type

☐ work with pie charts

☐ move a chart to a different location on a worksheet or its own chart sheet

☐ resize a chart to a different size or shape

☐ change the chart layout

☐ create, customize and remove a sparkline chart

☐ print a chart

Creating a Basic Chart

6.1

A chart is a pictorial representation of the data you enter in a worksheet. Often, a chart can be a more descriptive way of representing your data. As a result, those viewing the information provided by your spreadsheets may find it easier to examine and understand a chart rather than rows and columns of numbers.

Excel can display worksheet information in a variety of ways. Incorporating fonts, patterns, symbols, graphics and 3-D (three-dimensional) effects, Excel's charting feature is an extremely professional presentation tool.

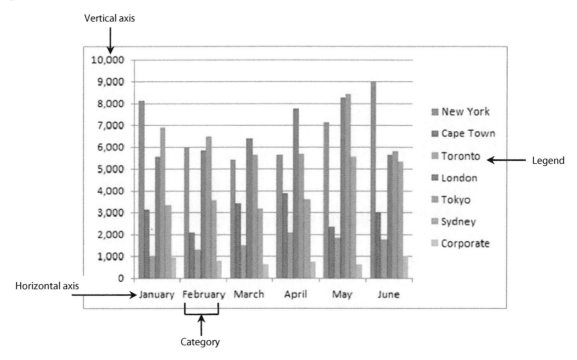

Each set of data in the chart is a *series*—for example, the six-month figures for the New York office comprise one series and the six-month figures for the Cape Town office comprise another series. The chart's horizontal axis is located at the bottom of the chart and the vertical axis is located at the left or right side of the chart. You will have the opportunity to apply labels for both axes. Excel will automatically include a legend with the chart to explain the meaning of each line in a line chart, or column in a column chart. Although you can remove the legend, it may be helpful to others to retain it if your chart has more than one data series.

The color charts that Excel creates are interesting to look at on the screen, but you may get very different results if you are printing using a black and white printer. To ensure that you get the best results, you should use gray shades and cross hatching to differentiate the data on your graph.

To create a chart, simply select the cells containing the data you want to chart and click the desired chart type. Once the chart appears in the worksheet, you will also see three different tabs for the **Chart Tools** that you can use to create or modify chart elements. You will learn about many of these as you progress through this lesson.

Learn the Skill

This exercise demonstrates how to create a chart in six (or fewer) easy steps.

1 Open the *Website Hits* workbook and save it as Website Hits - Student.

	A	B	C	D	E	F	G	H
1	Tolano Adventures							
2	Website Hits							
3								
4	Office	January	February	March	April	May	June	Total
5	New York	8,125	5,947	5,420	5,647	7,134	9,015	41,288
6	Cape Town	3,120	2,097	3,407	3,885	2,352	3,024	17,885
7	Toronto	1,017	1,281	1,512	2,107	1,825	1,761	9,503
8	London	5,530	5,852	6,366	7,760	8,257	5,619	39,384
9	Tokyo	6,905	6,471	5,648	5,665	8,412	5,808	38,909
10	Sydney	3,324	3,544	3,155	3,574	5,565	5,346	24,508
11	Corporate	904	804	641	772	632	998	4,751
12	Total	28,925	25,996	26,149	29,410	34,177	31,571	

This spreadsheet shows the number of times that potential customers of Tolano Adventures are accessing their website.

2 Select the range of cells from **A4** to **G11**.

Note that the row and column titles were included in this range, but the total values were not. If you wish, you can include the totals in the chart. In many cases, however, the purpose of creating a chart is to show any patterns in the data. Including the totals will actually reduce the visibility of the pattern because their presence causes the rest of the data to shrink in size.

3 On the **Insert** tab, in the **Charts** group, click **Column**.

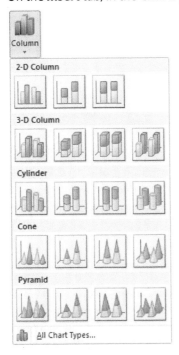

4 Click the **Clustered Column** option (left-most item in the **2-D Column** set).

The column chart now displays. Note that whenever you select the chart, the cells containing the source data are marked and three new tabs display under **Chart Tools**.

In the default chart, each row of data has been set up as the categories, and each column is a series. Assume that you need to exchange their positions so that each month is a category; you can do this very easily.

5   Under **Chart Tools**, on the **Design** tab, in the **Data** group, click **Switch Row/Column**.

The completed chart and worksheet should look similar to the following example:

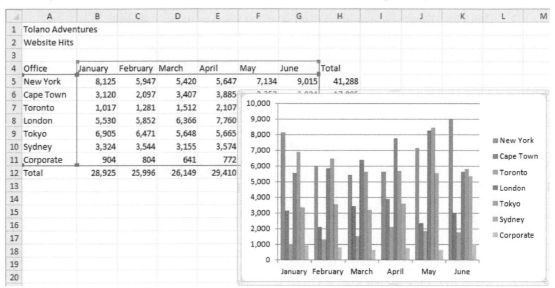

6   Save the workbook.

If the Total column (column H) had been included, then the chart would look like this example:

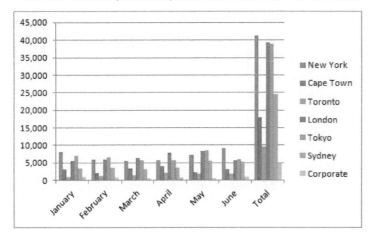

For the Total category, you can clearly see the difference in total hits between the different offices. However, the presence of the Total category overwhelms the patterns that emerge in the individual months.

Moving and Resizing Charts

You can move charts to any location on a worksheet. Typically, you place a chart next to its source data. To move a chart, simply use the mouse to drag it to its new location. While moving a chart, take care when placing the cursor to ensure that you are not moving a single component within the chart by mistake. To move an entire chart, you must click on a blank area of the chart where no chart components are located.

You can also make charts larger or smaller, or reshape them. To resize a chart, click and drag any of the handles around the chart. Every chart has eight of these handles: four in the corners and four at mid-points between the corners. Whenever you change the size or shape of a chart, the internal components will generally resize proportionately.

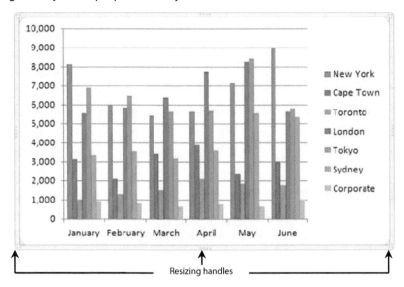

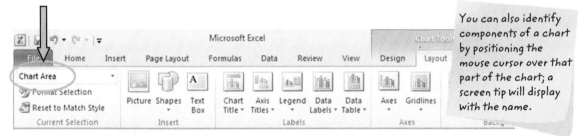

Resizing handles

MMM
Moving the
Chart Online
Exercise

You can also move charts to their own chart sheets. If you do this, the chart will automatically resize itself to fill the entire sheet.

Learn the Skill

This exercise demonstrates how to move and resize a chart and its components.

1   Make sure the *Website Hits - Student* workbook is active on the screen.

2   Click anywhere in the column chart to put it into editing mode.

3   Under **Chart Tools**, click the **Layout** tab.

4   Look in the **Chart Elements** box, located on the **Chart Tools Layout** tab, in the **Current Selection** group), which displays the name of the chart area that you clicked.

You can also identify components of a chart by positioning the mouse cursor over that part of the chart; a screen tip will display with the name.

5   If the **Chart Elements** box displays a name other than **Chart Area**, click another blank area of the chart until it does. Generally, any of the four corners of the chart are the best choices.

Use that spot to drag the chart to a new location on the worksheet.

6   Click that spot on the chart again and drag the chart so that it is directly below the data.

Make the chart bigger.

*You can also select **Chart Area** from the list box in the **Current Selection** group.*

7   Point to each of the four corners of the chart.

8   Click and drag the bottom right corner down and outwards to make the chart bigger.

9   Point to each of the mid-points of the chart corners, where the four dots (....) are located.

10   Click the middle handle at the bottom of the chart and drag it down to make the chart bigger.

You can also resize and move the components inside the chart. Imagine a square box around each of these components of the chart. To move the component, you click inside the box and move it to a new location.

11   Click in a blank area inside the legend to drag it to another location.

The completed chart and worksheet may look similar to the following example:

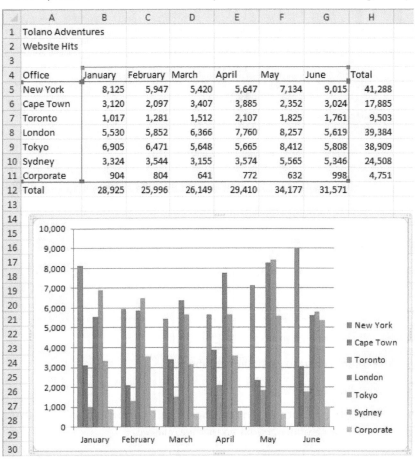

12   Save the workbook again.

Changing Chart Types

If the type of chart you select does not display the spreadsheet information appropriately, you can easily change it.

The type of chart to use will depend on what you are trying to show. Line charts are better for showing trends, column charts are better for showing volume and pie charts are better for showing portions of a total.

Excel provides a variety of chart types and several subtypes within each major type. The following explains the uses for some of the chart types:

Column	Use to compare values over time or across categories. This is a vertical presentation. The column shapes can be rectangular, cylindrical, conical or pyramid-shaped.

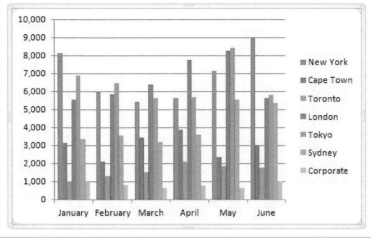

Line	Use to compare continuous trends.

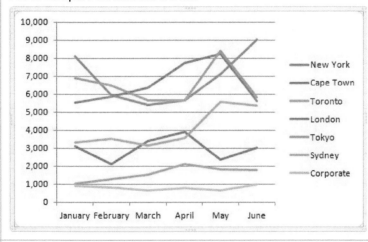

Pie	Use to compare values that make up the whole.

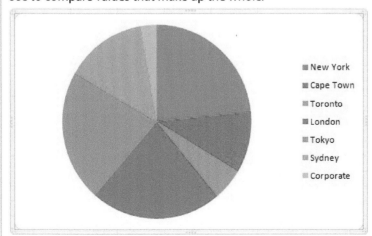

Bar

Use to compare values over time or categories. This is a horizontal presentation. As with the column chart type, you can choose from various bar shapes.

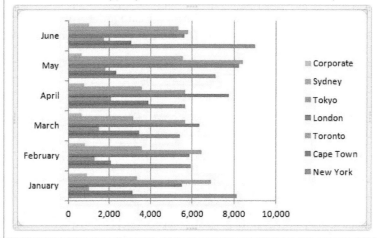

Area

Use to compare a continuous change in volume.

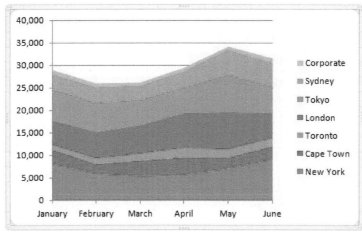

XY (Scatter)

Use to determine data patterns.

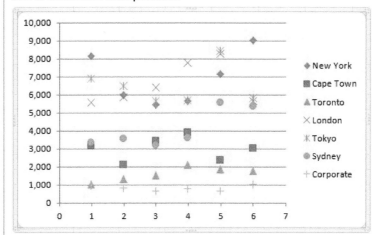

Stock	Use to display high-low-close data. To use this display, you must have at least three sets of data.
	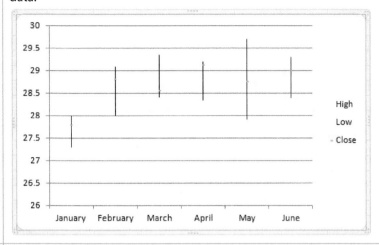

Surface	Use to display trends in values with a 3-D presentation and a continuous surface.
	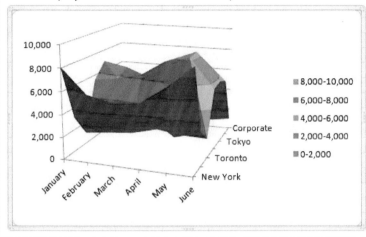

Doughnut	Similar to the pie chart, but for more than one set of data points.
	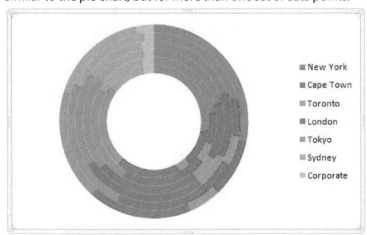

Bubble | Use to compare three values. This type of chart displays values similarly to a scatter chart, but the points are presented in bubbles.

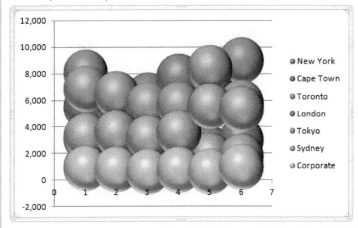

Radar | Use to determine patterns or trends with points matched up by lines.

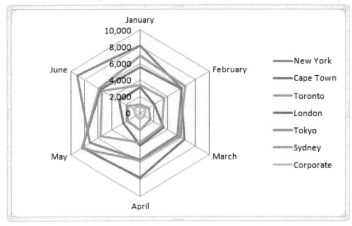

Most of these chart types also have two-dimensional and three-dimensional choices. Three-dimensional charts can be more interesting to look at, but may be more difficult to read because they tend to look crowded.

To change the chart type, click on the chart to go into chart mode and then use one of the following methods:

- Under **Chart Tools**, on the **Design** tab, in the **Type** group, click **Change Chart Type;** or
- right-click in any blank area of the chart and then click **Change Chart Type**.

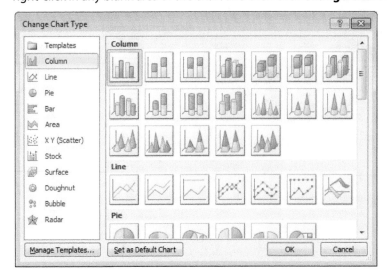

Working with Pie Charts

6.1

A pie chart is one of the chart type options that Excel provides. It is commonly used in business applications because it is particularly useful for displaying relative sizes (or percentages) of each piece of the total. For example, if you are writing a report about the importance of segments of your business, you may want to use the pie chart to show the various business segments.

Pie charts are not like the other chart types. For example, column and line charts are excellent choices for visually showing more than one data series—a table with multiple rows and columns of data. Pie charts only allow you to choose one data series, usually the totals for a table, or one row or column of that table.

You may wish to enhance your display further by exploding or moving out a portion of the pie. This draws the viewer's attention to that particular piece of the pie. You can only explode pie slices using the mouse; you cannot use the keyboard to do this.

Learn the Skill

This exercise demonstrates how to select different chart types for a worksheet.

1   Make sure the `Website Hits - Student` workbook is active on the screen.

2   Click anywhere inside the chart.

3   Under **Chart Tools**, on the **Design** tab, in the **Type** group, click **Change Chart Type**.

    The Change Chart Type dialog box appears, showing the different chart types from which to choose:

4   Click the **Line** option (the left-most one) in the **Line** section of the Change Chart Type dialog box and click **OK**.

Choose another chart type.

5   Under **Chart Tools**, on the **Design** tab, in the **Type** group, click **Change Chart Type**.

6   Click **Doughnut** in the chart type list on the left of the Change Chart Type dialog box. Click the **Doughnut** option and click **OK**.

Change the chart type back to a column chart.

7   Under **Chart Tools**, on the **Design** tab, in the **Type** group, click **Change Chart Type**.

8   Scroll up, click the **Clustered Column** option and click **OK**.

9   Save the workbook.

Learn the Skill

This exercise demonstrates how to create a pie chart and explode it.

1   Make sure the *Website Hits - Student* workbook is active on the screen.

First, create a new pie chart using only the total values for each month. The pie chart must include the category (X) titles as well as the total data in the chart, so you must highlight two rows that are not next to each other.

> *For this pie chart, the data series selected will be the total number of website hits for each office.*

2   Select cells **A5** to **A11**.

3   Hold down (Ctrl) and select cells **H5** to **H11**. Release (Ctrl).

4   On the **Insert** tab, in the **Charts** group, click **Pie** to display the various pie chart types.

If you want to create an exploded pie, you can choose this option. For the purpose of this exercise, you will start with a regular pie.

5   Click the **Pie** option in the **2-D Pie** section of the menu.

When selecting the data to show in a pie chart, you must take extra care to ensure you are selecting the correct cell range as your data series. This pie chart shows the total website hits for each office for all months. If you want to show the total website hits for each month for all offices, you must select cells **B4** to **G4**, and **B12** to **G12**.

You cannot use the pie chart to show the same data as the other chart types, such as the column chart. While other charts are able to show the statistics for each office for each month, a pie chart can only use one data series—in this case, total website hits (cells H5 to H11). If you want to show the hits per month per office, you must create separate pie charts for each row or column. Alternatively, you can show multiple data series in a circular pattern by using the doughnut chart type.

6   Click the pie part of the chart.

The selection blocks should appear on each of the pieces.

7   Click the **New York** pie piece (the one in the upper right).

The selection blocks should now appear only around this piece.

You can verify that you have selected the correct part of the chart by looking in the **Chart Element** box in the **Current Selection** group on the **Chart Tools – Layout** tab. At this point, the **Chart Element** box should read Series 1 Point "New York".

8   Click and drag the **New York** pie piece away from the rest of the pie. When you have the pie piece in the desired position, release the mouse button.

The pie chart should look similar to the following example:

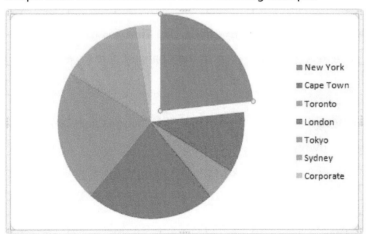

9   Move the pie chart to the right of the clustered column chart and then save the workbook.

Changing the Chart Layout and Location

With one click, Excel generates a chart using the standard defaults. You will typically want to modify the layout to create exactly the look you want. Excel also displays the **Chart Tools** option with tabs containing commands to manipulate items on the chart:

- The **Design** tab contains commands to help with the design of the chart, such as which data Excel will display in the chart or chart type.

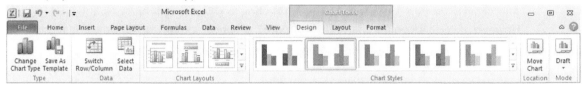

- The **Layout** tab contains commands to assist with the layout or position of items in the chart.

- The **Format** tab contains commands to format the appearance or position of text in the chart.

These layout components are commonly changed:

Chart Titles	Add a title for the chart.
Axis Titles	Add titles to the horizontal and vertical axes.
Legend	Include a legend and position it with the chart.
Data Labels	Include data labels on the chart.
Data Table	Display the chart data beneath the chart.
Axes	Modify the appearance of the horizontal and vertical axes.
Gridlines	Include gridlines on the chart.

Excel provides a variety of pre-built layouts that you can apply to your chart. You can further modify the chart with your own layout changes.

By default, Excel places the chart in the same worksheet where the source data is located. You can move this chart to its own chart sheet, back to its original worksheet or to a different worksheet.

Learn the Skill

This exercise demonstrates how to change different layout options for a chart.

1   Make sure the *Website Hits - Student* workbook is active on the screen.

2   Click in a blank area of the clustered column chart to put it into editing mode.

Choose different chart layouts and see how the chart is affected.

3 Under **Chart Tools**, on the **Design** tab, in the **Chart Layouts** group, click **Layout 3**.

4 Under **Chart Tools**, on the **Design** tab, In the **Chart Layouts** group, click **More** to display all layouts in the Gallery and choose another chart layout by clicking it.

5 Under **Chart Tools**, on the **Design** tab, in the **Chart Layouts** group, click **Layout 1**.

6 Click in the Chart Title box in the chart, highlight the default text *Chart Title* and type: Monthly Website Hits as the new title. Excel replaces the default text with your new title.

Alternatively for step 6, click on the Chart Title box to select it, type the new title and press Enter. However, if you click on the chart title box more than once, you will activate the edit mode for the text – as described in step 6 – and the selection box turns into dashed lines. When the title is in edit mode, you must delete the existing text ("Chart Title" in this case) and enter the new title. Although this method involves more steps, it works every time.

Add titles to each of the two chart axes.

7 Under **Chart Tools**, on the **Layout** tab, in the **Labels** group, click **Axis Titles** and click **Primary Horizontal Axis Title.** Click **Title Below Axis.**

8 Click in the horizontal axis title box in the chart, and type: Month as the new axis title.

9 In the **Labels** group, click **Axis Titles**, click **Primary Vertical Axis Title** and then click **Rotated Title.**

10 Click in the vertical axis title box in the chart and type: # of Hits as the new axis title.

If you click on a title text box only once before entering a new title, the changes will only appear in the Formula Bar. After you press the ENTER key, the text box will redisplay with the new title text.

Move the legend to the bottom of the chart.

11 Under **Chart Tools**, on the **Layout** tab, in the **Labels** group, click **Legend**, and then click **Show Legend at Bottom.**

Now move the chart into its own chart sheet.

12 Under **Chart Tools**, click the **Design** tab and, in the **Location** group, click **Move Chart**.

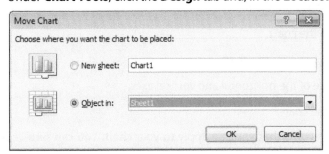

13 In the Move Chart dialog box, click **New sheet** and click **OK**.

14 Click the *Sheet1* worksheet.

The chart is no longer in this worksheet.

15 Click and drag the pie chart to a new position directly underneath the data; the upper left corner of the chart should be in cell **A14**.

16 Click the **Chart1** tab.

If Excel has not clustered the data series the way you want them, you can exchange them.

17 Under **Chart Tools**, on the **Design** tab, in the **Data** group, click **Switch Row/Column**.

The horizontal axis is now by office, with the months clustered together for each office. By changing how you cluster the data, you can see trends that were not obvious using the other grouping method.

18 Under **Chart Tools**, on the **Design** tab, in the **Data** group, click **Switch Row/Column** again.

The chart should look similar to the following example:

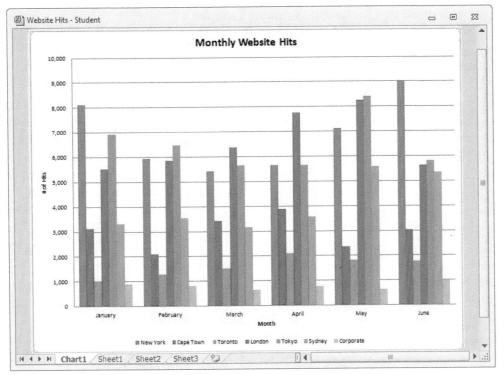

19 Save the workbook.

Learn the Skill

This exercise demonstrates how to change different layout options for a chart.

1 Open the *Eco Tours* workbook and save it as Eco Tours - Student.

2 Select the range from **A4** to **G12**.

Note that this range includes the titles but does not include the row containing the Total data.

3 On the **Insert** tab, in the **Charts** group, click **Bar**.

4   Click the **Stacked Bar in 3-D** option (middle item in the **3-D Bar** set).

Your chart should look similar to the following example:

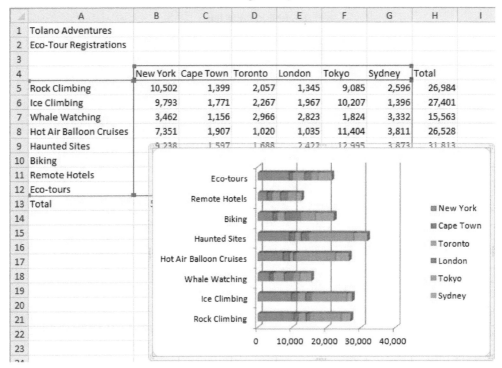

5   Under **Chart Tools**, on the **Design** tab, in the **Type** group, click **Change Chart Type**.

6   Click **Area** in the Chart type list on the left of the dialog box.

7   Click the **3-D Area** option (third from the right) and click **OK**.

The chart should now look similar to the following example:

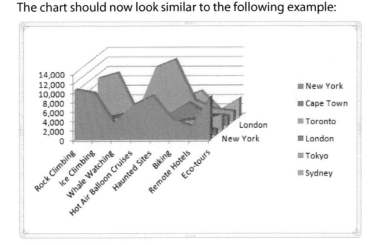

If the amount of space given to display a chart is too limited, Excel suppresses the display of some elements, such as some axis labels.

8   Right-click on any blank area on the chart and click **Change Chart Type**.

If the pop-up menu displays a **Change Series Chart Type** option, you must right-click again somewhere on a blank area of the chart. This menu option is displayed only if you right-click one of the data series.

9   Click the **Stacked Horizontal Cylinder** option in the **Bar** section of the dialog box and click **OK**.

Move the chart into its own chart sheet to make it bigger.

10   Under **Chart Tools**, on the **Design** tab, in the **Location** group, click **Move Chart**.

11   In the Move Chart dialog box, click **New sheet** and click **OK**.

The chart should now look similar to the following example:

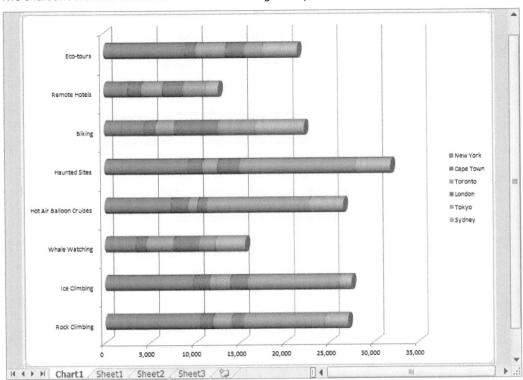

Switch the grouping of the data so that you can see the data by each Tolano Adventures office.

12   Under **Chart Tools**, on the **Design** tab, in the **Data** group, click **Switch Row/Column**.

Choose one of the standard layouts to put a title at the top of the chart and move the legend to the bottom.

13   Under **Chart Tools**, on the **Design** tab, in the **Chart Layouts** group, click **Layout 3**.

  Placing the legend at the bottom of this chart is appropriate because you have listed each of the eco-tour activities in the same sequence as the stacked bars.

14   Click in the chart title box in the chart, highlight the default text *Chart Title*, and type: Eco-Tour Registrations as the new title.

Add a title manually only to the horizontal axis, because the vertical axis shows the name of each Tolano Adventures office.

15   Under **Chart Tools**, on the **Layout** tab, in the **Labels** group, click **Axis Titles** and click **Primary Horizontal Axis Title**. Click **Title Below Axis**.

16   Type: # of Customers as the new axis title and press [Enter].

Try turning off the legend.

17   Under **Chart Tools**, on the **Layout** tab, in the **Labels** group, click **Legend** and then click **None**.

Look at how data labels appear on the chart.

18   Under **Chart Tools**, on the **Layout** tab, in the **Labels** group, click **Data Labels** and then click **Show**.

Look at how a data table will appear on a chart.

19   Under **Chart Tools,** on the **Layout** tab, in the **Labels** group, click **Data Table** and then click **Show Data Table**.

20   Under **Chart Tools**, on the **Layout** tab, in the **Labels** group, click **Data Labels** and then click **None**.

21 Under **Chart Tools**, on the **Layout** tab, in the **Labels** group, click **Data Table** and then click **Show Data Table with Legend Keys**.

The completed chart should now look similar to the following example:

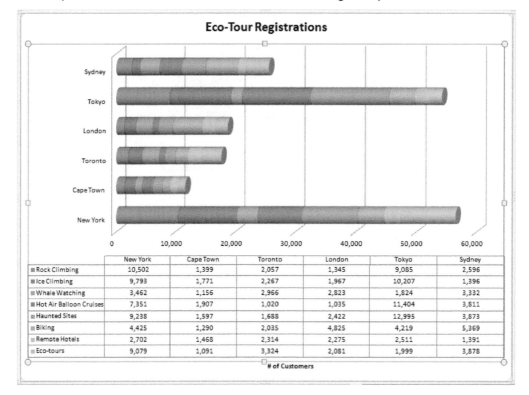

	New York	Cape Town	Toronto	London	Tokyo	Sydney
▥ Rock Climbing	10,502	1,399	2,057	1,345	9,085	2,596
▥ Ice Climbing	9,793	1,771	2,267	1,967	10,207	1,396
▥ Whale Watching	3,462	1,156	2,966	2,823	1,824	3,332
▥ Hot Air Balloon Cruises	7,351	1,907	1,020	1,035	11,404	3,811
▥ Haunted Sites	9,238	1,597	1,688	2,422	12,995	3,873
▥ Biking	4,425	1,290	2,035	4,825	4,219	5,369
▥ Remote Hotels	2,702	1,468	2,314	2,275	2,511	1,391
▥ Eco-tours	9,079	1,091	3,324	2,081	1,999	3,878

22 Save and close the workbook.

Using Sparklines

6.4

The Sparklines feature allows you to create a miniature chart inside a worksheet cell. This feature allows you to improve the visibility and readability of your worksheet without having to create one or more charts, which may take a lot of space. Like a regular chart, the sparkline displays a visual representation of each value in a horizontal or vertical range of cells. Because Excel displays the entire chart in a single worksheet cell, only the data points are shown without any chart components such as a legend, titles or axis.

There are three types of sparklines:

Line	Use this chart type to represent the values. The relative height of each point indicates the size of each value.	
Column	Use this chart type also to represent the values. The relative height of each column indicates the size of each value.	

Win/Loss	Create a series of bars, of which every bar is the same shape and size, and use the position of the bars to convey the information—positive values appear as higher bars and negative values appear as lower bars. The bars can only appear at one of two heights. Note that this example highlights negative values further by showing them in red. 

Sparkline charts have additional capabilities that you will not find in regular charts. Two examples are:

- You can display data in the regular way and with a sparkline chart at the same time in the same cells.

- You can activate markers in a sparkline chart, such as high, low, first, last and negative points. Without gridlines and axis markers, these markers help identify important points on the chart.

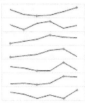

The Sparkline Tools Design tab offers a range of different settings and options to modify and customize sparkline charts.

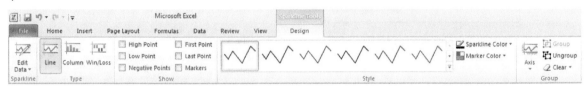

By default, a sparkline appears as just a raw chart without any title, legend or axis marker. The Axis option displays several formatting options, including a link to the column or row titles that are date values. If there are gaps in the dates, the sparkline chart shows corresponding gaps.

1-Jan	1-Feb	1-Mar	1-Jun		
8,125	5,947	5,420	9,015		
3,120	2,097	3,407	3,024		
1,017	1,281	1,512	1,761		
5,530	5,852	6,366	5,619		
6,905	6,471	5,648	5,808		
3,324	3,544	3,155	5,346		
904	804	641	998		

To remove the sparkline chart(s) from your worksheet, use the **Clear** button. To remove the sparkline from just one cell, use **Clear Selected Sparklines**. To remove the entire group, use the **Clear Selected Sparkline Groups**.

Learn the Skill

This exercise demonstrates how to insert a sparkline into a worksheet.

1   Make sure the *Website Hits - Student* workbook is active on the screen.

2   Select the *Sheet1* worksheet tab.

Widen the column so that Excel has more space in which to display the sparkline.

3   Click in any cell in column **I**. Then, on the **Home** tab, in the **Cells** group, click **Format** and then click **Column Width**.

4   In the **Column width** text box, change the value to 17 and click **OK**.

Choose different chart layouts and see how the chart is affected.

5   In cell I5, on the **Insert** tab, in the **Sparklines** group, click **Insert Line Sparkline**.

6   With the cursor in the **Data Range** text box, select the cell range **B5** to **G5** and click **OK**.

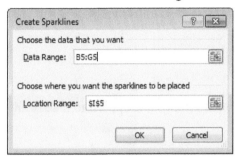

A sparkline chart now appears in cell I5. You can copy this to the other cells in column I.

7   With cell **I5** selected, click and drag the AutoFill handle in the lower right corner of cell **I5** down to cell **I11**.

After pasting the sparkline chart to the other cells, Excel automatically designates the entire range of cells as a sparkline group; therefore, a format change to one of those cells automatically applies to the other cells in the group. Whenever you select one or more cells in a sparkline group, a boundary line appears around the group to indicate that those cells belong together.

> To create a sparkline group at one time using the Create Sparklines dialog box, in step 5, you would select the entire cell range of B5 to G11 as the Data Range and cells I5 to I11 as the Location Range.

You can also use the copy and paste method to copy the sparkline chart from one cell to the other cells. When you use this technique, however, Excel does not treat the originating cell as a member of the sparkline group. Because of this, you should always use the AutoFill technique to create a sparkline group in adjacent cells; otherwise, you will have to manually add the originating cell to the sparkline group.

Have the sparkline charts display markers for the highest and lowest points.

8   Click on any cell in the range **I5** to **I11**, then click on the **Design** tab under **Sparkline Tools**.

9   Under the **Sparkline Tools**, on the **Design** tab, in the **Show** group, click the **High Point** and **Low Point** check boxes to turn them on.

Change the sparkline charts to the other types to see how they would look.

10 Under the **Sparkline Tools**, on the **Design** tab, in the **Type** group, click **Win/Loss** to change the sparkline to a group of columns.

11   Under the **Sparkline Tools**, on the **Design** tab, in the **Type** group, click **Column** to change the sparkline to a group of columns of varying heights.

To remove one or more sparkline charts within the sparkline group, use the **Clear Selected Sparkline** option. You can also remove the entire sparkline group at one time using the **Clear Selected Sparkline Groups** option.

12   Under the **Sparkline Tools**, on the **Design** tab, in the **Group** group, click the arrow next to **Clear** and click **Clear Selected Sparkline Groups**.

13   In the Quick Access Toolbar, click **Undo**.

The completed chart should now look similar to the following example:

	A	B	C	D	E	F	G	H	I
1	Tolano Adventures								
2	Website Hits								
3									
4	Office	January	February	March	April	May	June	Total	
5	New York	8,125	5,947	5,420	5,647	7,134	9,015	41,288	
6	Cape Town	3,120	2,097	3,407	3,885	2,352	3,024	17,885	
7	Toronto	1,017	1,281	1,512	2,107	1,825	1,761	9,503	
8	London	5,530	5,852	6,366	7,760	8,257	5,619	39,384	
9	Tokyo	6,905	6,471	5,648	5,665	8,412	5,808	38,909	
10	Sydney	3,324	3,544	3,155	3,574	5,565	5,346	24,508	
11	Corporate	904	804	641	772	632	998	4,751	
12	Total	28,925	25,996	26,149	29,410	34,177	31,571		

14   Save the workbook.

Printing Charts

1.2

You can print charts as part of a worksheet or on their own as individual chart sheet(s). Depending on the circumstances, each method offers advantages.

When you print a chart as part of a worksheet, you can display the chart with the data above, below or next to it. However, you cannot fit large charts onto one page; you must either reduce them in size or manually cut and paste them together on the paper you are using.

Learn the Skill

This exercise demonstrates how to print a chart either as part of a worksheet or as a separate chart sheet.

1   Make sure the *Website Hits - Student* workbook is active on the screen.

Preview the *Sheet1* worksheet for printing both the data and the pie chart.

2   Click any blank cell outside of the pie chart so that the chart is not selected.

3   Click **File** and then click **Print**.

4   Click **Portrait Orientation and** then click **Landscape Orientation** to change the orientation.

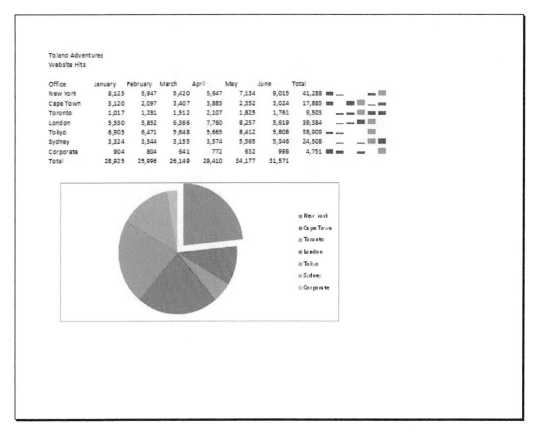

As long as a chart is not in edit mode, Excel prints the worksheet with all of the contents including any chart(s).

Now preview only the pie chart on its own for printing.

5   Click the **Home** tab.

6   Click in a blank area inside the pie chart to put it into edit mode.

7   Click **File** and then click **Print**.

8   If necessary, click **Portrait Orientation** and then click **Landscape Orientation** to change the orientation.

Preview the *Chart1* chart sheet for printing.

9   Click the **Home** tab and then click in a blank cell outside of the pie chart.

10   Click the *Chart1* worksheet tab.

11   Click **File** and then click **Print**.

12   Click the **Home** tab.

13   Save and close the workbook.

Lesson Summary

This lesson introduced you to working with charts. You looked at how to create a chart, how to change the type, layout and design of a chart, and how to manipulate a chart. You should now be able to:

☑ create charts

☑ change the chart type

☑ work with pie charts

☑ move a chart to a different location on a worksheet or its own chart sheet

☑ resize a chart to a different size or shape

☑ change the chart layout

☑ create, customize and remove a sparkline chart

☑ print a chart

Review Questions

MMM
Go online for
Additional
Review and
Activities

1. Provide examples of when you might want to use a chart to show the data in the worksheet.

2. List at least five different types of charts.

3. Describe the limitation you have when selecting data to create a pie chart, compared to other chart types.

4. Discuss the advantages and disadvantages of exploding pieces from the pie on a pie chart.

5. Provide examples of what changes you can make to the layout of a chart.

6. List the three different types of sparkline charts and provide examples of when you might use each type.

7. Provide an example of how printing charts differs from printing a worksheet that only contains data.

Microsoft®
Excel® 2010
Core Certification

Lesson 7: Working with Graphics

Lesson Objectives

In this lesson, you will learn to work with different types of graphics, including shapes, WordArt, pictures, clip art graphics and SmartArt. On successful completion of this lesson, you will be able to:

- ☐ draw different types of shapes on a worksheet
- ☐ move, resize and format shapes
- ☐ use WordArt objects
- ☐ insert clip art and pictures

- ☐ use the Image Editor tools
- ☐ insert screenshots
- ☐ resize, reshape and rotate graphics objects
- ☐ insert SmartArt objects

Drawing Shapes

6.2

As a core component of the MS Office Suite, Excel uses the same drawing tools found in MS Word and PowerPoint. In Excel, you can use these drawing tools to highlight significant parts of the worksheet or chart.

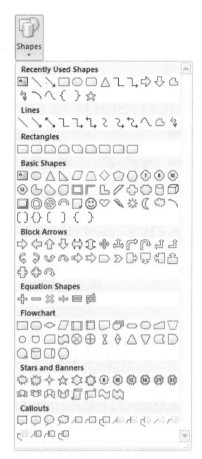

However, do not over-use the drawing tools. Excel is a spreadsheet, and its primary strength is the ability to perform many calculations quickly. While graphics in a text document or presentation can draw attention to important points, excessive use of graphics in a spreadsheet can have the opposite effect by drawing attention away from key data.

You can access shapes on the **Insert** tab, in the **Illustrations** group, under **Shapes**, as shown at right. The available shapes include basic rectangles, ovals and lines, as well as a variety of other commonly used shapes. Use the (Shift) key if you wish to ensure that your shapes are symmetrical, such as a square using the rectangle tool or a circle using the oval tool.

Note the following points about creating or working with shapes:

- You can create most shapes using the same method. Once activated, the mouse arrow changes to a + symbol. You can then click where you wish the top left corner of the object to begin and drag to the required size.

- Excel organizes groups of shapes by type, some of which are three-dimensional.

- When you use the Text Box feature, Excel changes the mouse cursor to a ↓ symbol. Click in the location where you want the text to begin and start typing.

While Excel's drawing capability provides numerous tools with which to create simple drawings, it is not the same as having a dedicated graphics program. If you need more features and flexibility when manipulating pictures or drawings, it is better to use a dedicated graphics program.

Moving and Resizing Shapes

After you have drawn the object, you can manipulate it in size and appearance. For instance, you will rarely be able to place a shape or object in exactly the right position on the worksheet in your first try. You may also need to adjust the size of your drawing to fit the space available.

To resize an object or shape, you must first select it; the shape or object then displays its eight handles (except lines, which only have two handles). By clicking and dragging these handles, you change the shape or object's size and proportion.

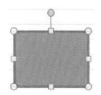

MMM
Moving and
Resizing
Shapes Online
Exercise

Clicking any of the corner handles enables you to change the length and width of the two adjoining sides. Dragging any of the midpoint handles resizes only that one side.

If you want to move a shape to a new position, you do not need to select it first. When you position the mouse cursor over the shape, the cursor changes to ⚓ to indicate that it is ready to move the shape directly underneath it. You can then drag the shape to another location on the worksheet.

To delete a shape object, click the shape to select it, then press (Delete).

Formatting Shapes

Excel creates shapes using the settings in the currently selected theme. After you draw the shape on the worksheet, you can customize it using the formatting options in the Ribbon.

Found under **Drawing Tools**, on the **Format** tab, the **Shape Styles** group includes several formatting tools:

Shape Fill	Select colors and patterns to fill the inside of the shape. By default, Excel uses the fill color for the current default theme. You can choose **No Fill** to make the shape transparent, leaving only the shape's border color. Instead of a solid color fill, you can choose a picture, gradient (where the shade intensity changes from one end of the object to the other) or texture to fill the inside of the shape.

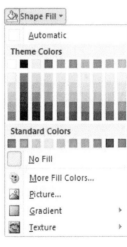

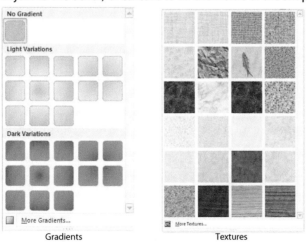

Gradients   Textures

Shape Outline	Select colors and patterns for the border(s) of the shape. As with **Shape Fill**, you can choose **No Outline** to make the border transparent. The **Weight** setting allows you to choose the thickness of the border, and the **Dashes** setting determines whether to use a solid line or a pattern of dots and/or dashes.

For line and arrow shapes, you can choose from several arrow patterns.

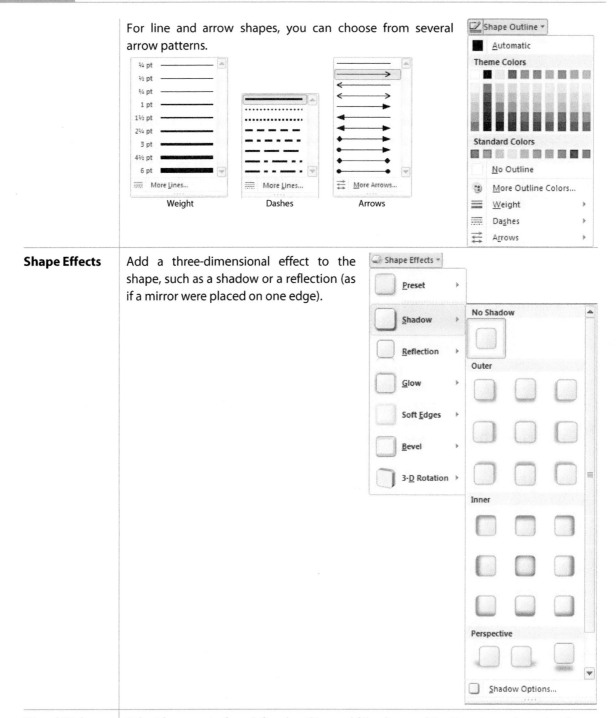

Weight	Dashes	Arrows

Shape Effects	Add a three-dimensional effect to the shape, such as a shadow or a reflection (as if a mirror were placed on one edge).
Visual Style	Select from a set of predefined outline and fill color combinations to apply to the shape.

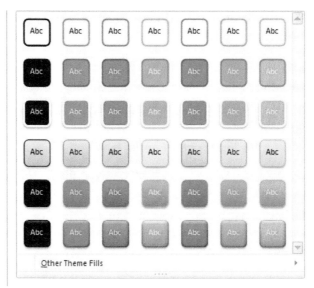

With these various drawing tools and formatting options, your only limits to creating colorful objects on your worksheet are your imagination and time. However, keep in mind that you use spreadsheets primarily for numbers, formulas and charts. You should therefore use the minimum number of graphical objects you need to focus the attention to those three parts of your worksheet.

Learn the Skill

This exercise demonstrates how to draw shapes, change their shape, move them around the worksheet and change their formatting.

1   Open the *Tour Prices* workbook and save as `Tour Prices - Student`.

	Travel Item	Group	Tour	Flight	Hotel	Misc.	Total Cost
	Tour Prices Breakdown (Average based on 7-day Trip)						
5	Kilimanjaro Climb	RC	4,000			1,000	5,000
6	Mt. Shasta Climb	RC	700				700
7	North Carolina	RC	500				500
8	Tucson, Mt. Lemmon, Cochise Stronghold	RC	350				350
9	Antarctica	E	4,000	3,000		1,000	8,000
10	Sydney Whale Watching (*Family of 4)	E	250				250
11	Vancouver Whale Watching (*Family of 4)	E	500			100	600
12	Maui Whale Watching (*Family of 4)	E	200	2,000	1,000		3,200
13	Bogota Cycling (*Two People)	Eco		1,500	1,500	200	3,200
14	Perth Cycling (*Two People)	Eco		4,000	3,500	500	8,000
15	Copenhagen Cycling (*Two People)	Eco		2,100	3,000	400	5,500

*You can also use the **Text Box** command from the **Text** group on the **Insert** tab.*

Add a text box to the worksheet.

2   On the **Insert** tab, in the **Illustrations** group, click **Shapes** and then click **Text Box** (located in the **Basic Shapes** section). The mouse cursor changes to a ↓ symbol to indicate that you can draw the text box on the worksheet.

3   Click and hold down the mouse button and drag the mouse to draw a box about 1 inch wide by 1 inch high to the right of the data.

4   Inside the text box, type: A Tolano Adventures exclusive!

Excel now displays the **Drawing Tools Format** tab because you have selected a shape (text box).

You can also add a new shape using the **Format** tab. However, Excel only displays the **Format** tab when you have selected another shape. Therefore, you can only add the first shape from the **Insert** tab. You can add subsequent shapes using either the **Insert** or the **Format** tabs.

5   Under **Drawing Tools**, on the **Format** tab, in the **Insert Shapes** group, click **Oval**. The mouse cursor changes to a + symbol.

6   Click and hold down the left mouse button above and to the left of cell **H9**. Then, while holding down the mouse button, drag the mouse cursor to a new position below and to the right of cell **H9**.

If you hold the SHIFT key while dragging the mouse to draw the shape, Excel creates a perfect circle. If you use the SHIFT key with the rectangle tool, Excel draws a square.

An oval shape now covers the area in and around cell **H9**. Make it transparent by turning off the fill option.

7   With the oval shape still selected, under **Drawing Tools**, on the **Format** tab, in the **Shape Styles** group, click **Shape Fill**. Click **No Fill**.

8   Point the mouse cursor to the edge of the oval; the mouse cursor changes to a ⬚ symbol. Click and drag the oval shape so that the 8,000 value in cell **H9** is in the center of the oval.

9   Point the mouse cursor at one of the four corner handles. Click and drag this handle to make the oval smaller or larger. If necessary, move the oval shape again to place the 8,000 value in the center.

Draw an arrowed line from the text box to the oval shape.

10   Under **Drawing Tools**, on the **Format** tab, in the **Insert Shapes** group, click **Arrow**.

11   Point the mouse cursor at the left middle handle of the text box. Notice that the four middle handles turn red when the mouse cursor is nearby.

12   Click and drag the mouse from the handle in the text box to one of the red handles on the oval.

Make the arrowed line thicker and darker.

13   Under **Drawing Tools**, on the **Format** tab, in the **Shape Styles** group, click **Shape Outline**. Click **Weight** and then click **1½ pt**.

14   Under **Drawing Tools**, on the **Format** tab, in the **Shape Styles** group, click **Shape Outline**. Click **Blue, Accent 1, Darker 25%** (fifth column from the left, second from the bottom) in the **Theme Colors** section.

When you drew the line from the text box to the oval shape, you connected all three objects together by starting and ending on one of the connection handles. This connection stays in place, even when you move the shape.

15   Click on the oval shape. The handles should appear around the oval shape, but not around any other shape.

16   Click and drag the oval shape to encompass the Antarctica text in cell **B9**.

Add color around the edges of the text box.

17 Click anywhere in the text box to select it again.

18 Under **Drawing Tools**, on the **Format** tab, in the **Shape Styles** group, click **Shape Effects**. Click **Glow**, and then click one of the **Glow Variations**, such as **Olive Green, 11 pt glow, Accent color 3**.

The completed worksheet should look similar to the following:

	Travel Item	Group	Tour	Flight	Hotel	Misc.	Total Cost			
	Tour Prices Breakdown (Average based on 7-day Trip)									
Kilimanjaro Climb	RC	4,000			1,000	5,000				
Mt. Shasta Climb	RC	700				700				
North Carolina	RC	500				500				
Tucson, Mt. Lemmon, Cochise Stronghold	RC	350				350				
Antarctica	E	4,000	3,000		1,000	8,000				
Sydney Whale Watching (*Family of 4)	E	250				250				
Vancouver Whale Watching (*Family of 4)	E	500			100	600				
Maui Whale Watching (*Family of 4)	E	200	2,000	1,000		3,200				
Bogota Cycling (*Two People)	Eco		1,500	1,500	200	3,200				
Perth Cycling (*Two People)	Eco		4,000	3,500	500	8,000				
Copenhagen Cycling (*Two People)	Eco		2,100	3,000	400	5,500				

A Tolano Adventures exclusive!

19 Save the workbook.

Using WordArt

WordArt is a special type of text shape that allows you to display text characters in a variety of imaginative ways. Unlike a text box, WordArt is bold and colorful, with the letters twisted and turned at different angles.

To insert WordArt, on the **Insert** tab, in the **Text** group, click **WordArt**.

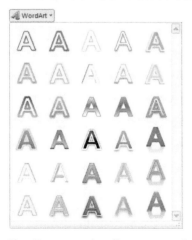

The **Format** tab offers many of the same formatting options as graphical shapes, such as fill, outline, effects and visual styles. You can therefore choose most of the same colors, patterns and dashes as graphical shapes.

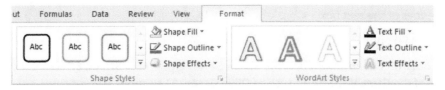

However, some of the options underneath are different. For example, **Text Effects** has a **Transform** option that is not available under **Shape Effects,** and is not practical for graphical shapes such as ovals and rectangles. With WordArt, you can twist and twirl the text characters in different directions.

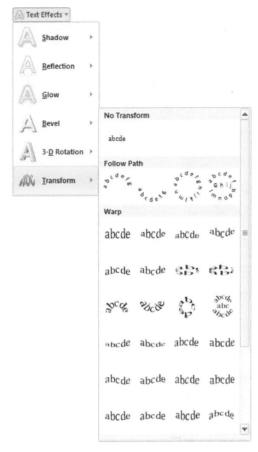

To remove a WordArt object, select it and press (Delete).

Learn the Skill

This exercise demonstrates how to use WordArt in a worksheet.

1   Make sure the *Tour Prices - Student* workbook is open on the screen.

2   Scroll down the worksheet to the blank area below the data.

3   On the **Insert** tab, in the **Text** group, click **WordArt**.

4   Click the **Fill – Red, Accent 2, Warm Matte Bevel** (second row from the bottom, third from the left).

    Excel now displays the WordArt object on your worksheet with the default text.

5   Ensure the WordArt object is selected and replace the default text with: Limited Time Specials.

6   Position the mouse cursor over one of the WordArt object edges (the mouse cursor changes to ⛭) and move the object to a blank area of the worksheet with at least three rows below the data.

7   Also be sure that you have selected the WordArt object by noting whether Excel has framed it with a solid border with the eight handles, similar to the following:

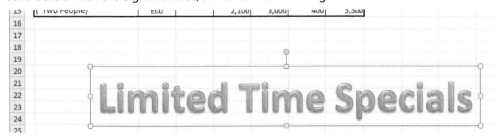

8   Under **Drawing Tools**, on the **Format** tab, in the **WordArt Styles** group, click the **More** button for the **Visual Styles**.

9   Position the cursor over various visual styles of your choice and observe the Live Preview effect on the WordArt object.

10 Click in a blank area away from the **Visual Styles** menu box to close it. If necessary, click on the edge of the WordArt object so that Excel selects it again, as shown by a solid border.

11 Under **Drawing Tools**, on the **Format** tab, in the **WordArt Styles** group, click **Text Fill**. Then position the cursor over various fill colors to observe the Live Preview effect.

12 Click in a blank area away from the **Text Fill** menu box to close it. If necessary, click on the edge of the WordArt object to select it again (as shown by a solid border).

You can also use the Shape Styles group to format the background fill and outline of the WordArt object.

13 Under **Drawing Tools**, on the **Format** tab, in the **Shape Styles** group, click the **More** button for the **Visual Styles**.

14 Click in a blank area away from the **Visual Styles** menu box to close it. If necessary, click on the edge of the WordArt object to select it again.

15 Under **Drawing Tools**, on the **Format** tab, in the **WordArt Styles** group, click **Text Effects**. Click **Transform** and select a transformation pattern of your choice.

The completed worksheet may look similar to the following:

16 Save the workbook again

Inserting Pictures and Clip Art

6.2

Excel can insert pictures, photographs, and clip art images into worksheets. It will accept pictures in any of the common image formats, such as bmp, gif, jpg, png and tif.

There is also a vast number and variety of clip art images that you can import into Excel worksheets and other Microsoft Office documents. You can obtain these images from the Microsoft Office Web site, among others.

To insert a picture into a worksheet, on the **Insert** tab, in the **Illustrations** group, click **Picture**. The Insert Picture dialog box then enables you to search for and select a picture file to insert.

To insert a clip art image into the worksheet, on the **Insert** tab, in the **Illustrations** group, click **Clip Art**. The Clip Art task pane then displays, enabling you to search your local computer and/or the Microsoft Web site for available clip art images.

Learn the Skill

This exercise demonstrates how to add a clip art image to your worksheet.

1   Make sure the *Tour Prices - Student* workbook is open on the screen.

First, add the company logo at the top of the worksheet.

2   Click in cell B1.

3   On the **Insert** tab, in the **Illustrations** group, click **Picture**.

4   In the Insert Picture dialog box, navigate to the folder where the *tolano logo.jpg* file is located.

5   Select the *tolano logo.jpg* file and click **Insert**.

6   Click and drag the bottom right corner handle up and reduce the size of the logo image to the height of two worksheet rows.

Now add a clip art image.

7   On the **Insert** tab, in the **Illustrations** group, click **Clip Art**.

The Clip Art task pane appears at the right side of the screen. The number of graphics that appear in the list depends on whether other pictures were on the system before the installation of Microsoft Office, or if any graphics had been downloaded from Microsoft's web site.

8   In the **Search for** text box of the Clip Art task pane, type: travel.

9   Verify that you have set the **Results should be** box to **All media file types**.

10 Click the **Include Office.com content** check box to turn it on and click **Go**.

Office.com is a Microsoft Office Web site where a large number of clip art images are available for download.

As the search progresses, Excel displays clip art images in the task pane.

If your computer does not have the same images appearing in the task pane, choose one from those available to you.

11 Click in an empty cell of the worksheet below the text box containing the words "A Tolano Adventures exclusive!" There should be a lot of empty cells below and to the right.

12 Scroll through the list of clip art images displayed, and click one of the images to insert it into the worksheet.

When you insert a picture or clip art image into a worksheet, Excel displays it with handles around it, in the same way it displays an object when selected. You can size or move the picture as you would an object, although you cannot manipulate the color or actual picture.

13 Reduce the size of the image to about 1 inch in height and width.

Now add another picture to the worksheet.

14 Click in an empty cell below the clip art image to insert the new picture there.

15 On the **Insert** tab, in the **Illustrations** group, click **Picture**.

16 In the Insert Picture dialog box, navigate to the folder where the *Ice Climbing.jpg* file is located.

17 Select the *Ice Climbing.jpg* file and click **Insert**.

18 Click and drag the bottom right corner handle up to reduce the size of the logo image to a height of 2 inches.

Your worksheet and chart should look similar to the following:

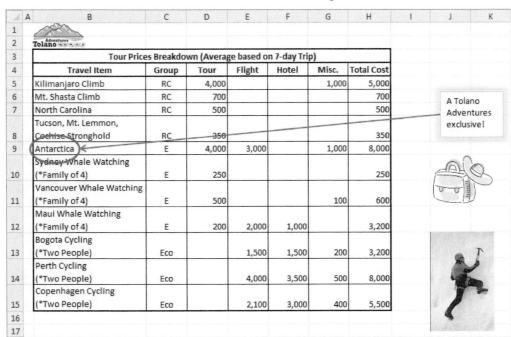

MMM
Inserting
Pictures and
Clip Art Online
Exercise

19 Close the Clip Art task pane.

20 Save the workbook.

Using the Image Editor

6.3

Excel provides several image-editing tools to allow you to adjust and correct photographs and clip art objects on your worksheet. When you add or select a picture or clip art, Excel displays this Format tab:

Some image-editing tools on the tab include:

Remove Background	Remove the background surrounding the main subject within the photograph. If this tool is selected, Excel displays another tab to help you identify the areas of the photograph to keep or remove. 
Corrections	Change the brightness and contrast settings, and adjust the sharpness of the edges around the various objects within the picture or clip art. 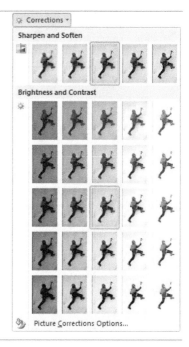

Color	Adjust the color saturation and color tone settings, or change the color of the picture or clip art.	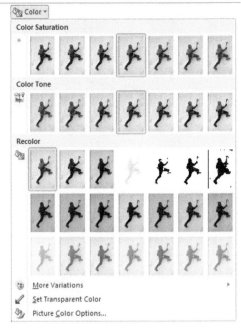
Artistic Effects	Modify the photograph using various filters to achieve special effects.	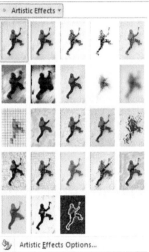
Picture Border	Set the color, weight and dashes options for the border around the picture or clip art object. These are the same options as for drawing shapes.	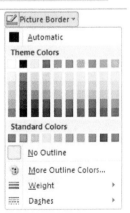

Picture Effects	Set various three-dimensional picture effects. These are the same options as for drawing shapes.	
Picture Layout	Crop or resize the picture or clip art to a shape (such as a circle or square), and possibly add a text box.	
Visual Styles	Apply a predefined set of borders or a three-dimensional effect to the picture or clip art. Excel also crops it to fit the shape used.	
Crop	Hide the outer parts of the picture or clip art to achieve a stronger focus on the main subject.	
Shape Height, Shape Width	Manually set the height and width of the picture or clip art.	

As with drawing shapes, you should not overuse photographs or clip art images in your worksheet in order to avoid distracting readers from the main data.

Learn the Skill

This exercise demonstrates how to do image editing with pictures and clip art graphics.

1   Make sure the *Tour Prices - Student* workbook is open on the screen.

Select one of the pictures and try some of the editing options in the **Adjust** group on the **Format** tab. These editing options apply to the inside of the picture.

2   Click on the Ice Climbing picture. Excel displays handles around its edges.

3   Under **Picture Tools**, on the **Format** tab, in the **Adjust** group, click **Corrections**.

4   Position the mouse cursor over some of the options available and observe the Live Preview effect on the picture. Click in a blank area away from the **Corrections** drop-down menu.

5   Under **Picture Tools**, on the **Format** tab, in the **Adjust** group, click **Color**.

6   Position the mouse cursor over some of the options available and observe the Live Preview effect on the picture. Click in a blank area away from the **Color** drop-down menu.

7   Under **Picture Tools**, on the **Format** tab, in the **Adjust** group, click **Artistic Effects**.

8   Position the mouse cursor over some of the options available and observe the Live Preview effect on the picture. Click in a blank area away from the **Artistic Effects** drop-down menu.

The **Picture Styles** group on the **Format** tab offers another set of editing tools that apply to the outside edge of the picture.

9   Under **Picture Tools**, on the **Format** tab, in the **Picture Styles** group, click the **More** button next to the **Visual Styles**.

10   Position the mouse cursor over some of the options available and observe the Live Preview effect on the picture. Click in a blank area away from the **Visual Styles** drop-down menu.

11   Under **Picture Tools**, on the **Format** tab, in the **Picture Styles** group, click **Picture Layout**.

12   Position the mouse cursor over some of the options available and observe the Live Preview effect on the picture. Click in a blank area away from the **Picture Layout** drop-down menu.

Select a clip art graphic and observe which editing tools you can use.

13   Click the clip art graphic to select it.

Excel grays out some of the editing options for clip art, such as the **Artistic Effects** and **Remove Background**.

14   Under **Picture Tools**, on the **Format** tab, in the **Picture Styles** group, click the **More** button next to the **Visual Styles**.

15   Position the mouse cursor over some of the options available and observe the Live Preview effect on the picture. Click in a blank area away from the **Visual Styles** drop-down menu.

Now remove the background for one of the pictures.

16   Click the Ice Climbing picture again.

17   Under **Picture Tools**, on the **Format** tab, in the **Adjust** group, click **Remove Background**.

Excel displays a marker box to identify the main subject in the picture.

18 On the **Background Removal** tab, in the **Close** group, click **Keep Changes**.

The completed worksheet should now look similar to the following example:

	Travel Item	Group	Tour	Flight	Hotel	Misc.	Total Cost
3	Tour Prices Breakdown (Average based on 7-day Trip)						
5	Kilimanjaro Climb	RC	4,000			1,000	5,000
6	Mt. Shasta Climb	RC	700				700
7	North Carolina	RC	500				500
8	Tucson, Mt. Lemmon, Cochise Stronghold	RC	350				350
9	Antarctica	E	4,000	3,000		1,000	8,000
10	Sydney Whale Watching (*Family of 4)	E	250				250
11	Vancouver Whale Watching (*Family of 4)	E	500			100	600
12	Maui Whale Watching (*Family of 4)	E	200	2,000	1,000		3,200
13	Bogota Cycling (*Two People)	Eco		1,500	1,500	200	3,200
14	Perth Cycling (*Two People)	Eco		4,000	3,500	500	8,000
15	Copenhagen Cycling (*Two People)	Eco		2,100	3,000	400	5,500

A Tolano Adventures exclusive!

19 Save and close the workbook.

Inserting Screenshots

6.2

Excel can also take screenshots of any part of your current screen to insert pictures, photographs, and clip art images into worksheets. It will accept pictures in any of the common image formats, such as bmp, gif, jpg, png and tif.

There is also a vast number and variety of clip art images that you can import into Excel worksheets and other Microsoft Office documents. You can obtain these images from the Microsoft Office Web site, among others.

To insert a screenshot into a worksheet, on the **Insert** tab, in the **Illustrations** group, click **Screenshot**. Then click one of the following:

- One of the thumbnail icons displaying in the drop down menu, or
- **Screen Clipping** to capture a rectangular area of your screen.

Learn the Skill

This exercise demonstrates how to add a screenshot to your worksheet.

1 Open a new blank workbook.

2 On the **Insert** tab, in the **Illustrations** group, click **Screenshot**.

A drop down box will appear containing thumbnail icons of the windows currently displayed on your screen.

Notice how there is nothing in the drop down list as you have no other programs open other than Excel.

Suppose you want to capture how the market is doing today at this moment in time.

3   Click anywhere in the new worksheet to close this option.

4   Start the Web browser installed on the computer system you are using.

5   In the address bar, type: www.dowjones.com and press (Enter).

6   Switch back to Excel and on the **Insert** tab, in the **Illustrations** group, click **Screenshot**.

7   Click the Web browser screen in the list.

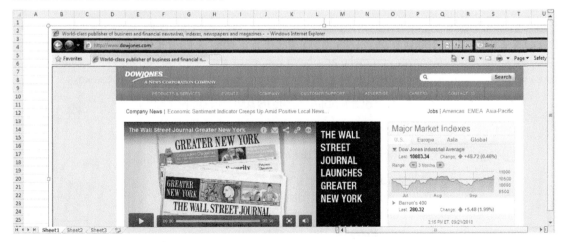

Notice Excel inserts a screen of the entire window for the web browser. However, all you want to show is the current market value.

8   Press (Delete) to remove this picture.

9   On the **Insert** tab, in the **Illustrations** group, click **Screenshot** and then click **Screen Clipping**.

Excel minimizes at this point and you should be viewing the Web browser. In fact, the Web browser should also show a white foreground in front of the page contents.

Hint: The contents of Web pages change frequently so you may need to find the Market Indexes box if it is not clearly visible as shown in the previous screen. You will need to perform this step prior to performing step 9 onwards.

10   Position the cursor at the top left of the Major Market Indexes box and drag to select the entire box.

Notice as you drag to select the box that the contents of this box become visible so you can identify which areas you want to include in the screenshot.

You now have a copy of the values you wanted to show for the current date in an Excel worksheet that you could use as reference for the rest of the worksheet.

11   Close the workbook and discard the changes.

Modifying Graphics Objects

Resizing, Reshaping and Scaling Objects

6.2

The mouse is usually the fastest method of changing the size, shape and position of an object.

In some cases, you may not want the unrestrained freedom to make certain kinds of changes, such as changing the proportion of the height to the width, which we refer to as *aspect ratio*. You can choose to lock this ratio whenever you make an object bigger or smaller. You can also temporarily lock the position or aspect ratio when you use the mouse to resize an object by using one of these keys:

Ctrl   Lock the center of the object while its size and shape changes.

Shift   Lock the aspect ratio of the object while its size changes.

Ctrl + Shift   Lock both the position and the aspect ratio of the object.

In addition, you can reshape many objects. When you select one of these objects, Excel displays an adjustment handle in the form of a small yellow diamond. By clicking and dragging this handle, you can modify the shape of one part of the object without changing the shape of the rest of it.

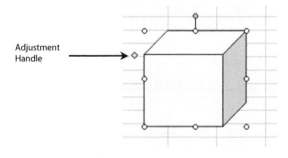

Rotating Objects

Rotating an object refers to changing its angle. However, you cannot rotate some objects, such as lines, because they are straight. You can make them diagonal simply by dragging an end handle to the required angle.

Use one of the following methods to rotate a selected object in Excel:

- Click and drag the green handle at the top of the object in the direction for the rotation angle.

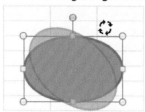

- Under **Drawing Tools**, on the **Format** tab, in the **Arrange** group, click **Rotate**.

- Under **Drawing Tools**, on the **Format** tab, in the **Size** group, click the **Dialog box launcher**. In the **Size** category of the Format Shape dialog box, enter the angle in the **Rotation** field.

- Right-click the object and click **Size and Properties**. In the **Size** category of the Format Shape dialog box, enter the angle in the **Rotation** field.

You cannot rotate text boxes with the green rotate handle. You can rotate the angle of lines and arrow line objects by changing the position of the two ends at any time.

Learn the Skill

This exercise demonstrates how to resize, reshape and rotate shapes and pictures.

1   Create a new blank workbook.

2   On the **Insert** tab, in the **Illustrations** group, click **Shapes**. Then draw a cube (located in Basic Shapes) approximately 1.5" wide by 1.5" high (or 4 cm wide by 4 cm high).

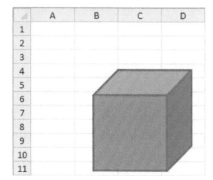

3   Under **Drawing Tools**, on the **Format** tab, in the **Size** group, click on the spin buttons for both the **Shape Height** and **Shape Width** boxes until both are 1.5" (or 4 cm).

First, change the size and shape of the cube to make it wider using the **Shape Width** text box.

4   Click the spin button for the **Shape Width** until the value is 3" (or 8 cm).

The square cube is now rectangular.

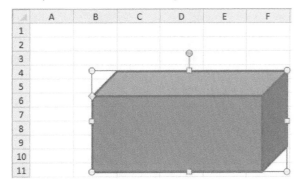

You can also type the new values directly into the text boxes. This may be easier than using the mouse to change the length or width of a shape.

Change the size and shape of a cube by using the mouse.

5   Click **Undo** in the Quick Access Toolbar.

6   With the cube selected, click and drag the bottom right corner handle downward and to the right. Move to the right more than downward so that the cube is no longer square. Release the mouse button.

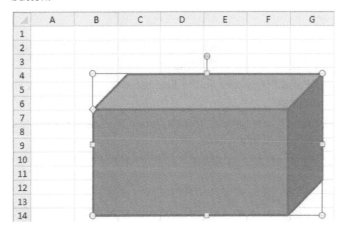

Now change the size of the cube using the mouse again, but lock the aspect ratio so that it stays a cube.

7   Click **Undo** in the Quick Access Toolbar.

8   Hold down the (Shift) key, and click and drag the bottom right corner handle downward and to the right. Release the mouse button.

Notice that the new shape remains a cube even if you try to move the mouse in different directions. Also, the top left corner (the opposite end of the handle you are moving) does not move as the shape grows. This is the effect of using the (Shift) key while resizing the shape.

Change the size of the cube again, but lock the center position of the shape.

9   Click **Undo** in the Quick Access Toolbar.

10   Hold down the (Ctrl) key, and click and drag the bottom right corner handle to the right. Release the mouse button when the left edge of the shape has moved past the left edge of the worksheet.

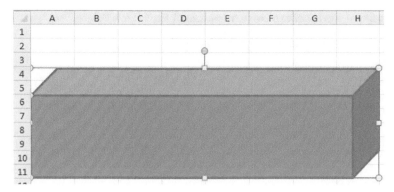

Notice that, while dragging the mouse, the center of the shape does not move. Therefore, the width of the shape grows equally on both the left and right side as you drag the handle to the right. This is the effect of using the Ctrl key while resizing the shape.

Because the left edge of the shape moved past the left edge of the worksheet, Excel cuts the left edge of the shape back when you release the mouse button. This is the exception to the rule of using the Ctrl key to lock the center of the shape in the same position.

Now rotate an object manually using the rotate handle.

11   Click **Undo** in the Quick Access Toolbar.

12   Position the cursor over its rotate handle.

Excel replaces the cursor symbol with the rotate symbol (↻).

13   Click and drag the rotate handle clockwise by 45°.

14   Under **Drawing Tools**, on the **Format** tab, in the **Arrange** group, click **Rotate**. Then click **More Rotation Options**.

Excel displays the Format Shape dialog box, showing the many shape formatting options.

Drag the green handle toward the position of the top right corner handle. This may not be 45° exactly but it is approximate.

15   Change the **Rotation** value to 45° by clicking the increment or decrement buttons, then click **Close**.

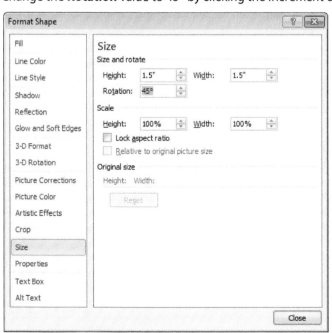

You can enter a number directly into the Rotation text box. You can also enter negative values and angles greater than 360°.

16   Click **Undo** in the Quick Access Toolbar twice to move the cube back to its original position.

17   Under **Drawing Tools**, on the **Format** tab, in the **Arrange** group, click **Rotate**. Position the mouse cursor over each of the four menu options and observe the Live Preview effects on the shape.

18   Click on any blank area of the worksheet to close the menu.

Now change the shape of the cube using the adjustment handle.

19   Click and drag the adjustment handle (◇) in different directions to see how the cube changes shape.

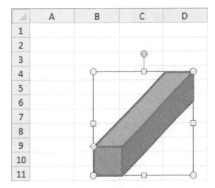

20   Close the workbook without saving it.

Using SmartArt Graphics

6.2

Shapes—text, lines, arrows, boxes, circles, and so on—are elemental graphics objects that you can combine to make more complex objects. SmartArt graphics give you a powerful visual-presentation tool within Excel rather than having to create graphics using other software and import them into your worksheet. SmartArt graphics provide an instant, easy-to-use set of objects to help you communicate ideas quickly—a useful feature in a fast-paced business environment.

When you are in edit mode, SmartArt graphics show a Text pane at the left into which you can enter text bullets. Each bullet then appears in the SmartArt graphic as a shape, which varies depending on which layout you have selected. You can choose from several layout types, as shown in the following illustrations:

List

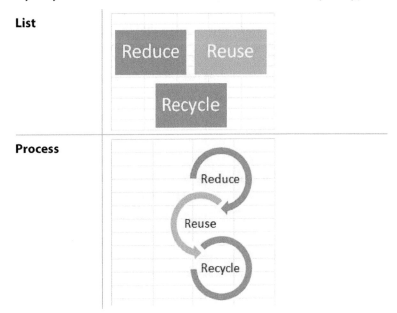

Process

Cycle	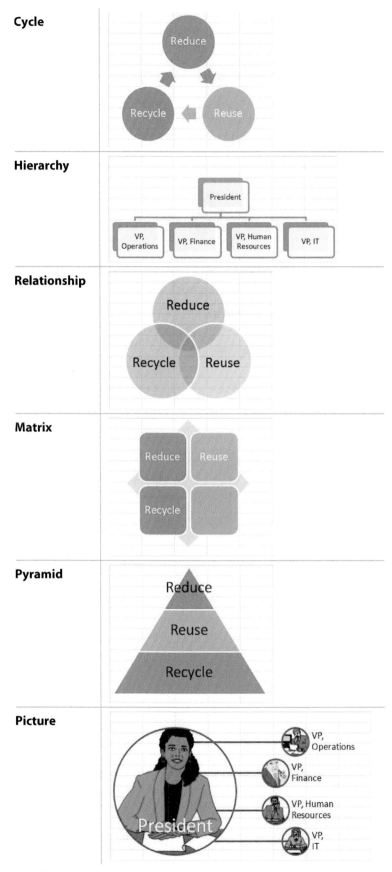
Hierarchy	
Relationship	
Matrix	
Pyramid	
Picture	

Excel automatically resizes the shape and text font to maintain the symmetrical appearance of the graphic, overall, as you enter each line. You can enter additional lines by pressing (Enter), and delete extraneous lines by using (Delete); Excel realigns the SmartArt graphic to accommodate the changed number of lines.

As with PowerPoint, you can demote or promote bulleted lines to organize similar ideas together. Excel automatically modifies the SmartArt graphic; however, each SmartArt type shows these demoted bullets differently.

It is important to note that you cannot use Excel formulas to reference cell data from within a SmartArt graphic.

This same SmartArt graphics tool is included in the other Microsoft Office products: PowerPoint, Word and Outlook. You can also copy and paste SmartArt graphics as images into other programs. Furthermore, if you paste SmartArt graphics into PowerPoint presentations, you can add animation features to them.

Learn the Skill

This exercise demonstrates how to create and format a SmartArt graphic.

1   Create a new workbook and save as Eco Tourism Strategy - Student.

2   On the **Insert** tab, in the **Illustrations** group, click **SmartArt**.

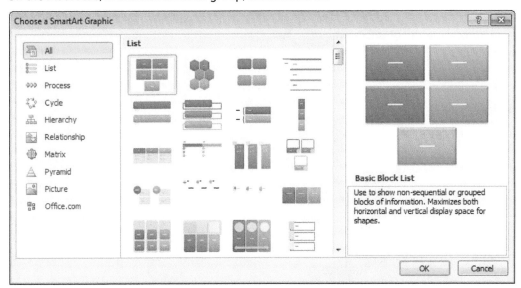

Excel displays a large list of SmartArt layouts. You can select one of the categories on the left side to see only those types of layouts.

3   With the **Basic Block List** diagram selected, click **OK**.

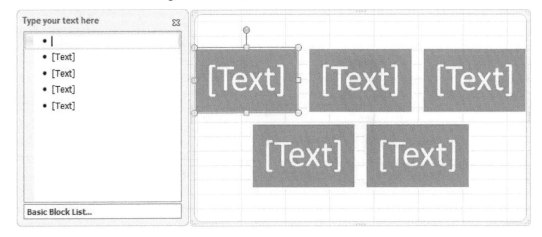

Excel now displays the Text pane and the SmartArt graphic. The Text pane contains five placeholder text lines, each corresponding to one box in the SmartArt graphic.

4   In the first line of the Text pane, type: `Promote responsible tourism`.

5   Click in the next line of the Text pane.

6   For each of the placeholder text lines, repeat steps 4 and 5 with the following text:
> `Promote eco-education`
> `Promote eco-friendly tourism operators`
> `Offer unique and different tours`
> `Ensure customers enjoy themselves`

To insert a new line into the graphic, simply add a new shape. Since each of these lines form a separate SmartArt shape, adding a new shape to the group adds a new line of text.

7   Click anywhere in line two. Then, under **SmartArt Tools**, on the **Design** tab, in the **Create Graphic** group, click **Add Shape**.

Alternatively, you can add a new blank line by moving to the end of the line and pressing ENTER.

8   In this new line, type: `Reduce footprint of tourism activities`.

The worksheet should now look similar to the following example:

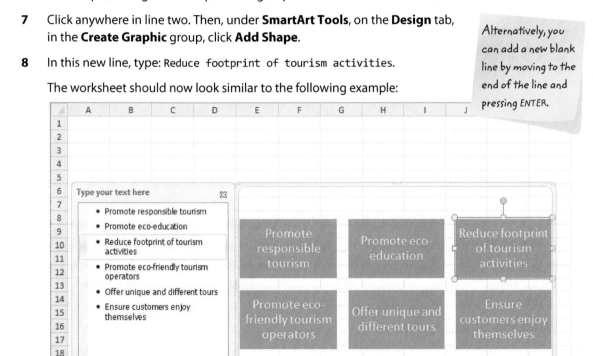

SmartArt graphics will allow you to convert any line into sub-bullets underneath the previous line.

9   Click anywhere in the fourth line of text and then, under **SmartArt Tools**, on the **Design** tab, in the **Create Graphic** group, click **Demote**.

The fourth line of text is now a sub-bullet of the third line of text. Repeat this for the other lines of text.

10   Repeat step 9 for the third and second lines of text.

Add a new shape and demote the remaining lines below it.

11   Click at the end of fourth line of text, press `Enter` to add a new blank line and type: `Operate a viable business`.

> To convert the sub-bullets back to their previous positions, under **SmartArt Tools**, on the **Design** tab, in the **Create Graphic** group, click **Promote**. Or press `Shift`+`Tab` on each of these lines.

Alternatively, you can demote a line of text by pressing TAB, and promote a line of text by pressing SHIFT+TAB.

12   With the cursor still in the new line of text, press `Shift`+`Tab`.

13   Click in the last two lines of text, and press `Tab` in each of those lines.

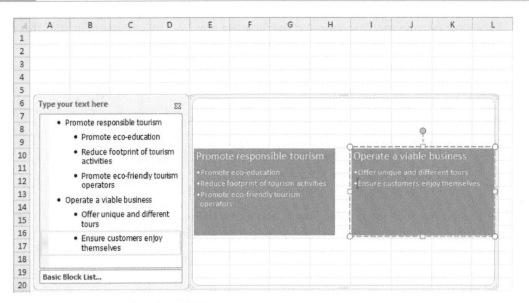

Use the Ribbon to turn the Text Pane off and on.

14   Under **SmartArt Tools**, on the **Design** tab, in the **Create Graphic** group, click **Text Pane** to close the Text Pane.

15   Under **SmartArt Tools**, on the **Design** tab, in the **Create Graphic** group, click **Text Pane** again to display it again.

You can move each of the panes around independently of the other ones. You can also resize SmartArt graphics as a group or individually.

16   Click on the Text Pane header (the gray area at the top of the Text Pane) and drag it to the right side of the SmartArt Pane.

17   Position the mouse over one of the four edges of the SmartArt Pane and drag it to the upper left corner of the worksheet. If necessary, drag the Text Pane to a new position to the right of the SmartArt Pane.

You can also change the color pattern.

18   Under **SmartArt Tools**, on the **Design** tab, in the **SmartArt Styles** group, click **Change Colors**. Click on a theme color of your choice.

19   Under **SmartArt Tools**, on the **Design** tab, in the **SmartArt Styles** group, click the **More** button next to the **Visual Styles**. Click on a visual style of your choice.

The worksheet may look similar to the following example (except for the visual style and theme color):

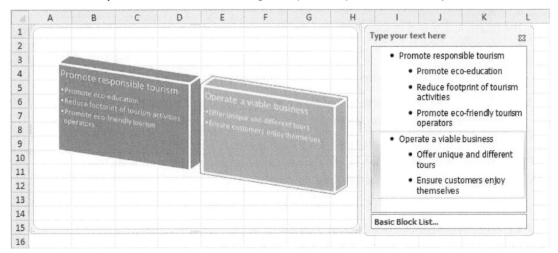

You can also change the layout without losing any of the text.

20 Under **SmartArt Tools**, on the **Design** tab, in the **Layouts** group, click the **More** button next to the **Visual Styles**. Click **More Layouts**.

Excel displays the Choose a SmartArt Graphic dialog box again.

21 Scroll down and choose another layout of your choice and click **OK**. If desired, choose a different visual style.

22 Click in a blank area of the worksheet outside of the SmartArt Pane and the Text Pane.

The completed worksheet may look similar to the following (except for the layout, theme color and visual style):

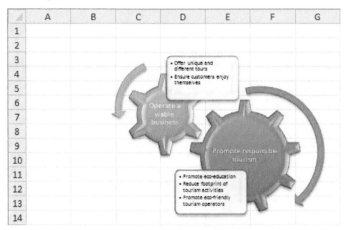

23 Click on one of the SmartArt graphics to reactivate the SmartArt Pane and Text Pane.

24 Save and close the workbook.

Lesson Summary

In this lesson, you learned to work with different types of illustrations, including shapes, WordArt, pictures, clip art graphics and SmartArt. You should now be able to:

☑ draw different types of shapes on a worksheet

☑ move, resize and format shapes

☑ use WordArt objects

☑ insert clip art and pictures

☑ use the Image Editor tools

☑ insert screenshots

☑ resize, reshape and rotate graphics objects

☑ insert SmartArt objects

Review Questions

1. Explain how you would draw a shape such as a rectangle. Begin with selecting it and continue to drawing it on the worksheet.

2. Provide at least two examples of what you can do after you have selected a graphic object.

3. Give examples of the types of formatting you can apply to a graphic object.

4. Provide an example of how you might use WordArt in a worksheet.

5. Explain why you might want to use the Copy option with a clip art graphic instead of inserting it directly into the worksheet.

6. Provide at least four examples of the types of formatting that you can apply to both pictures and clip art.

7. Provide examples of when you might want to use SmartArt in a workbook.

8. Provide an example of why you would use the Text pane for a SmartArt diagram.

MMM
Go online for
Additional
Review and
Activities

Microsoft®
Excel® 2010
Core Certification

Lesson 8: Analyzing, Organizing and Sharing Workbooks

Lesson Objectives

In this lesson, you will look at various methods of analyzing, organizing, linking and sharing workbooks. On successful completion of this lesson, you will be able to:

☐ sort data

☐ use the AutoFilter feature to find specific data

☐ create, modify and delete range names

☐ create, modify and delete hyperlinks

☐ create and delete comments

☐ import and export data with other programs

☐ change workbook document properties

☐ use Office BackStage to share workbooks with others

Sorting Data

8.2

Worksheets with a large amount of data are often difficult to understand. Excel provides a sorting tool that enables you to change the sequence of the data based on the values in selected columns. After sorting, the data becomes more readable. You can sort and re-sort the data as many times as required, using different columns each time. You can sort the data by columns or rows, but the most common method is sorting by rows (with column headers and the data extending downwards).

Sorting by Single-Level Data

The Ribbon offers the quickest method of sorting your data, but you are limited to sorting by one column. The Ribbon has two ready-to-use buttons for this:

- on the **Home** tab, in the **Editing** group, click **Sort & Filter** and then click **Sort A to Z** or **Sort Z to A**, or
- on the **Data** tab, in the **Sort & Filter** group, click **Sort A to Z** or **Sort Z to A**.

MMM
Finding a Tour
Online
Exercise

Sorting by Multi-Level Data

In many cases, you will need to sort by more than one column to handle situations with multiple rows with the same value (e.g., a list of names where several people have the same last name). Excel allows you to choose the custom sort option, which displays the sort dialog box.

This dialog box provides a comprehensive set of options for sorting your data:

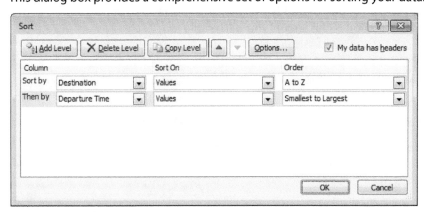

Add Level, Delete Level, Copy Level	Add, delete or copy sort columns or rows. Note that the topmost sort key is the highest (primary) sorting level, followed by the remaining levels in descending order.
Move up / Move down	Move the selected sort level higher or lower in the sorting sequence.
Options	Sort by columns or rows, and choose whether to be case-sensitive.
My data has headers	Tell Excel to treat the first row of cells as data or field labels.
Column/Row	Identify the column or row to be used for a sort level.
Sort On	Includes (cell data) *Values*, *Cell Color*, *Font Color*, or *Cell Icon*.

Order	Sort data in ascending (*A to Z, Smallest to Largest*) or descending (*Z to A, Largest to Smallest*) order.
Sort by	Determine the first column or row Excel will use to sort the database—the primary sort level.
Then by	Determine the next columns or rows for sorting, if necessary. When there are multiple rows that match the primary sort key, this determines the sort order within the first column grouping.

With the Sort dialog box, if the primary sort level contains repeating values, you can choose up to 64 columns or rows as sort levels. You can sort the data in each sort level in ascending or descending sequence. Each sort level can also be sorted using the cell data, fill color, font color or by cell icon.

If the range of cells being sorted does not contain column or rows headers, turn off the **My data has headers** option. Use this option to prevent sorting the header data together with the other data—they will remain in their place as headers.

Learn the Skill

This exercise demonstrates how to sort a table of data using one column, and then multiple columns, as sort keys.

1   Open the *Flights* workbook and save it as `Flights - Student`.

First, sort the data using a column containing text data.

2   Select any cell in the *Airline* column.

3   On the **Home** tab, in the **Editing** group, click **Sort & Filter** and then click **Sort A to Z**.

You have now sorted the data by airline name. Look closely to see how Excel has sorted the data for each group of rows with the same airline name.

> *Be sure to select a cell below the header row — Excel determines how to sort for the column based on the type of data in the selected cell.*

> *This sort button is also available in the **Data** tab.*

	A	B	C	D
1	Airline	Flight #	Destination	Departure Time
2	Aer Lingus	104	Dublin (DUB)	5:45 PM
3	Aer Lingus	110	Shannon (SNN)	6:30 PM
4	Aer Lingus	108	Dublin (DUB)	9:50 PM
5	Aeroflot	316	Moscow (SVO)	7:00 PM
6	AeroMexico	405	Mexico City (MEX)	9:00 AM
7	AeroMexico	5279	Mexico City (MEX)	9:05 AM
8	AeroMexico	5878	Rome (FCO)	5:30 PM
9	AeroMexico	5904	Barcelona (BCN)	5:35 PM
10	AeroMexico	403	Mexico City (MEX)	5:50 PM
11	AeroMexico	5760	Richmond, VA (RIC)	6:35 PM
12	AeroMexico	5610	Albany, NY (ALB)	7:00 PM
13	AeroMexico	5388	Norfolk, VA (ORF)	7:30 PM

Now sort a column containing numbers in descending order (largest values at the top to the smallest values at the bottom).

4   Select any cell in the *Flight #* column.

5   On the **Home** tab, in the **Editing** group, click **Sort & Filter** and then click **Sort Largest to Smallest**.

Now try sorting by a column containing time data in ascending order.

6   Select any cell in the *Departure Time* column.

7   On the **Data** tab, in the **Sort & Filter** group, click **Sort Smallest to Largest**.

	A	B	C	D
1	Airline	Flight #	Destination	Departure Time
2	US Airways	5211	Seoul (ICN)	12:30 AM
3	United Airlines	1069	Seoul (ICN)	12:30 AM
4	Asiana Airlines	221	Seoul (ICN)	12:30 AM
5	Delta Air Lines	7928	Seoul (ICN)	12:50 AM
6	Korean Airlines	86	Seoul (ICN)	12:50 AM
7	American Airlines	8297	Mexico City (MEX)	12:55 AM
8	Delta Air Lines	6870	Bogota (BOG)	12:55 AM
9	Avianca	285	Bogota (BOG)	12:55 AM
10	Mexicana	1	Mexico City (MEX)	12:55 AM
11	Caribbean Airlines Limited	425	Port-of-Spain (POS)	1:05 AM
12	Delta Air Lines	383	Georgetown (GEO)	1:10 AM
13	Prince Edward Air	9743	Hamilton (YHM)	1:15 AM
14	ICL Express	941	Liege (LGG)	1:30 AM
15	Korean Airlines	258	Anchorage, AK (ANC)	3:43 AM
16	Asiana Airlines	587	Brussels (BRU)	3:55 AM
17	American Intl.	543	Amsterdam (AMS)	4:00 AM
18	United Airlines	5317	San Salvador (SAL)	4:42 AM
19	US Airways	4933	San Salvador (SAL)	4:42 AM
20	Taca Airlines	567	San Salvador (SAL)	4:42 AM
21	El Al Israel	8147	Miami, FL (MIA)	5:30 AM
22	American Airlines	1229	Miami, FL (MIA)	5:30 AM

Now sort the data using two columns.

8   Ensure that the active cell is anywhere within the data range, then on the **Home** tab, in the **Editing** group, click **Sort & Filter** and then **Custom Sort**.

Excel displays the Sort dialog box.

9   Ensure that you have selected **My data has headers**.

10   Click the arrow next to the **Sort by** field and click **Destination**.

The Destination column is the primary sort key. Use the Departure Time column as the secondary sort key.

11   Click **Add Level** to add another sort key.

12   Click the arrow for **Then by** and then click **Departure Time**.

13   Click **OK**.

> *You can also open the Sort dialog box from the Data tab.*

Now add a third sort key.

14   On the **Data** tab, in the **Sort & Filter** group, click **Sort**.

15   Click on the **Then by** row to select that row. The best area to click is on the **Then by** text so that you do not click in any of the selection fields.

16   Click **Add Level** to add another sort key below the existing rows.

17   Click the arrow for the second **Then by** and then click **Airline**.

18   Click the arrow next to the **Order** field for the second **Then by** and click **Z to A** to sort this field in descending order.

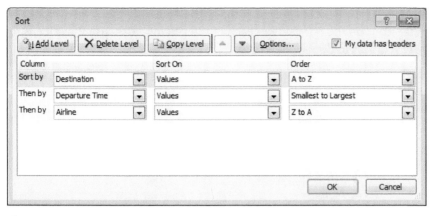

19 Click **OK**.

Delete the middle sort sequence.

20 On the **Data** tab, in the **Sort & Filter** group, click **Sort**.

21 Click on the first **Then by** row to select that row.

22 Click **Delete Level** and click **OK**.

The list is now sorted first by destination in ascending order and then by airline in descending order. The worksheet now looks similar to the following example:

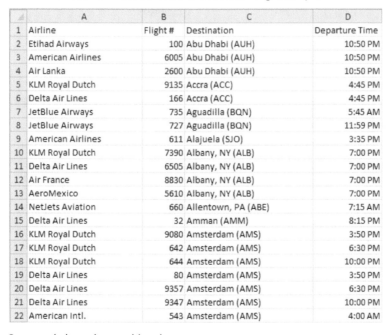

	A	B	C	D
1	Airline	Flight #	Destination	Departure Time
2	Etihad Airways	100	Abu Dhabi (AUH)	10:50 PM
3	American Airlines	6005	Abu Dhabi (AUH)	10:50 PM
4	Air Lanka	2600	Abu Dhabi (AUH)	10:50 PM
5	KLM Royal Dutch	9135	Accra (ACC)	4:45 PM
6	Delta Air Lines	166	Accra (ACC)	4:45 PM
7	JetBlue Airways	735	Aguadilla (BQN)	5:45 AM
8	JetBlue Airways	727	Aguadilla (BQN)	11:59 PM
9	American Airlines	611	Alajuela (SJO)	3:35 PM
10	KLM Royal Dutch	7390	Albany, NY (ALB)	7:00 PM
11	Delta Air Lines	6505	Albany, NY (ALB)	7:00 PM
12	Air France	8830	Albany, NY (ALB)	7:00 PM
13	AeroMexico	5610	Albany, NY (ALB)	7:00 PM
14	NetJets Aviation	660	Allentown, PA (ABE)	7:15 AM
15	Delta Air Lines	32	Amman (AMM)	8:15 PM
16	KLM Royal Dutch	9080	Amsterdam (AMS)	3:50 PM
17	KLM Royal Dutch	642	Amsterdam (AMS)	6:30 PM
18	KLM Royal Dutch	644	Amsterdam (AMS)	10:00 PM
19	Delta Air Lines	80	Amsterdam (AMS)	3:50 PM
20	Delta Air Lines	9357	Amsterdam (AMS)	6:30 PM
21	Delta Air Lines	9347	Amsterdam (AMS)	10:00 PM
22	American Intl.	543	Amsterdam (AMS)	4:00 AM

23 Save and close the workbook.

Filtering Information

8.1

Worksheets are often used to store large amounts of data. Finding information in large worksheets is often difficult because of the sheer volume. Sorting the rows is one way of making it easier to find information; however, you still have to look through many if not all the rows in the worksheet. Another way to locate information quickly is to use a filter to hide the rows you are not interested in viewing. Filtering does not change the content of your worksheet or the sequence of the rows (like the way sorting does), only what you see of your worksheet.

The quickest and easiest way to filter data in Excel is to use the AutoFilter tool. When you activate this tool, Excel places AutoFilter icons on the right side of each of the column titles. Use these icons to specify the selection criteria that Excel uses to display the records.

In its simplest form, the AutoFilter finds and displays the rows where the value in the selected column is equal to a specific value.

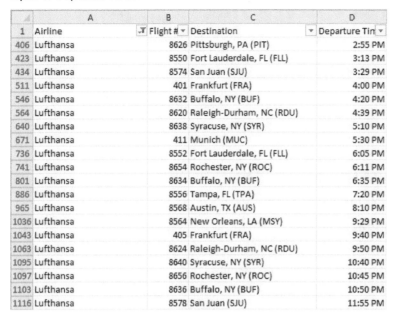

	A	B	C	D
1	Airline	Flight #	Destination	Departure Tin
406	Lufthansa	8626	Pittsburgh, PA (PIT)	2:55 PM
423	Lufthansa	8550	Fort Lauderdale, FL (FLL)	3:13 PM
434	Lufthansa	8574	San Juan (SJU)	3:29 PM
511	Lufthansa	401	Frankfurt (FRA)	4:00 PM
546	Lufthansa	8632	Buffalo, NY (BUF)	4:20 PM
564	Lufthansa	8620	Raleigh-Durham, NC (RDU)	4:39 PM
640	Lufthansa	8638	Syracuse, NY (SYR)	5:10 PM
671	Lufthansa	411	Munich (MUC)	5:30 PM
736	Lufthansa	8552	Fort Lauderdale, FL (FLL)	6:05 PM
741	Lufthansa	8654	Rochester, NY (ROC)	6:11 PM
801	Lufthansa	8634	Buffalo, NY (BUF)	6:35 PM
886	Lufthansa	8556	Tampa, FL (TPA)	7:20 PM
965	Lufthansa	8568	Austin, TX (AUS)	8:10 PM
1036	Lufthansa	8564	New Orleans, LA (MSY)	9:29 PM
1043	Lufthansa	405	Frankfurt (FRA)	9:40 PM
1063	Lufthansa	8624	Raleigh-Durham, NC (RDU)	9:50 PM
1095	Lufthansa	8640	Syracuse, NY (SYR)	10:40 PM
1097	Lufthansa	8656	Rochester, NY (ROC)	10:45 PM
1103	Lufthansa	8636	Buffalo, NY (BUF)	10:50 PM
1116	Lufthansa	8578	San Juan (SJU)	11:55 PM

The AutoFilter has the flexibility to help you build more complex queries, which you can use to narrow down the results and avoid selecting rows that you do not want. For example, you can select criteria that examine two or more columns, or that are equal to one of two or more values. In addition, Excel provides powerful selection criteria that are specific to columns containing text, numbers or dates, such as the following:

Numbers   Evaluate data in the selected column with the commonly used comparison operators (equals, greater than, less than, greater than or equal to, between and so on) as well as the Top 10 values (or rows with values above or below the average of all values in the column).

Dates	Evaluate date-type data using special criteria that are specific for dates, such as comparing the date of today with tomorrow, yesterday, this/next/last week, this/next/last month, this/next/last quarter, this/next/last year or year to date.	Equals... Before... After... Between... Tomorrow Today Yesterday Next Week This Week Last Week Next Month This Month Last Month Next Quarter This Quarter Last Quarter Next Year This Year Last Year Year to Date All Dates in the Period ▶ Custom Filter...
Text	Evaluate text data using special criteria that are specific to text, such as begins or ends with (text), or contains or does not contain (text).	Equals... Does Not Equal... Begins With... Ends With... Contains... Does Not Contain... Custom Filter...

Learn the Skill

This exercise demonstrates how to use AutoFilters in various ways on a worksheet.

1   Open the *Flights* workbook.

Do a quick visual scan of the worksheet to see how many rows are in it.

2   Scroll down to the bottom of the data (row 1121), then scroll back to the top.

Activate the AutoFilter and select all rows for a specific airline.

3   Select any cell in the data (between cells **A2:D1121**).

4   On the **Data** tab in the **Sort & Filter** group, click **Filter**.

> *Another way of activating the AutoFilter icons is on the **Home** tab, in the **Editing** group, click **Sort & Filter** and click **Filter**.*

AutoFilter arrows now appear next to each field name:

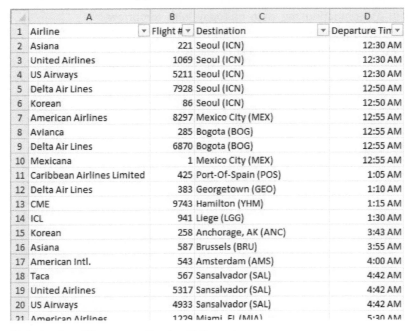

5   Click the AutoFilter arrow for the *Airline* column.

The AutoFilter menu displays a list of every unique value in this column. You set the filter by turning the check box on or off for the value(s) you want.

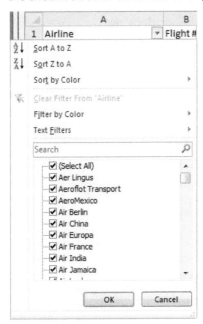

6   Click **Select All** to turn it off.

7   Scroll down the list, click *Lufthansa* to turn it on and click **OK**.

Notice the row numbers of the records that remain displayed from the database. Excel hides the rows that do not meet the criteria and displays only records that have a matching value in the filtered field. Excel also changes the AutoFilter icon to indicate that it is using a field to limit the records displayed.

Now redisplay all records.

8   Click the AutoFilter arrow for the *Airline* column and click **Clear Filter From "Airline"**.

The conditions you select are called **filter criteria.** You can also set up criteria for date, time and numeric values.

9   Click the AutoFilter arrow for the *Departure Time* column, click **Select All** to turn it off. Click *6:00 AM* to turn that check box on and click **OK**.

You can set date, time and numeric AutoFilters to look for a range of values using comparison operators such as greater than, less then, between and more. Suppose you want to find all flights departing between 2 PM and 3 PM. Text fields contain a similar set of comparison operators.

10   On the **Data** tab, in the **Sort & Filter** group, click **Clear**.

11   Click the AutoFilter arrow for the *Departure Time* column, click **Number Filters and** then click **Between**.

12   Select the departure time values as shown in the following example screen:

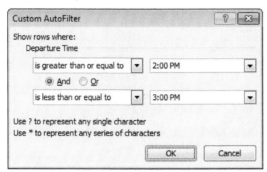

13   Click **OK**.

The results should look similar to the following example:

	A	B	C	D
1	Airline	Flight #	Destination	Departure Tim
363	American Airlines	4655	Raleigh-Durham, NC (RDU)	2:00 PM
364	British Airways	5519	Raleigh-Durham, NC (RDU)	2:00 PM
365	Delta Air Lines	7854	Seoul (ICN)	2:00 PM
366	Jet Airways	5105	Raleigh-Durham, NC (RDU)	2:00 PM
367	Korean	82	Seoul (ICN)	2:00 PM
368	MALEV Hungarian Airlines	4122	Raleigh-Durham, NC (RDU)	2:00 PM
369	Saudi Arabian	24	Jeddah (JED)	2:00 PM
370	SouthAfrican	7451	Washington, DC (IAD)	2:04 PM
371	United Airlines	7112	Washington, DC (IAD)	2:04 PM
372	JetBlue Airways	821	Santo Domingo (SDQ)	2:17 PM
373	Alaska Airlines	4273	Boston, MA (BOS)	2:20 PM
374	American Airlines	4638	Boston, MA (BOS)	2:20 PM
375	Japan Airlines	5650	Boston, MA (BOS)	2:20 PM
376	Jet Airways	5102	Boston, MA (BOS)	2:20 PM
377	MALEV Hungarian Airlines	4121	Boston, MA (BOS)	2:20 PM
378	JetBlue Airways	615	Jacksonville, FL (JAX)	2:23 PM
379	JetBlue Airways	143	West Palm Beach, FL (PBI)	2:29 PM

The AutoFilter selection menu includes a search field that you can use to find the filter values you are looking for quickly instead of scrolling up and down the list. In effect, you are applying a filter to the filter values. Suppose now that you want to find flight 8778. You can search for 8778. You can also use shorter search criteria, which will find all filter values that contain this search value in it.

14   On the **Data** tab, in the **Sort & Filter** group, click **Clear**.

15   Click the AutoFilter arrow for the *Flight #* column. Then type 87 in the Search text box (located above the Select All check box) to display a list of all values with 87 in it.

16 Click the **Select All Search Results** check box to turn it off. Then click the *8778* check box to turn it on and click **OK**.

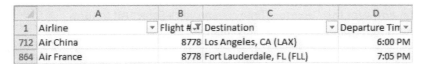

	A	B	C	D
1	Airline	Flight #	Destination	Departure Tim
712	Air China	8778	Los Angeles, CA (LAX)	6:00 PM
864	Air France	8778	Fort Lauderdale, FL (FLL)	7:05 PM

Excel does not limit you to selecting rows using only one value; you can also select multiple values for a single column.

17 On the **Data** tab, in the **Sort & Filter** group, click **Clear**.

18 Click the AutoFilter arrow for the *Airline* column and click **Select All** to turn it off. Click *KLM Royal Dutch* and *Lufthansa* to turn them on and click **OK**.

The results should look similar to the following example:

	A	B	C	D
1	Airline	Flight #	Destination	Departure Tim
33	KLM Royal Dutch	9362	Atlanta, GA (ATL)	6:00 AM
68	KLM Royal Dutch	5790	San Francisco, CA (SFO)	7:00 AM
69	KLM Royal Dutch	8342	Los Angeles, CA (LAX)	7:00 AM
70	KLM Royal Dutch	9356	Salt Lake City, UT (SLC)	7:00 AM
128	KLM Royal Dutch	9555	Chicago, IL (ORD)	8:10 AM
162	KLM Royal Dutch	9259	Buffalo, NY (BUF)	8:30 AM
163	KLM Royal Dutch	9734	Pittsburgh, PA (PIT)	8:30 AM
196	KLM Royal Dutch	5049	Burlington, VT (BTV)	9:00 AM
203	KLM Royal Dutch	5124	Detroit, MI (DTW)	9:05 AM
281	KLM Royal Dutch	7311	Chicago, IL (ORD)	11:20 AM
284	KLM Royal Dutch	9401	Minneapolis, MN (MSP)	11:25 AM
309	KLM Royal Dutch	9609	Detroit, MI (DTW)	12:20 PM
337	KLM Royal Dutch	9331	Tokyo (NRT)	1:10 PM
339	KLM Royal Dutch	9367	Rochester, NY (ROC)	1:20 PM
389	KLM Royal Dutch	7269	Buffalo, NY (BUF)	2:40 PM
406	Lufthansa	8626	Pittsburgh, PA (PIT)	2:55 PM
423	Lufthansa	8550	Fort Lauderdale, FL (FLL)	3:13 PM
427	KLM Royal Dutch	9285	Toronto (YYZ)	3:15 PM
431	KLM Royal Dutch	9382	Washington, DC (DCA)	3:25 PM

You may also select criteria across multiple fields. For example, try selecting all rows where the destination is Fort Lauderdale and the airline is KLM or Lufthansa.

19 Click the AutoFilter arrow for **Destination**, click **Select All** to turn it off and then click *Fort Lauderdale, FL (FLL)* to turn only that check box on. Click **OK**.

	A	B	C	D
1	Airline	Flight #	Destination	Departure Tim
423	Lufthansa	8550	Fort Lauderdale, FL (FLL)	3:13 PM
503	KLM Royal Dutch	9342	Fort Lauderdale, FL (FLL)	3:55 PM
736	Lufthansa	8552	Fort Lauderdale, FL (FLL)	6:05 PM
877	KLM Royal Dutch	7370	Fort Lauderdale, FL (FLL)	7:05 PM

This list shows that there are four flights departing today for Fort Lauderdale.

Now turn off the AutoFilter feature.

20 On the **Data** tab, in the **Sort & Filter** group, click **Filter**.

21 Close the workbook and discard the changes.

MMM
Filtering the
Tour List
Online
Exercise

Working with Named Ranges
Creating Named Ranges

When developing spreadsheets, you will find that they quickly become very large and it becomes difficult to keep track of all the cells. One feature in most spreadsheet programs is the ability to create a name for a cell or range of cells. It is much easier to understand the formula *=Revenues-Expenses* than a cryptic formula such as *=C7-C16*.

To define a range with a name, select the range and then use one of the following methods:

- On the **Formulas** tab, in the **Defined Names** group, click **Define Name**; or
- click in the **Name Box** and type the name; or
- right-click the selected range and then click **Define Name**.

Once you define a name for a cell or a range of cells, you can use that name when creating formulas. Excel also provides tools for applying range names to your existing formulas.

You can also quickly jump to a named range by using **Go To** or by selecting the named range from the **Name Box** list to the left of the Formula bar.

In addition to making spreadsheets easier to read, range names can make the process of entering cell data easier. Simply changing the range defined by a range name updates all formulas that use that range name; therefore, there is no need to edit every formula in the spreadsheet.

Range names can be from 1 to 255 characters in length. They may contain alphabetic or numeric characters (alphanumeric), underscores (_), backslashes (\), periods (.) and question marks (?). You cannot use spaces in range names. The first character must be alphanumeric, an underscore or a backslash.

Modifying and Deleting Named Ranges

You can use the Name Manager to modify and delete range names or change the cell range references.

Be cautious when deleting named ranges. When you delete a named range, any formula that refers to this name no longer displays the correct value. Deleting a range name may also cause a domino effect with other formulas that indirectly refer to this formula.

Learn the Skill

This exercise demonstrates how to create range names and set up formulas using those range names.

1   Open the *Income Statement* workbook and save as Income Statement - Student.

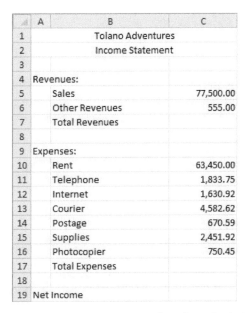

Now create a range name to use in sales calculations.

Excel can use either row or column headers as range names. However, this is not a good practice because formulas using this range name will often not recalculate correctly if you (or someone else) add more data. You should explicitly create range names instead.

2   Select cells **C5:C6**.

3   On the **Formulas** tab, in the **Defined Names** group, click **Define Name**.

The New Name dialog box displays with the cell range entered.

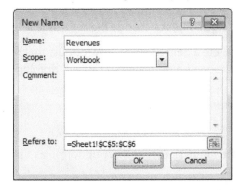

4   In the **Name** field, type: Revenues and click **OK**.

From now on, whenever you select these two cells, the range name **Revenues** displays in the **Name Box**, which appears to the left of the Formula Bar. If you click the arrow at the right side of the Name Box and select a range name, Excel will select that range of cells.

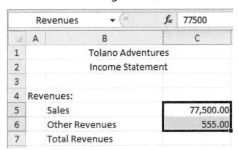

5   Select each of the cells in the cell range **C5:C6** and observe what displays in the Name Box.

6   Select the cell range **C5:C6** and observe what displays in the Name Box.

7   Select cells **C10:C16**. On the **Formulas** tab, in the **Defined Names** group, click **Define Name**.

8   In the **Name** field, type: Expenses and click **OK**.

Now enter summary formulas using this range name.

9   Select cell **C7**.

10 Type: =SUM(Revenues) and press ⌷Enter⌷.

Range names are not case sensitive.

Notice that as you type the first one or two characters of the range name, a quick tip box appears, showing you this name and other functions with similar names. You can double-click the range name in the quick tip box to select it

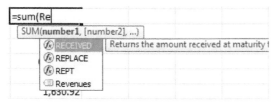

11 Select cell **C17**, type: =SUM(Expenses) and press ⌷Enter⌷.

You can also create a range name by selecting the desired cell(s) and clicking in the **Name Box** on the Formula bar. Then type the desired name and press ⌷Enter⌷.

12 Select cells **B7:C7**.

13 On the **Formulas** tab, in the **Defined Names** group, click **Create from Selection**.

14 Click **Left column** to turn it on and click **OK**.

15 Select cell **C7**.

Note that the range name in the Name Box is **Total_Revenues**.

Create a range name for the *Total Expenses* cell, but this time using the Name Manager.

Excel does not permit blank spaces in range names. You can use the underscore character between the words in a multi-word range name.

16 Select cell **C17**.

17 On the **Formulas** tab, in the **Defined Names** group, click **Name Manager**.

The Name Manager dialog box is now displayed.

18 In the Name Manager dialog box, click **New** to create a new range name.

19   Verify that the **Name** is Total_Expenses and that the **Refers to** field contains the formula =Sheet1!$C$17. Click **OK**.

If the New Name dialog box is blocking access to the worksheet behind it, you can minimize it temporarily by clicking the **Expand** button to the right of the **Refers to** field. You can then select a range of cells from the worksheet.

The Name Manager dialog box now has this new range name added, similar to the following example:

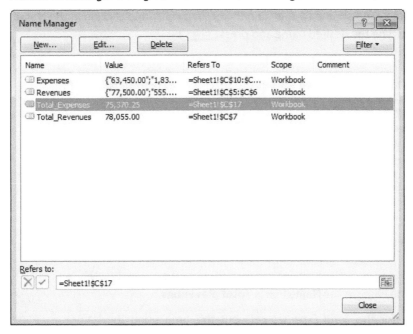

20   Click **Close** to close the Name Manager dialog box.

Enter the formula to calculate the Net Income, using the range names.

21   Select cell **C19**, and type: =

22   On the **Formulas** tab, in the **Defined Names** group, click **Use in Formula**.

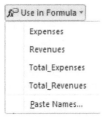

23   Click Total_Revenues, then press ⊖ to indicate that you are going to perform a subtraction.

24   On the **Formulas** tab, in the **Defined Names** group, click **Use in Formula**. Click Total_Expenses and press ⌅ Enter .

The completed worksheet will look similar to the following example:

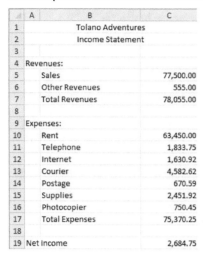

A common situation is adding more rows to a named range. As long as you add the rows inside the range, Excel automatically includes the new data as part of the range. If you add the new data below the range, you will need to expand the range to include the new row(s).

25 Click the gray header for row 17 to highlight the entire row. Right-click in the highlighted row and click **Insert** in the menu.

26 Select cell **B17**, type: Travel and press (Tab).

27 In cell **C17** type: 1400 and press (Enter).

Note that none of the figures in the report changed because the new entry sits outside of the named range Expenses. Now expand the named range to include the new entry.

When you first created the range name, you could have included additional blank cells for future growth. Then, as you add new entries to the list, Excel automatically recalculates the total expenses formula.

28 On the **Formulas** tab, in the **Defined Names** group, click **Name Manager**.

29 In the Name Manager dialog box, click the *Expenses* row to select it.

30 In the **Refers to** text field, change the range to **=Sheet1!$C$10:$C$17** as the range.

31 Click **Update** (the checkmark) to the left of the field to update the changes, and click **Close**.

The worksheet should now show the correct calculations for each of the functions, similar to this example:

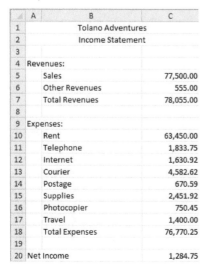

Try deleting a named range and see how it affects the worksheet.

32 On the **Formulas** tab, in the **Defined Names** group, click **Name Manager**.

33 Click the *Revenues* row and then click **Delete**.

Excel displays a message box asking you to confirm the deletion of this range name.

34 Click **OK** for the confirmation message box and then click **Close** to close the Name Manager dialog box.

As shown in the following example, when you remove a named range, Excel displays an error indicator regarding any formulas that depend on that name. Note also that the change has affected the formula in cell **C20** as well, even though it does not use the range name Revenues directly.

	A	B	C
4	Revenues:		
5		Sales	77,500.00
6		Other Revenues	555.00
7		Total Revenues	#NAME?
8			
9	Expenses:		
10		Rent	63,450.00
11		Telephone	1,833.75
12		Internet	1,630.92
13		Courier	4,582.62
14		Postage	670.59
15		Supplies	2,451.92
16		Photocopier	750.45
17		Travel	1,400.00
18		Total Expenses	76,770.25
19			
20	Net Income		#NAME?

35 In the Quick Access Toolbar, click **Undo**.

36 Save and close the workbook.

Using Hyperlinks

2.3

A hyperlink is a clickable element in an electronic document that you can use to jump to or open another document. The World Wide Web consists of web pages (which are essentially documents) containing text, images, videos and hyperlinks to other web pages. You can insert hyperlinks into workbooks to enable the same capability of launching web pages from the Internet or an internal corporate intranet, or open documents located on any computer within your local area network.

A hyperlink can be text or a picture on a page that links you from where you are to another location. This allows you to "jump" to that location, which may be in the same document, another document, a document or page on another Web site or an e-mail address.

Inserting Hyperlinks

By clicking a hyperlink, you can display the referenced document. Each hyperlink contains a code in the form of a Uniform Resource Locator (URL), which is the unique address for this document or page at this particular location on the Internet or intranet.

URLs can be stored in Excel worksheets or workbooks and used as hyperlinks to jump to other documents on the Internet or intranet, other Excel workbooks or other Microsoft Office documents.

To insert a hyperlink, use one of the following methods:

- On the **Insert** tab, in the **Links** group, click **Hyperlink**; or
- right-click on a cell and click **Hyperlink**; or
- press Ctrl + K.

The displayed Insert Hyperlink dialog box allows you to insert one of four types of hyperlinks:

Existing File or Web Page	Used to link to workbooks, files, or documents stored on a local or networked hard drive, or on the intranet or the Internet.

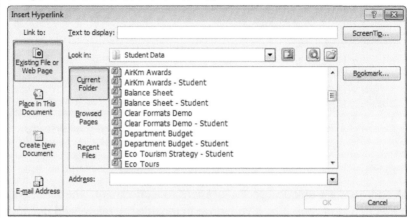

Place in This Document	Used to link to a cell or named range of cells in the current workbook, either in the current worksheet or another worksheet.

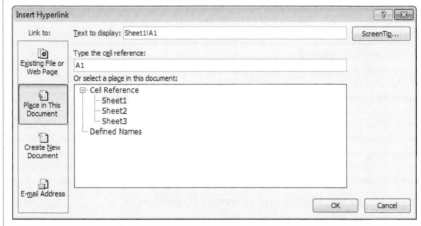

Create New Document	Used to create a new workbook using the name that you specify in the **Name of new document** text box and located in the folder specified under **Full path**.

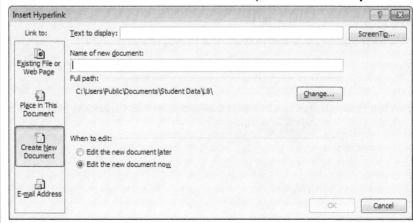

E-mail Address	Used to launch the e-mail program (e.g. Outlook) installed on the local computer, and create a new e-mail message using the e-mail address and subject line specified in this dialog box.

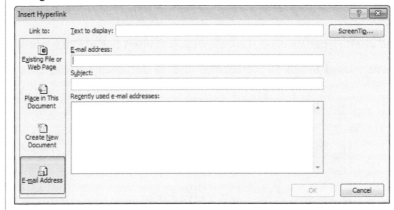

A **mailto** URL is a special type of URL used by e-mail systems.

Modifying and Deleting Hyperlinks

Hyperlink addresses are unique, specific locations to a document, whether it is stored on the Internet, the local intranet or a local computer. If you move or rename the referenced document, you must change the hyperlink.

You may also want to change the text displayed in the worksheet for the hyperlink or add a custom ScreenTip.

When you no longer need the hyperlink, you can remove the reference. The text displayed for the hyperlink remains in the cell.

To modify a hyperlink in the worksheet, use one of the following methods:

- Right-click the hyperlink and then click **Edit Hyperlink**; or

- move the cell pointer to the cell containing the link and then, on the **Insert** tab, in the **Links** group, click **Hyperlink** to display the Edit Hyperlink dialog box. Make the necessary changes and close the dialog box.

To delete a hyperlink in the worksheet, use one of the following methods:

- Right-click the link and then click **Remove Hyperlink**; or

- move the cell pointer to the cell containing the link and then, on the **Insert** tab, in the **Links** group, click **Hyperlink** to display the Edit Hyperlink dialog box. Click **Remove Link**.

Learn the Skill

This exercise demonstrates how to create and modify hyperlinks in an Excel workbook.

1   Open the *Financial Statements* workbook and save it as Financial Statements – Student.

▲	A	B	C	D
1	Tolano Adventures			
2				
3	Website:			
4				
5	Income Statement:			
6				
7	Balance Sheet:			

Insert a hyperlink to a website in cell **B3**.

2   Select cell **B3**.

3   On the **Insert** tab, in the **Links** group, click **Hyperlink**.

4   Click in the **Address** field and type: `http://tolanoadventures.com`.

5   Click in **Text to display** and change the contents to: `Tolano Adventures`.

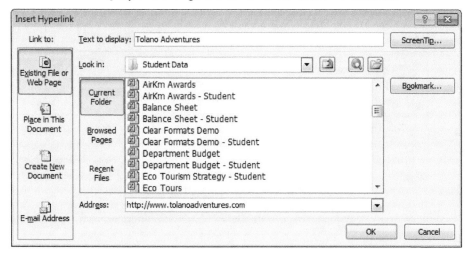

6   Click **OK**.

Now insert two hyperlinks to other workbooks.

7   Select cell **B5.**

8   On the **Insert** tab, in the **Links** group, click **Hyperlink**.

9   Scroll down and select the *Income Statement* workbook. If necessary, select a different folder in the **Look in** list where the data files are located, as directed by the instructor.

10   Click **OK**.

11   Right-click in cell **B7**, then click **Hyperlink**.

12   Scroll down and select the *Balance Sheet* workbook and click **OK**.

Test one of the hyperlinks by clicking on it.

13   Position the mouse cursor over the hyperlink in cell **B5;** the cursor changes to a white pointing hand.

Notice that a screen tip will appear with the URL for the *Income Statement* workbook.

14   Click the *Income Statement* hyperlink.

The *Income Statement* workbook is now open on top of the *Financial Statements* workbook.

15   Close the *Income Statement* workbook.

The color of the hyperlink has changed to indicate that it has been used. The worksheet should look similar to the following example:

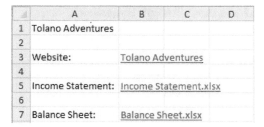

Now manually change one of the hyperlinks to point at a different workbook.

16   Right-click the *Income Statement* hyperlink in cell **B5** and then click **Edit Hyperlink**.

17   In the Edit Hyperlink dialog box, scroll down and select the Income Statement – Student workbook.

18   Click **Text to display**, and change the contents to: Link to Income Statement - Student.

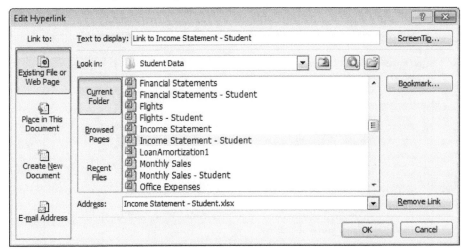

19   Click **OK**.

You can change the hyperlink text directly on the worksheet without having to launch the Edit Hyperlink dialog box. However, if you click on the cell containing the hyperlink, the workbook will open. The next two steps will show you how to work around the problem.

20   Click in cell **A7 and** then press the ➔ key to make cell **B7** into the active cell without activating the hyperlink.

> You can select any nearby cell and then use the cursor keys on the keyboard to select the cell.

21   Press the F2 key to switch to edit mode, change the link text to Balance Sheet workbook and press Enter.

There are two other ways of selecting a cell without activating the hyperlink, by holding down the Ctrl key while clicking on the cell, or by clicking and holding down the left mouse button on the cell for a few seconds, until the mouse pointer changes from a hand to a white cross. Release the left mouse button and press the F2 key to go into edit mode.

The worksheet should now look similar to the following:

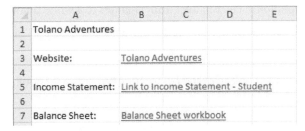

Now enter a custom ScreenTip for one of the hyperlinks.

22   Right-click the *Balance Sheet* hyperlink in cell **B7** and then click **Edit Hyperlink**.

23   In the Edit Hyperlink dialog box, click **ScreenTip**.

24   In the Set Hyperlink ScreenTip dialog box, type: This is the link to the Balance Sheet workbook and click **OK**.

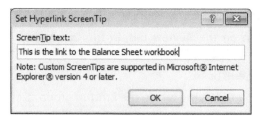

25 In the Edit Hyperlink dialog box, click **OK**.

26 Position the cursor over the hyperlink in cell **B7** to view the ScreenTip.

Test the change to the Balance Sheet hyperlink to make sure that it is working properly.

27 Click the hyperlink in cell **B7**.

28 Close the *Balance Sheet* workbook.

Now delete one of the hyperlinks.

29 Right-click the hyperlink in cell **B7** and click **Remove Hyperlink**.

The hyperlink in cell B7 has now changed to plain text.

30 Save and close the workbook.

Using Comments

Comments are like "sticky" notes on a hard-copy document. You typically use them so that several users who are sharing a workbook can annotate the spreadsheet with their various comments. Excel automatically adds the current user's name (as shown in the Excel Options dialog box located in the Backstage) at the top of the comment text box. The final reviewer can then act on each comment and follow up with the originator, if necessary.

In non-workgroup situations, you can use comments to remind yourself about things you need to do or to record detailed information about formulas you have used for future reference. Spreadsheets typically contain large volumes of numbers, titles and formulas to produce the desired results. Comments often help with explanations. The traditional way of adding comments is to enter free-form text into cells on the worksheet. Although this method is simple and works well with smaller spreadsheets, it does not work well with large spreadsheets where the space available may be far away and you have to draw lines from your comments to the cells to which you are referring. Embedded comments are better because you can insert them directly into the cells and display them only when you want to see them.

To insert a comment into a worksheet, use one of the following methods:

- Select the cell where the comment will be inserted, then on the **Review** tab, in the **Comments** group, click **New Comment**; or
- press (Shift)+(F2); or
- right-click the cell where the comment will be inserted and then click **Insert Comment**.

To temporarily display the contents of an individual comment, position the cursor over a cell containing the (**Comment Symbol**). When you move the cursor away, only the Comment Symbol displays.

To force a comment to remain displayed, use one of the following methods:

- Select the cell containing the comment, then on the **Review** tab, in the **Comments** group, click **Show/Hide Comment**; or
- right-click the cell containing the comment and click **Show/Hide Comment**.

To display the contents of all comments in a worksheet, on the **Review** tab, in the **Comments** group, click **Show All Comments**.

To delete a comment, use one of the following methods:

- Select the cell containing the comment, then on the **Review** tab, in the **Comments** group, click **Delete**; or
- right-click the cell and then click **Delete Comment**; or
- select the cell containing the comment, then on the **Home** tab, in the **Editing** group, click **Clear**, and then click **Clear Comments**.

Learn the Skill

In this exercise, you will insert comments into a worksheet.

1   Open the *Income Statement - Student* workbook.

2   Select cell **C6**.

3   On the **Review** tab, in the **Comments** group, click **New Comment**.

4   In the comment box, type: Revenue source was sales of souvenir T-shirts.

The worksheet appears as follows with the comment displayed.

	A	B	C	D	E	F
1		Tolano Adventures				
2		Income Statement				
3						
4	Revenues:					
5		Sales	77,500.00			
6		Other Revenues	555.00			
7		Total Revenues	78,055.00			
8						
9	Expenses:					
10		Rent	63,450.00			
11		Telephone	1,833.75			
12		Internet	1,630.92			
13		Courier	4,582.62			
14		Postage	670.59			
15		Supplies	2,451.92			
16		Photocopier	750.45			
17		Travel	1,400.00			
18		Total Expenses	76,770.25			
19						
20	Net Income		1,284.75			

Comment on cells C5–C7: `<student 1>: Revenue source was sales of souvenir T-shirts.`

5   Click anywhere on the worksheet away from the comment.

Excel displays a ◤ **(Comment Symbol)** in this cell to remind you that you have inserted a comment there; otherwise, the comment would remain hidden until you placed the cursor over that cell.

6   With the current active cell elsewhere on the worksheet, move the cursor over cell **C6**.

The comment box reappears and continues to display until you move the cursor elsewhere.

7   Select cell **C20** and, on the **Review** tab, in the **Comments** group, click **New Comment**.

8   In the comment box, type: Net income needs to be improved!

9   Click elsewhere on the worksheet.

If necessary, you can display all comments on a worksheet at one time. You may want to do this if you are seeing the worksheet for the first time, or if others have added many comments since you last opened the workbook.

10 Select cell **C20** again and then, on the **Review** tab, in the **Comments** group, click **Show/Hide Comment**. Click elsewhere on the worksheet.

You can now hide the comment again.

11 Select cell **C20 and** then, on the **Review** tab, in the **Comments** group, click **Show/Hide Comment** again.

You can also make all the comments in the worksheet display at the same time.

12 On the **Review** tab, in the **Comments** group, click **Show All Comments**.

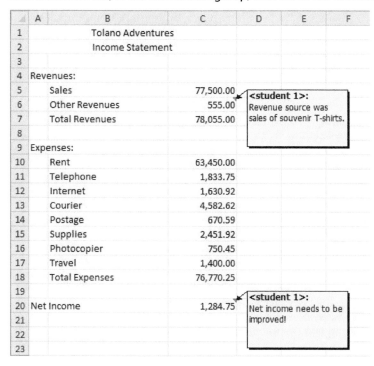

13 On the **Review** tab, in the **Comments** group, click **Show All Comments** again to hide all comments.

14 On the **Review** tab, in the **Comments** group, click **Next**.

15 Click the **Next** button two more times until Excel displays a message box.

16 Click Cancel to close the message box and click elsewhere on the worksheet.

You can delete a comment from a cell when you no longer need it.

17 Select cell **C6**. Then on the **Review** tab, in the **Comments** group, click **Delete**.

18 Save and close the workbook.

Importing and Exporting Data

Importing Data Files

1.3

Most businesses use various specialized computer systems for their operations. Typically these systems reside on servers, other PCs, or even mainframe computers. The challenge has always been trying to move data from one system to another without having to manually re-enter the data. Almost all of these systems have the ability to export data into files, and the text data file format is the most commonly used.

Because Excel uses a customized binary format for its own workbook data, it has to convert external data files by importing them.

On the **Data** tab, in the **Get External Data** group are four icons used for importing external data:

The **From Other Sources** button shows a drop down menu for the remaining options for importing data:

These import options are as follows:

From Access	Imports directly from a Microsoft Access database.
From Web	Imports data that is displayed in specific locations of a web page.
From Text	Imports data from a file containing numeric and alphabetic data in text format.
From SQL Server	Imports data from a Microsoft SQL Server database.
From Analysis Services	Imports data from the Analysis Services module, a component of Microsoft SQL Server.
From XML Data Import	Imports data from a XML-formatted file. The XML format is rapidly becoming a standard format for exchanging data between different systems.
From Data Connection Wizard	Imports data using a data connection (such as ODBC) to another system.
From Microsoft Query	Imports data using the Microsoft Query module.

The text format has at least three sub-formats:

- Delimited: The text data is separated by a pre-defined character such as comma, tab, semi-colon, blank space, or possibly other characters. Excel uses this delimiter to separate the line of text into separate values to be inserted into each worksheet cell.

- Fixed width: Each value has a specific start and end position in every line of text. Excel uses the position of the text to separate the data into each worksheet cell.

Learn the Skill

In this exercise, you will import a comma delimited text file into a worksheet.

1   Create a new blank workbook.

2   On the **Data** tab, in the **Get External Data** group, click **From Text**.

The Import Text File dialog box is displayed.

3   Locate and select the *Eco Cruises.txt* file and click **Import** in the Import Text File dialog box.

The Text Import Wizard will start automatically.

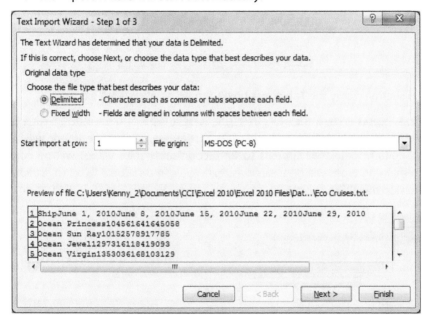

The **Original data type** section has two options: **Delimited** and **Fixed width**. Use the **Delimited** option if the data is compressed together with no gaps between the values, and delimiter characters (such as commas and tab characters) to separate each value from the next. Use **Fixed width** if the values are vertically aligned, and blank spaces are inserted into the data where necessary. The Preview section at the bottom of this Wizard shows the data in each line pushed together, so it is obviously not a **Fixed width** type.

The **File origin** text box allows you to select whether the data originated from a computer using the Macintosh, DOS, Windows (ANSI), or a variety of foreign language formats.

4   Verify the **Original data type** is **Delimited**, and **Start import at row** is **1**, then click **Next**.

In Step 2 of the Text Import Wizard, you specify the delimiter character from the list of options: **Tab**, **Semicolon**, **Comma**, **Space**, or **Other**. You can select more than one type of delimiter character.

You also specify the type of **Text qualifier**: double-quote (") or single quote ('). Text qualifiers are used to identify text characters that belong together. For this data file, none of the data is using any text qualifier.

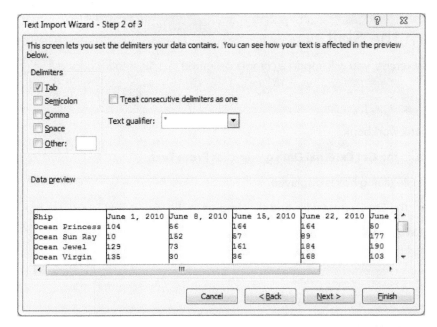

5   In the **Delimiters** section, verify the **Tab** check box is turned on and click **Next**.

Step 3 of the Text Import Wizard tries to guess the correct type of data used in each column. The default type is **General**, in which a column with data that appears to be all numeric will be converted into a number. Similarly, data that appears to be recognizable date values will be converted into dates, and any remaining types will be treated as text. You can also force Excel to accept columns as date or text, or to skip the entire column.

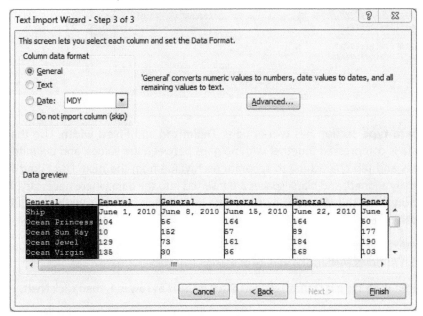

6   Click **Finish**.

7   Click **OK**.

The worksheet should appear similar to the following:

	A	B	C	D	E	F	G
1	Ship	1-Jun-10	8-Jun-10	15-Jun-10	22-Jun-10	29-Jun-10	6-Jul-10
2	Ocean Princess	104	56	164	164	50	58
3	Ocean Sun Ray	10	152	57	89	177	85
4	Ocean Jewel	129	73	161	184	190	93
5	Ocean Virgin	135	30	36	168	103	129
6	Ocean Dancer	75	143	96	144	169	81
7	Ocean Radiance	150	18	106	111	158	70

8 Save the workbook as Eco Cruises - Student and close it.

Exporting Data from Excel

Excel provides an easy-to-use method of exporting data to other systems. In the Save As dialog box, the **Save as type** drop down list includes an extensive list of different formats for saving the worksheet data:

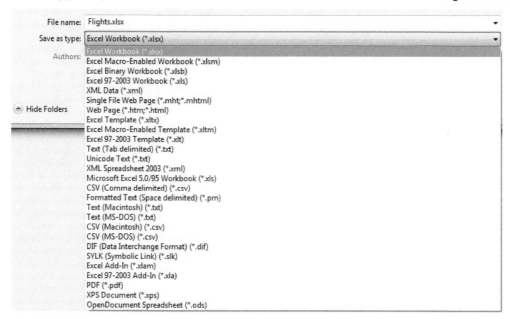

Another method of sending data to another Windows program is to use the Windows Clipboard. To use it, simply copy the data from Excel into the Clipboard, and paste the data into the other Windows program. The target software will usually offer several options, such as copying the data formatting as well.

Learn the Skill

In this exercise, you will export worksheet data to a comma-delimited text file, and copy and paste the data to a Microsoft Word document.

1 Open the *Flights* workbook.

Export this worksheet to an external CSV data file.

2 Click the **File** tab, then click **Save As**.

3 Click the arrow at the far right of the **Save as type**, and select **CSV (Comma delimited) (*.csv)**.

4 With the **File name** as *Flights.csv*, click **Save**.

A warning message box appears to inform you that the data from only the current worksheet will be exported to the data file.

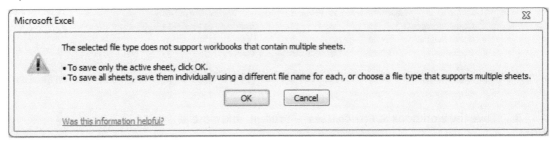

5   Click **OK**.

A second warning message box appears to inform you of possible data incompatibilities. Do not be overly concerned about the warning—you can just verify the output to make sure that the data looks correct.

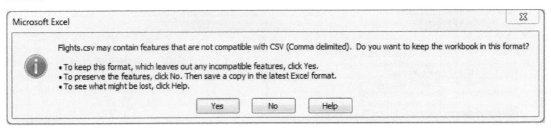

6   Click **Yes**.

Use MS Notepad to check the contents of the output file.

7   Start up Notepad from the Windows **Start** button.

8   In Notepad, click **File**, **Open** from the menu.

9   Change the document type from **Text Documents (*.txt)** to **All Files (*.*)**.

10   Locate and select the *Flights.csv* file and click **Open**.

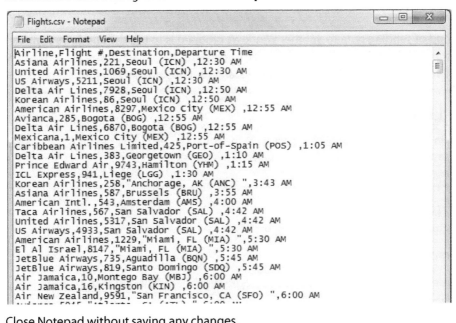

11   Close Notepad without saving any changes.

12   Go back to Excel and close the *Flights.csv* file.

Now try copying and pasting the worksheet data to Microsoft Word using the Clipboard.

13 Open the *Flights* workbook.

14 Select columns A, B, C, and D, and on the **Home** tab, in the **Clipboard** group, click **Copy**.

15 Start up Microsoft Word with a new blank document.

16 In Word, on the **Home** tab, in the **Clipboard** group, click the arrow under **Paste**, and click **Paste Special**.

17 Select **Formatted Text (RTF)** and click **OK**.

18 Save and close the Word document as *Flights - Student*.

19 Go back to Excel and close the *Flights* workbook without saving any changes.

Changing Workbook Properties

1.3

Another useful tool for workgroups is the ability to display a workbook's properties prior to opening it. This is useful when there are many workbooks stored on the network server, often with very similar names. The properties display will help distinguish each of the workbooks from each other.

These same benefits apply in non-workgroup situations as well.

It is good practice to view the document properties before saving your workbook for the first time or sending it to others. Sometimes the document properties may contain confidential data about you or your company that you should not be sharing with others.

Learn the Skill

In this exercise, you will display and change the workbook properties.

1 Open the *Financial Statements - Student* workbook.

2 Click the **File** button, click **Info**, and then click **Properties**, and click **Show Document Panel**.

The Document Properties panel is displayed above the workbook.

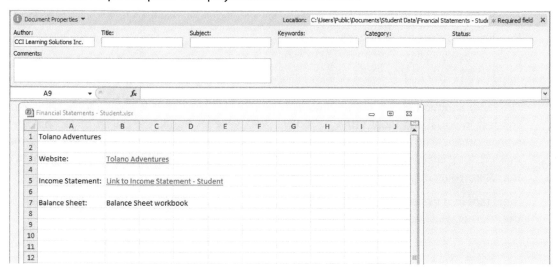

3   Type the following:

Author: \<your own name\>
Title: Tolano Adventures
Subject: financial statement
Keywords: links, website, income statement, balance sheet
Category: financial
Status: Draft

4   Click **Document Properties** and then **Advanced Properties**.

5   Click each of the tabs and you will see that entering the information in the Document Properties panel is the same as with Windows, except that you can see the contents of the document at the same time, which enables you to enter more precise details about the document.

6   Click **OK** to close the dialog box.

7   Close the Document Properties panel.

8   Save and close the workbook.

Sharing Workbooks

7.1

The rapid adoption of the Internet into everyday life demonstrates how communication helps people to connect in social and work settings. Today's workplace leverages the power of technology to increase worker productivity in creating, analyzing and sharing data, leading to faster and more informed decision-making. Most office workers now have at least one computer, and almost every one of them connects to the others using the corporate local area network.

Excel taps into this pervasive connectivity with its built-in ability to send workbooks to others using e-mail, the Internet, and Microsoft SharePoint.

Using E-mail

One way of sharing workbooks quickly with others is to send them by e-mail. The downside of using e-mail is that every recipient gets his or her own copy of the workbook. These individuals often make changes or add comments to their copy of the workbook and send it back. The originator must then merge these copies together.

To send a workbook using e-mail from within Excel, do the following steps:

1.   Open the workbook.

2.   On the **File** tab, click **Save & Send**.

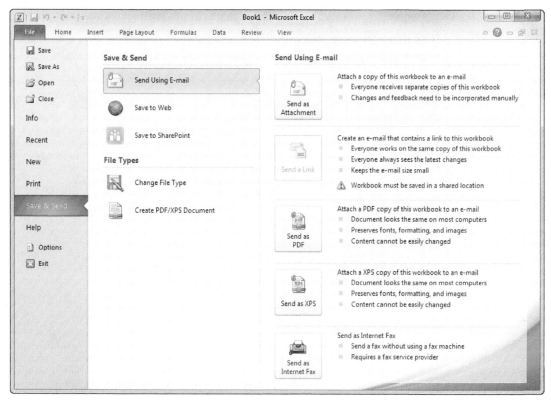

3.   Ensure **Send Using E-mail** is selected and then click one of the following buttons:
     a.   Send as Attachment
     b.   Send a Link
     c.   Send as PDF
     d.   Send as XPS
     e.   Send as Internet Fax

Send as Attachment   Create a new e-mail message with your workbook included as an attachment, as demonstrated in the following example:

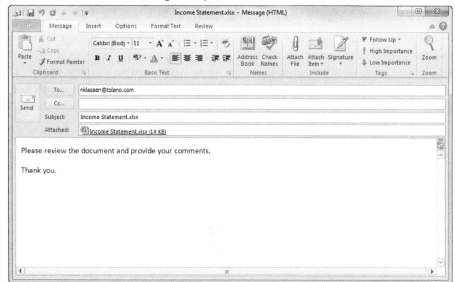

	When you click the **Send** button, Outlook sends the e-mail and the attached workbook to the intended recipient.
Send as Link	Launch Outlook with a new e-mail message containing a hyperlink to your workbook. Unlike **Send as Attachment**, **Send as PDF** or **Send as XPS**, your recipients do not receive any file; instead, they open the original workbook by clicking on the hyperlink in the e-mail. Note that your workbook must be stored in a shared location (e.g., a network drive) where your recipients can access it from wherever they are located.
Send as PDF	Convert the workbook into a PDF (Portable Document Format) before you send it. Then Outlook creates a new e-mail message with this PDF file included as an attachment, as demonstrated in the following example: 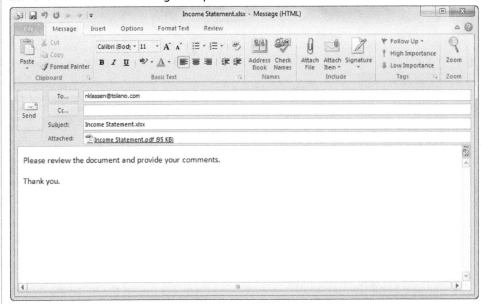 The PDF format allows the recipient to view and print the workbook, but it does not permit them to make changes.
Send as XPS	Convert the workbook into XPS format before sending. As with **Send as PDF**, Excel converts the workbook and then Outlook creates a new e-mail message with this XPS file included as an attachment; recipients can view and print the workbook but they cannot make changes to it.
Send as Internet Fax	Convert the workbook into an electronic fax file and send it to the internet fax software installed on your local computer.

Of these alternatives, you should select **Send as Link** as your preferred method when sharing with co-workers within the same organization. Avoid sending a workbook as an attachment because you will simply create more work for yourself when your co-workers make changes to their copies of the workbook, possibly at the same time as you are doing so. If instead you put the workbook into a shared location and send out a link, everyone (including you) is always updating the same workbook.

The **Send as PDF** or **Send as XPS** are useful alternatives if you want to prevent the recipients from making changes to the workbook.

Save to Web

Another way of sharing workbooks with others is to use a web-based storage service such as the Microsoft SkyDrive. SkyDrive is one of the components of the Microsoft's Windows Live group of online services. Every registered Windows Live user has a SkyDrive with 25 GB of storage space at no cost. By default, you have two main folders: My Documents and Public. Anyone with a Windows Live ID can access any files in the Public folder at any time; any files you put into the My Documents folder are only accessible by you, except for the ones that you designate your contacts can share. You can also add other online web-based (e.g. Internet) storage services to store your workbooks.

To save a workbook to the SkyDrive from within Excel, do the following:

1. Open the workbook.

2. On the **File** tab, click **Save & Send**.

3. Under **Save & Send**, click **Save to Web**.

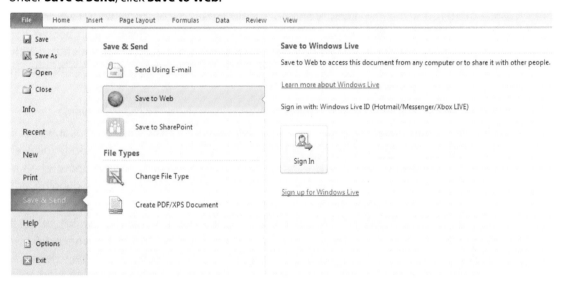

4. If necessary, click **Sign In** to access the SkyDrive.

5. Enter your login ID and password in Windows Live.

    Excel then displays the folders in your SkyDrive.

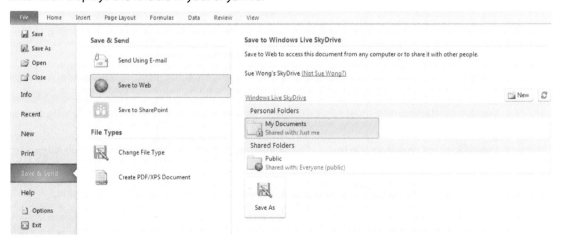

6. Click one of the SkyDrive folders (e.g. *Public* or *My Documents*) and then click **Save As**.

The Save As dialog box appears (there may be a short wait while the connection is completed with the SkyDrive). Although it looks like any other folder on your computer or a network drive, it is actually a remote drive provided as part of your Windows Live account. If you want to share your workbook with others, be sure to select the *Public* folder.

7. If desired, change the **File name** and/or **Save as type**.

8. Click **Save**.

9. If necessary, make any other changes to the workbook and save these changes. Note that, any time you save changes, you are saving them directly to the workbook in the SkyDrive, not to your local computer.

10. Close the workbook.

The workbook is now accessible from the SkyDrive.

Using SharePoint

Another method of sharing Excel workbooks (and other documents) with co-workers is by using SharePoint. Recognizing that people working together are more productive than people working alone, Microsoft designed SharePoint to facilitate document sharing within an organization and with authorized users in partner organizations. The term *web-based collaborative environment* refers to this kind of online sharing.

SharePoint brings together the many different tools that people use to share, including:

*   **Shared network drives to store files and documents**—In the past, a company or IT department would designate specific computers to store these files. Access security quickly followed to ensure protection of confidential files. However, the demand for shared storage space in an organization usually exceeds the space available after a few years, representing an ongoing administrative nightmare for most IT departments.

*   **Document version control**—A collaborative environment brings a new set of challenges and headaches, primarily the dispersal of ownership and loss of control over changes made, which often leads to uncontrolled and haphazard changes. For example, someone may delete a document accidentally or make changes that conflict with another person's changes. Version control ensures that only one person enters their changes at any one time. If someone accidentally deletes a document or makes unwanted changes, this feature allows you to restores a previous version easily.

*   **Workflow control**—You can designate documents to be funneled through workflow processes, such as approving purchase requisitions or media releases. The system then automatically routes the document to the next person in the workflow when the current approver has completed his or her work.

*   **Social networking**—Facebook is an example of social networking.

*   **E-mail**—Announcements, notices and other types of team communication, which are often sent by e-mail, can be quickly lost in the daily volume of other e-mail. An effective collaboration site has a section containing the most relevant communications to the team without having to wade through e-mails.

*   **Other shared communications**—These include things such as corporate or team calendars, surveys and polls.

To save a workbook to SharePoint from within Excel, do the following:

1. Open the workbook.

2. On the **File** tab, click **Share**.

3. Under **Share**, click **Save to SharePoint**.

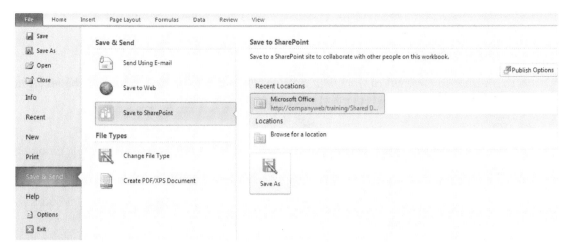

4. If necessary, click **Browse for a location**.

The Excel Save As dialog box now appears, allowing you to navigate to the SharePoint site where the document is to be stored.

A SharePoint site can be designed in many different ways; the following illustration shows one example where documents of various types are stored.

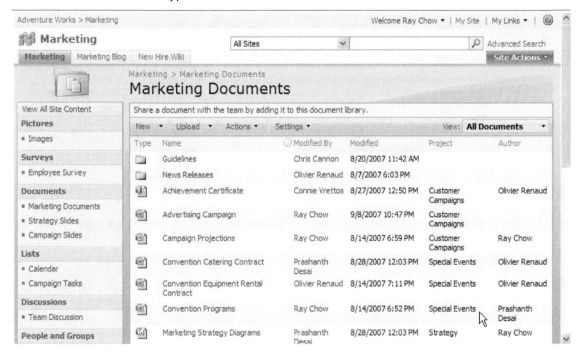

Lesson Summary

In this lesson, you learned to work with different types of illustrations, including shapes, WordArt, pictures, clip art graphics and SmartArt. You should now be able to:

☑ sort data

☑ use the AutoFilter feature to find specific data

☑ create, modify and delete range names

☑ create, modify and delete hyperlinks

☑ create and delete comments

☑ import and export data with other programs

☑ change workbook document properties

☑ use Office BackStage to share workbooks with others.

Review Questions

MMM
Go online for
Additional
Review and
Activities

1. What is the difference between sorting and filtering?

2. What can you use the AutoFilter tool for in a worksheet?

3. Why do you need to tell Excel whether you have headers in the data?

4. Provide examples of when you might set up multiple levels for sorting.

5. Give examples of why you might want to name cell ranges instead of using the cell references.

6. What restrictions are in place regarding range names?

7. What can you use the Name Manager for?

8. Give an example of when you might insert a hyperlink into a worksheet.

9. What can you use comments for in a worksheet?

10. What is the preferred method of sharing a workbook with your co-workers, and why?

Microsoft®
Excel® 2010
Core Certification

Appendices

Appendix A
Courseware Mapping

Appendix B
Glossary of Terms

Appendix C
Index

Appendix A: Courseware Mapping

Skills Required for the Microsoft® Office Specialist Excel 2010 Core Exam 77-882:

	Objective Domain	Lesson
1	**Managing the Worksheet Environment**	
1.1	Navigate through a worksheet	1
1.2	Print a worksheet or workbook	5, 6
1.3	Personalize environment by using Backstage	1, 5, 8
2	**Creating Cell Data**	
2.1	Construct cell data	1, 2
2.2	Apply AutoFill	2
2.3	Apply and manipulate hyperlinks	8
3	**Formatting Cells and Worksheets**	
3.1	Apply and modify cell formats	2, 4
3.2	Merge or split cells	4
3.3	Create row and column titles	1
3.4	Hide and unhide rows and columns	2, 4
3.5	Manipulate Page Setup options for worksheets	5
3.6	Create and apply cell styles	4
4	**Managing Worksheets and Workbooks**	
4.1	Create and format worksheets	2, 4
4.2	Manipulate window views	5
4.3	Manipulate workbook views	1, 5
5	**Applying Formulas and Functions**	
5.1	Create formulas	3
5.2	Enforce precedence	3
5.3	Apply cell references in formulas	3
5.4	Apply conditional logic in a formula (<,>,=)	3
5.5	Apply named ranges in formulas	8
5.6	Apply cell ranges in formulas	3
6	**Presenting Data Visually**	
6.1	Create charts based on worksheet data	6
6.2	Apply and manipulate illustrations	7
6.3	Create and modify images by using the Image Editor	7
6.4	Apply Sparklines	6
7	**Sharing worksheet data with other users**	
7.1	Share spreadsheets by using Backstage	8
7.2	Manage comments	8
8	**Analyzing and Organizing Data**	
8.1	Filter data	8
8.2	Sort data	8
8.3	Apply conditional formatting	4

Appendix B: Glossary of Terms

Alignment – The positioning of the contents of a cell; e.g. left, right, or centered.

AutoFill – A method of copying data and formulas or creating data series by dragging the lower right corner of a cell or range.

AutoFit – A feature that will automatically adjust the width of a column or the height of a row so that the cells are just wide or high enough to display the values in all of those cells.

AutoFilter – See Filter.

AutoFormat – A feature that enables you to apply many different formatting characteristics with a single command by choosing from a selection of format templates; see Cell Styles also.

AutoSum – A tool that will quickly insert a SUM function into the current cell, and determine the appropriate cell range to be used.

Backstage – Introduced in the Microsoft Office 2010 suite, replacing the Office button. The Office Backstage is a single view that allows you to manage the workbook, including printing, opening and saving in different formats, and changing the metadata.

Bold – Dark or highlighted text.

Borders – The feature that enables you to add lines or surrounding borders to the selected cells in the worksheet.

Built-in Functions – Pre-programmed formulas to do specific calculations. You can either type these functions in or use the Insert Function wizard to assist.

Cell Styles – A feature that enables you to apply many different formatting characteristics to one or more cells with a single command by choosing from a selection of format templates; see AutoFormat also.

Center – To place text in the center of a cell.

Chart Wizard – The automatic feature that Excel provides to help you create a chart in a step-by-step process.

Chart – A pictorial representation of the data you enter in a worksheet.

Circular References – A type of error that occurs when one or more cells refer to each other directly or indirectly.

Clear – Removes information (and/or formatting and comments) from selected cells and leaves the cells blank.

Column – A vertical arrangement for text or numbers, separated from other columns by a grid line and denoted with alpha letters per column. Excel has a maximum of 256 columns, denoted from A to IV.

Comma delimited text file – The format of the data exported from a program such as Excel. All data in this file is of variable length. Each cell value is followed by a comma, except for the last value in each row. See also Fixed width text file.

Comments – Similar to a post-it note where you can enter information for yourself or others to review.

Copy – An editing function used to duplicate selected cells.

Cut – The editing process of transferring selected cells to the Clipboard so that you can move them from one location and place them into another.

Data Table – A table that displays one or two input variables and the result of a calculation using the input variables.

Data Validation – A feature that helps you set up validation checks in the cells, e.g., numbers only, list of inventory items available, etc.

Database – Used for compiling and sorting (typically large) lists of data.

Digital certificate – A code sequence that can be applied to any document or macro. Excel is able to read and display these certificates so that the user can assure themselves that the document is safe to use. Digital certificates may be issued by a commercial certification authority or created by individuals.

Document Inspector – A tool to assist in removing any personal or hidden information you don't want others to see when they open this file.

Error Checking – An auditing tool to assist in checking any errors that may exist in the formulas. Any errors are marked with a dark green triangle in the upper left corner of a cell.

Excel Services – A component of Microsoft SharePoint that is used to Excel data to others, whether they have Excel installed on their computer or not. It is used in business intelligence applications to help users analyze business data.

Filter – A feature that will suppress the display of data that do not meet the filter criteria.

Fixed width text file – The format of the data exported from a program such as Excel. All data in the same column have the same length, usually the defined width of the column. Cells that have less data than the defined width will have extra blank spaces added at the right side of the cell. See also Comma delimited text file.

Font – A specific typeface and point size.

Footer – Text that repeats at the bottom of every page and may include automatic page numbers.

Format – Instructions to Excel as to how it should display and number styles, fonts, colors, etc.

Formula Bar – A field on the screen that displays the formula in the active cell. It can also be used to make entries into the worksheet.

Formula – Used in a cell to calculate new result values to be displayed. Composed of values, cell references, arithmetic operators and special functions. These results may be used in other formulas located in other cells.

Function – A feature designed by Excel that enables you to perform quickly a calculation or formula using a specialized function.

Graphics – Illustrations that can be inserted into a worksheet such as pictures, clip art, charts, text boxes, shapes, etc.

Header – Text that repeats at the top of every page and may include automatic page numbers.

HTML – Acronym for Hyper Text Markup Language. It is the underlying language for the set of instructions used by web browsers to display information on a web page.

Hyperlink – A link to another document. It is usually stored in the form of a Uniform Resource Locator (URL), which is the unique address to find this document; e.g. on the Internet, the intranet, folder on local or network hard drive, location in current document or workbook.

Insert Function – The feature that Excel provides to help you select the desired function to perform calculations.

Insert – An editing function that enables you to add text between other text, including entire columns or rows.

Insert Worksheet Tab – The tab at the end of the worksheet tabs on the lower left corner of a workbook to assist in inserting/creating a new worksheet at the current location.

Justification – The formatting function that determines how Excel will align the data within a cell or cells.

Legend – A box on a chart that explains the meaning of each line in a line chart, or bar in a bar chart.

Linking – The process of referencing cells or worksheets in one file to another, so that changes made on one file will automatically change in the linked file.

Macro – A feature that "records" keystrokes for future use. Macros save time in operations where the same series of commands is repeated.

Margin – The white space or area from the edge of the paper to the text.

Name Box – This box displays the cell address of the active cell. It is located on the left below the toolbar.

Page Break – The division between two pages.

Page Setup – The feature that determines how Excel will display and/or print the worksheet — e.g., margins, headers/footers, gridlines, etc.

Paste – The editing function of placing cut or copied data into a new location.

Pick List – A type of data validation that ensures only valid information is entered by allowing the user to select only from a predefined list of items.

Quick Access Toolbar – A toolbar that is displayed in the upper left part of the Excel window. It is customizable to give you ready access to commands that you want to use frequently without having to select a tab in the Ribbon.

Ribbon – The collection of commands grouped under different tabs across the top of the Excel screen. Each tab is aimed at a type of activity, such as page layout or inserting items into a worksheet. Some tabs are only shown when appropriate.

Series – Each set of data used in a graphical chart.

Shared Workbook – A feature in Excel which enables more than one user to update a workbook at the same time. If the same cell(s) are updated by different people, Excel will display the conflicts and allow one of the values to remain.

SharePoint – A Microsoft software product that allows multiple users (usually within an organization) to collaborate by sharing documents, files, and workbooks. This concept is that end products are better through team work.

SkyDrive – A file storage and sharing service that is part of the Windows Live range of online services. All Window Live users are given 25 GB of free personal storage.

SmartArt – A type of illustration with a variety of diagrams to show progress or flow of information.

Solver – A tool designed to reach a solution, by changing a number of variables.

Style – A combination of formatting features you can save and apply as a set.

Table Styles – A feature that enables you to apply many different formatting characteristics to a table with a single command by choosing from a selection of format templates; see AutoFormat also.

Template – A pre-designed workbook that may already contain data, formulas, and other objects, thereby saving you time and effort in entering these items.

Tracing Errors – An audit tool that draws arrows to help you find or trace formula errors in cells that are precedents or dependents of the current cell.

Tracking Changes – A process that displays all changes made to the worksheet, including editing actions and formatting changes.

Trendline – A common method of analyzing data using charts or graphs based on the data in a worksheet.

What-if analysis – The ability to pursue an almost endless cycle of trial-and-error use of base numbers in formulas and therefore be able to make important decisions quickly.

Workspace – A file that contains the references to the workbooks, file locations, window sizes, and screen positions.

X-axis – The horizontal edge of a chart, marking the scale used there.

Y-axis – The vertical edge of a chart, marking the scale used there.

Appendix C: Index